I0137252

BABYLONIAN WITCHCRAFT LITERATURE

Program in Judaic Studies
Brown University
BROWN JUDAIC STUDIES
Edited by
Jacob Neusner
Wendell S. Dietrich, Ernest S. Frerichs, William Scott Green,
Calvin Goldscheider, David Hirsch, Alan Zuckerman

Project Editors (Project)

David Blumenthal, Emory University (Approaches to Medieval Judaism)
William Brinner (Studies in Judaism and Islam)
Ernest S. Frerichs, Brown University (Dissertations and Monographs)
Lenn Evan Goodman, University of Hawaii (Studies in Medieval Judaism)
(Studies in Judaism and Islam)
William Scott Green, University of Rochester (Approaches to Ancient Judaism)
Marc L. Raphael, Ohio State University (Approaches to Judaism in Modern Times)
Norbert Samuelson, Temple University (Jewish Philosophy)
Jonathan Z. Smith, University of Chicago (Studia Philonica)

Number 132
BABYLONIAN WITCHCRAFT LITERATURE
Case Studies

by
I. Tzvi Abusch

BABYLONIAN WITCHCRAFT LITERATURE
Case Studies

by
I. Tzvi Abusch

Scholars Press
Atlanta, Georgia

BABYLONIAN WITCHCRAFT LITERATURE
Case Studies

Library of Congress Cataloging-in-Publication Data

Abusch, I. Tzvi.
Babylonian witchcraft literature : case studies / I. Tzvi Abusch.
p. cm. -- (Brown Judaic studies)
Based on author's thesis (Ph. D.)--Harvard University, 1972.
Bibliography: p.
ISBN 1-555-40191-0
1. Incantations, Assyro-Babylonian. 2. Magic, Assyro-Babylonian.
3. Witchcraft--Iraq--Babylonia. I. Title. II. Series.
PJ3791.A28 1987
492'.1--dc19 87-28539
CIP

ISBN-13: 978-1-930675-40-7 (alk.paper:paper)

Printed in the United States of America
on acid-free paper

In honor of my mother

and

In memory of my father

Contents

Part II: *Maqlû* I 1-36: An Interpretation

Preface

The essays in this volume were composed in response to several major problems that I uncovered when I undertook the study of Mesopotamian magical and medical texts centering on witchcraft and sorcery. They address difficulties that I noted when I tried to sort the texts into coherent categories and to understand individual prayers and incantations. Hence, the studies in this volume focus on individual texts and suggest solutions to complications and intricacies in the material. In the process, useful approaches were developed for the understanding of magical texts generally. Part One follows a diachronic approach, Part Two a synchronic one. In this sense, the studies are to be viewed broadly: while unravelling knots in individual texts, they highlight certain issues and exemplify some solutions for common problems in traditional Mesopotamian therapeutic literature.

In Part One, I examine such well known Akkadian incantations and prayers as *KAR*[1] 226 IV 3ff. and related texts (Chapter 1), *Maqlû* VII 119-146 and related texts (Chapter 2), and *KAR* 26 and *BMS* 12 (Chapter 3). This examination grew out of my various attempts to determine the limits of the witchcraft corpus and to categorize the many texts that display divergent and sometimes contradictory textual features. These texts contain indicators that suggest that they were used not only to combat witchcraft but also for other purposes as well. Some of these texts had been labelled "Universal Beschwörungen". I found that adaptation and change had occurred in these texts and that, at different times, these texts were used for different purposes. Such changes resulted in the appearance of disjointed and/or contradictory statements and of features pointing to multiple and often unrelated uses of the text. Accordingly, I have argued that a determination of the stages of development of such compositions is necessary for an understanding of the text[2] and is

[1] In the main, the abbreviations used are those of W. von Soden, *Akkadisches Handwörterbuch* (Wiesbaden, 1959-81) and of the *Assyrian Dictionary of the Oriental Institute of the University of Chicago* (Chicago, 1956-). In citing Akkadian and Sumerian, h/H represent ḫ/Ḫ.

[2] Obviously a full understanding of the text requires analysis on both the diachronic and synchronic levels and the synthesis of the results of both forms

one way to decide whether a text should be included in, or excluded from, the corpus.

Part Two focusses on an individual incantation, *Maqlû* I 1-36, an address to the gods of the night sky. Although this opening incantation in *Maqlû* is a famous and oft-cited example of magical literature, my initial study of the text raised new questions and revealed unexplained details. I found it necessary to construct a coherent and comprehensive statement of the meaning and function of the incantation. Accordingly, I subjected this incantation to a detailed and sustained analysis. The painstaking examination of the individual elements of an incantation and of their relationship to each other is laborious, but at least in this case it resulted in a fuller understanding of the text and of its place in *Maqlû*. Moreover, this type of analysis showed the incantation to be the product of a literary creativity that draws together magical and legal imagery for the purpose of creating an indictment in which social and moral dimensions of the witchcraft accusation come into play.

This nocturnal invocation was probably recited on the rooftop, and like prayers of divination, it probably anticipated some oracular response. In light of the analysis, I would render the incantation as follows:

The speaker calls upon the court of the heavenly gods of Anu to convene and hear his plaint; he first lays out the facts that justify his right to a hearing (1-14):

1 *I have called upon you Gods of the Night;*
2 *With you I have called upon Night, the veiled bride;*
3 *I have called upon Twilight, Midnight, and Dawn.*
4 *Because a witch has bewitched me,*
5 *A deceitful woman has accused me,*
6 *Has (thereby) caused my god and goddess to be estranged from me (and)*
7 *I have become sickening in the sight of those who behold me,*
8 *I am (therefore) unable to rest day or night,*

---

of analysis. However, all too often applications that purport to be rooted in aesthetic and/or formal theory are ahistorical and much too removed from the meaning of the text.

9 *And a gag continually filling my mouth*
10 *Has kept food distant from my mouth and*
11 *Has diminished the water which passes through my drinking organ,*
12 *My song of joy has become wailing and my rejoicing mourning—*
13 *Stand by me ye Great Gods and give heed to my suit,*
14 *Judge my case and grant me an (oracular) decision!*

Only then does the plaintiff present his accusation and claim that the witch has treated him wrongly (15-20):

15 *I have made an image of my warlock and witch,*
16 *Of my conjuror and sorceress,*
17 *I have set it at your feet and plead my case:*
18 *Because evil did she perform against me and baseless charges has she conjured up against me,*
19 *May she die, but I live!*
20 *Verily are her bewitchments, enchantments, and charms released!*

The speaker now takes an oath and establishes his own innocence of any charge (21-26):

21 *The tamarisk ... shall clear me!*
22 *The date palm ... shall release me!*
23 *The soapwort ... shall cleanse me!*
24 *The pine cone ... shall release me!*
25 *In your presence have I become pure like grass,*
26 *Clean and innocent like nard.*

Having thus proved that the accusations made against him by the witch are false and motivated by malice, the plaintiff states that her accusation has been refuted and she is therefore unable to level charges again (27-28):

27 *Her spell being that of an evil witch,*
28 *Her word has been turned back into her mouth and her tongue constricted.*

Given the falseness of the accusation, the court is called upon to label her acts as witchcraft, to charge her with the crime of performing this evil deed, to release its consequences, and to destroy the very organs that the witch used in her plot and which make her dangerous (29-33):

29 *On a(c)count of her witchcraft, may the Gods of the Night strike her;*
30 *May the three watches of the night release her evil enchantments.*
31 *Her mouth be tallow, her tongue be salt:*
32 *May that (i.e., her mouth) which uttered evil against me melt like tallow!*
33 *May that (i.e., her tongue) which performed witchcraft against me dissolve like salt!*

The final stanza informs us of the court's decision (34-36):

34 *Her bonds are broken, her deeds nullified;*
35 *Her accusations are dismissed—*
36 *By the verdict pronounced by the Gods of the Night!*

It seems that the speaker felt himself to have been accused of an unspecified but serious crime, accused, that is, of having in some way violated societal norms, thus becoming the object of shame in the opinion and judgment of the public. He deals with this threat by turning on his accuser, who is the personification of moral reprobation; he asserts his own innocence and directs against his accuser the accusation of witchcraft.[3]

[3]Such psychological- social dynamics may perhaps be better understood when viewed in the comparative light of explanations such as those offered by K. Thomas, "The Relevance of Social Anthropology to the Historical Study of English Witchcraft," in *Witchcraft Confessions and Accusations*, ed. M. Douglas, pp. 61ff. (London/New York, 1970) or D. L. O'Keefe, *Stolen Lightning: The Social Theory of Magic* (New York, 1982), pp. 414ff.

The studies included in this monograph were written in 1970-71 and completed as part of the requirements for the degree of Doctor of Philosophy in the Department of Near Eastern Languages and Literatures, Harvard University, 1972.[4] These studies treated only a limited number of problems and used selected forms of textual inquiry. Since they were originally intended to be part of a much larger work and represented even then only a fraction of my reconstruction and interpretation of the witchcraft corpus, I delayed their publication. I have continued working on the witchcraft corpus, searching for new texts especially among the unpublished materials of the British Museum (photographs and Geers' copies)[5] but also elsewhere, and preparing editions of the compositions. Recently, I have resumed my work of exposition of the corpus.[6] Having not

---

[4] The original dissertation was entitled "Studies in the History and Interpretation of Some Akkadian Incantations and Prayers Against Witchcraft." Th. Jacobsen and W. L. Moran served as dissertation advisors. Portions of Part One were read before the 180th meeting of the American Oriental Society, 1970. The ritual nature of *Maqlû* has been established in my "Mesopotamian Anti-Witchcraft Literature: Texts and Studies, Part I: The Nature of *Maqlû* : Its Character, Divisions, and Calendrical Setting," *JNES* 33 (1974) 251-262. A version of Part One, note 69, was published as "Dismissal by Authorities: *Šuškunu* and Related Matters," *JCS* 37 (1985) 91-100. The study mentioned in Part Two, note 94, appears in *HTR* 80/1 (1987) under the title "*Alaktu* and *Halakhah*: Oracular Decision, Divine Revelation." I am indebted to Scott Magoon and his staff in the Department of Research and Academic Computing, Brandeis University, for the production of the camera ready copy of this monograph. The actual work was done by Jussi Eloranta. I am deeply grateful to Kathryn Kravitz, Joel Hunt, and James McMann for their generous assistance proofreading and correcting computer generated copy.

[5] I again express my indebtedness to the late A. Leo Oppenheim and the Oriental Institute for permission to study the late F. W. Geers' copies. All joins of British Museum materials made through 1976 were communicated to C. B. F. Walker at regular intervals. I remain grateful to him for checking the joins, answering my questions, recording the various texts that I was to edit, and arranging for the production of photographs. Some of my joins have been registered by R. Borger, *Handbuch der Keilschriftliteratur*, Vol. II (Berlin/New York, 1975), pp. 331ff., and idem, "Zur Kuyunjik-Sammlung: Nachträge zu HKL II, s. 331-395," *AfO* 25 (1975-77) 411ff. I communicated suggested joins of British Museum materials to Franz Köcher in 1978 for his use.

[6] For an updated, if concise, statement of some of my views about *Maqlû*, see the article "*Maqlû*" in a forthcoming fascicle of *Reallexikon der Assyriologie und vorderasiatischen Archäologie* (Berlin/New York).

yet completed the larger work, I have decided to make these studies available to the broader scholarly community in their original form. Here and there, corrections can be made and bibliographical citations updated.[7] But I have decided not to rewrite the studies, in part because my style and interests have changed somewhat over the years. Today, I might prefer to incorporate somewhat different lines of inquiry, kinds of solutions, and styles of argumentation. To have revised the essays would have meant rewriting them completely and producing studies quite different from those contained herein. Since the present studies retain most of their original merit, there is little reason for discarding them and replacing them at this time with new studies of the same texts or with similar studies of different texts.

The studies in their present form have been found useful by several specialists who have had access to them[8]; they represent attempts to make sense of magical texts, and provide working examples of productive approaches to the material. I ask the reader to overlook those errors that might have been rectified by a thorough revision in the belief that the benefit of placing the studies in the public domain outweighs some minor annoyances. I hope they will be of some interest and use to other scholars working on cuneiform literature, generally, and therapeutic texts, specifically.

---

[7] In addition to the dictionaries, cf., e.g., the information in the following books: M.-J. Seux, *Hymnes et prières aux dieux de Babylonie et d'Assyrie* (Paris, 1976) (note the review by Werner Mayer, *Or*NS 46 [1977] 386-392, esp. pp. 391f. for *BMS* 12 and *KAR* 26); Werner Mayer, *Untersuchungen zur Formensprache der babylonischen "Gebetsbeschwörungen"* (Studia Pohl: Series Maior 5; Rome, 1976); W. Farber, *Beschwörungsrituale an Ištar und Dumuzi* (Wiesbaden, 1977); E. von Weiher, *SpBTU* II. Note also volumes containing SB therapeutic texts such as *BAM* IV-VI, *CT* 51, *SpBTU* I-II, *UET* 7, nos. 118ff., Loretz/Mayer, *Šu-ila-Gebete* (AOAT 34). Elsewhere, I will provide updated information about the exemplars, joins, and readings of compositions treated or cited in my studies. (For example, I have since identified and joined more fragments to, and augmented the text of, the Marduk composition cited in Part Two, n. 21.) I should note here, moreover, that when I wrote these studies I was still relying on published copies and editions and on Geers' unpublished copies. Subsequently, I expanded the number of texts that comprise the corpus, and examined photographs of most of the tablets, including unpublished Mss of various compositions. This examination has resulted in some corrections and in a more systematic and fuller listing of variants for some of the compositions cited in these studies.

[8] See, for example, W. Farber, *op. cit.*, pp. 42-53.

There is one possible source of error that to my mind, at least, is not minor; however, there is little point in trying to rectify the situation at this time. I refer to my reading of the broken text *KAR*, no. 269, rev.(?). In Part One, Chapter 2, I attempt to explain how a composite incantation like *Maqlû* VII 119-146 came into existence. After identifying *KAR* 269 rev. as a parallel to *Maqlû* VII 119-146, I prepared a working transliteration of *KAR* 269 rev. and subjected *Maqlû* VII 119ff., *KAR* 269 rev., and other relevant texts to a detailed comparison using this transliteration. *KAR* 269 rev. played an important role in the analysis and determined some of the details of the overall reconstruction.

Unfortunately, *KAR* 269 rev. is quite broken, and some of my readings are restorations and conjectures. Sometime after the study was composed, I began to entertain alternative readings for some of the traces and breaks in the tablet as a result of several suggestions made by Thorkild Jacobsen. In some instances, these readings seem preferable to, or at least cast some doubt on, my original readings; moreover, several of these readings would require some changes in the details of the historical reconstruction. But given the broken state of the text, some form of collation was required to reach any degree of certainty; there was no point in revising the detailed argumentation – especially since the analysis was clear and simple – prior to collation. Unfortunately, collation has not proved possible for me.

When it became clear in 1974-75 that there was little chance of my visiting Berlin in the foreseeable future, I asked (8/75) the authorities of the Staatliche Museen zu Berlin for photographs of *KAR* 269 (VAT 11119) as well as of some other texts. Correspondence with the late G.R. Meyer followed, but in April 1976 Dr. Liane Jakob-Rost most graciously sent me a photograph of *KAR* 269. Upon examination, I noted that the photograph contained only the left side of the obverse (?) and the top left piece of the reverse (?) (parts of lines 1′-5′). What for my purposes was the crucial piece was detached and not on the photograph. Although only one museum number was designated in the publication, *KAR* 269 was presumably the result of a join. I communicated this information and asked if a search could be undertaken for the missing piece. Unfortunately, the piece was lost; in a letter of 4 June 1976, Dr. Jakob-Rost informed me that "das fehlende Stück der Tafel VAT 11119 offenbar durch die Kriegswirren verlorengegangen ist." I conclude, therefore, that while other readings may be preferable, a fundamental revision of my reconstruction of the literary history of *Maqlû* VII 119-146 is best deferred to a time when the reading of *KAR* 269 rev. can be checked against an original.

Still, here we should at least note a few of the alternative readings and their effects. Possible changes in *KAR* 269 rev., lines 1′-6′[9] as well as in Meier's edition of *Maqlû* VII 119-146[10] have little bearing on our analysis. But alternative restorations of *KAR* 269 rev., line 7′[11] or line 11′[12] are another matter. If our original reading of line 7′ is rejected, this would surely affect the statements about and inferences drawn from the occurrence of the generic catch-phrase (*mimma lemnu mimma lā ṭābu* ...) before the witchcraft entry.

Here it may also be noted that a duplicate of R. Caplice, *Or*NS 39 (1970) 149:22′ff., a Namburbi included in our treatment of *Maqlû* VII 140ff., is R. Caplice, *Or*NS 42 (1973) 509:16ff. Line 22 of this duplicate provides the correct reading of *Or*NS 39 (1970) 149:26′,[13] and indicates that also that line (*lippašrā idāti ittāti lemnēti ša iššaknāni*) should be included in our discussion, for it as well as *Maqlû* VII 144 (*lippašrū* ...) begin with forms of the N precative plural of *pašāru* (cf. *AMT* 23/9). Accordingly, line 144—or rather an earlier non-witchcraft form of 144—should probably be treated together with the preceding lines (140-143). This suggests a slight modification of my historical reconstruction. In no way, however, does this invalidate our claim that *Maqlû* VII 140ff. derives from the Namburbis rather

---

[9]Probably restore .ME rather than .MEŠ in lines 1′-2′ on the basis of .ME in line 2; but cf. the use of .MEŠ in lines 7′ff. Perhaps restore line 1′ on the basis of *Maqlû* VII 123, *LKA* 128 obv. 5f., etc.: the visible ME would then either be the plural mark in Á].ME or part of G]I[SK]IM! (<.ME>) [. In line 3′, perhaps restore SIZKUR instead of *ni-qi*. In line 4′, perhaps restore [*ba*]-⌈*ru*⌉-[*ti šá*] instead of [LÚ.HAL-*ti*] ⌈x⌉ [.

[10]E.g., in lines 133f., probably restore *tazimti* [*ilī*] and delete one occurrence of *nīš ilī*.

[11]E.g., ⌈*di*⌉-*li*-⌈*ip!*⌉-[*tú*/*d*]*a-li*-⌈*ih*⌉-[*tú* N]U DÙG.GA.[(MEŠ) UZ]U.MEŠ *á*[*r-rat* DINGIR.MEŠ] *ta*(?)-x [(=*tazimti*?); or ... UZ]U.MEŠ-*i*[*a* NU DÙG.G]A! ŠÀ x [/(consider also G]AZ ŠÀ x [).

[12]E.g., *a-na* UGU *d*[*i-na*]-*ni*

[13]See already R. Caplice, *Or*NS 40 (1971) 182.

than the reverse; if anything, it may even strengthen that claim. In any case, it provides additional support for the contention that lines 140ff. should be treated as a unit, and, thereby, strengthens further the argument for the absence of lines 140-141 in the original framework of the text from which the incantation *Maqlû* VII 119ff. derives. In support of this latter point, note further that lines 140-141 are absent in the *Maqlû* VII Ms K 7476+.

Obviously, some details of our analysis and reconstruction of the emergence of *Maqlû* VII 119-146 and related texts require modification. Perhaps, at a later date, we will be able to provide a revised historical reconstruction. At that time, moreover, we might also wish to consider other interpretations of the evidence,[14] with the almost certain result, however, of more – rather than less – complicated stemmata. The analysis, moreover, would be further refined – probably not modified – by a close comparison of the individual Mss of *Maqlû* VII 119-146. Still, the thrust of our argument stands: *KAR* 269 rev. is some form of parallel of *Maqlû* VII 119-146. In gross terms, the historical scheme seems to be sound. Even if an alternative reconstruction is to be preferred, our attempt will have highlighted some developments that magical texts underwent and changes to which they were subjected. Most important, the study still serves to exemplify the type of textual development it set out to document. The principle enunciated and exemplified remains documented; namely, that texts like *Maqlû* VII 119-146 are the end product of a series of changes and adaptions and that some of the logical and contextual difficulties encountered in reading these texts are the result of changes introduced into the composition at various points of its development.

One further comment: It may be recalled that this reconstruction was among the first of a growing number of attempts at producing the detailed history of a magical text.[15] It is possible that in my desire to understand how such texts came into being and to find, thereby, a satisfactory way of reading them, I may have simplified

[14] E.g., that the Namburbi lists of evils in *KAR* 269 rev. and *Maqlû* VII 119ff. were derived independently from variant forms of the list.

[15] Note that our attempts are concerned with SB incantations, and we do not assume OB prototypes.

matters by creating overly logical schemes and solutions. In the process, I may not have accorded sufficient weight to the vagaries of the transmission of cuneiform texts and to the formulaic nature of some of the phrases and blocks in incantations and prayers. Such considerations may render precise historical reconstruction and stemma less cogent or compelling. Still, at this stage of the study of Standard Babylonian literature, I prefer the excesses of the historical-analytical approach. I proceed as if all elements of a text have significance and stand in meaningful relationships to each other. But if strict coherence or integration seems absent, I then attempt to define the difficulty and, when appropriate, to isolate additions and revisions and determine the manner of, the motivation behind, and the effect of the inclusion. It is not easy to read a composite and inconsistent text. Even if structural(ist) or stylistic artifices are detectable, we should first execute the historical operations so that we know what we are doing when we construct a harmonistic or selective reading that is often the only way to comprehend the composite.

I should like to express my gratitude and affection to Thorkild Jacobsen and William L. Moran. They were my teachers and have been good friends even during difficult times. Marvin Fox has been both mentor and colleague; he has created the circumstances for renewed productivity. Calvin Goldscheider of Brown University suggested and facilitated the publication of this work in the *Brown Judaic Studies*, and offered the encouragement and advice of a dear friend. I am grateful to Jacob Neusner for graciously accepting this volume into the series.

My wife Susan and my sons David and Ra'anan have shared life with me. They have been constant sources of love, joy, and knowledge. They grow more precious by the day. I owe them a great debt.

When I was writing these studies, I intended to dedicate them to my parents. Now, perforce, I would dedicate them to my mother with love and prayers that old-age be kind to her, and to the loving memory of my father.

I. Tzvi Abusch

Brandeis University
August 1986

Introduction

The written remains of ancient Mesopotamia preserve a partial record of the life and thought of that civilization, a record composed of documents of diverse forms and varied concerns. A significant portion of these documents constitutes a rich and complex magical and medical literature. This literature, which is part of the mainstream of the Mesopotamian cultural tradition, comprises descriptions of symptoms, diagnoses, ritual and medical prescriptions, incantations, and prayers, and is recorded in a variety of formally distinct textual types. In modern terms, the magical and medical texts describe the beliefs and behavior associated with pathological disorders, personal and social crises, and culturally determined anxieties of the individual, and they prescribe the self-administered and professionally-administered measures undertaken to restore the afflicted individual to a normal life. These texts reflect suffering, fears, and anxieties common to all men, and are among the most important sources for our knowledge of the personal and religious life of the ancient Mesopotamian.

Although much progress has been made as a result of the work of a small number of devoted scholars, the study of this branch of cuneiform literature is still in its infancy, and much remains to be done in the areas of publication, systematization, and interpretation of the texts. Because of the size and complexity of the materials, significant advances can best be made by the intensive study of topically related segments of the magical and medical corpus. This procedure is far from new, and several segments of the corpus have already been investigated. However, although there has been a growing realization–since the pioneering works of Evans-Pritchard and Kluckhohn–of the importance of the role of witchcraft in the cultural and social life of many primitive and western societies, no comprehensive study of the Mesopotamian texts which deal with witchcraft has been attempted. This lack is surprising in view of the existence of a large number of relevant cuneiform texts, some of which have been known since almost the beginning of cuneiform studies, and of the mention of witchcraft in a number of general works on Mesopotamian religion, magic, and literature.

Accordingly, in the spring of 1968, we undertook the study of that segment of the Mesopotamian magical and medical corpus which deals with witchcraft. This project has consisted in (1) the collection of all Sumerian and Akkadian texts in which witchcraft plays a role, to which end all of the magical and medical texts previously published as well as Geers' copies of several thousand unpublished British Museum tablets have been examined, and (2) the systematization and analysis of the texts for the purposes of tracing their history and ascertaining their meaning and of reconstructing Mesopotamian beliefs and behavior relating to witchcraft. In view of the richness both in quality and in quantity of the materials, it is not surprising that this investigation has resulted in a number of new finds, some of which have already been presented in several papers to the American Oriental Society, communicated to the authorities of the British Museum, and shared with interested colleagues in the field. While this is not the place to summarize all these finds, two results should be mentioned here, though they will be presented in detail and substantiated elsewhere.

During the preparation, for eventual publication, of an edition of the textual materials which form the witchcraft corpus, many new texts, duplicates, and joins were identified, and, thereby, new compositions were discovered and previously known ones were either wholly or partially restored or provided with a fuller collection of variants. In this context, the importance of the Geers collection should be emphasized.

The single most important result of the investigation, however, has been registered not in the area of text publication, but in that of interpretation. The ritual and incantation series *Maqlû*, which series was edited originally by Tallqvist and more recently by Meier, still remains the single most important source for the study of Mesopotamian witchcraft. In the course of an intensive examination of *Maqlû*, it was found that this series, far from being a collection of incantations brought together because of a common theme, represents a consecutive and unified ceremony whose incantations were recited and whose rituals were performed in the order given in the series, and that the ritual tablet of the series, far from being a simple catalog, is the manual for the complete ceremony. As a long and complex ceremony, *Maqlû* is divided into three major parts. These three divisions, each of which displays an inner unity and is definable on the basis of internal and formal criteria, were performed in sequence: the first two being performed during the night and the third during the following morning. These divisions are tablets I-V, VI-VII 57, and VII 58-VIII.

The length and complexity of the series are due to a number of changes introduced into the ceremony in the course of its evolution and to the accompanying developments in the body of the text. The stages of growth of *Maqlû* can still be traced, and the series can be shown to have originated in a short sequence of ten incantations. Contrary to previous opinion, the *Maqlû* incantations which are listed by incipit in *BBR* 26 V and in *PBS* 1/1 13 rev. // K 15234 + 16344 (confirmed) are not an extract from the "canonical" *Maqlû*; rather they constitute the historical nucleus out of which tablets I-V, the oldest division in the series, emerged through a conscious process of adaptation, repatterning, and expansion.

While the short original version and the expanded final version of I-V differ from each other in respect to size and time of performance (the former was performed in the morning), the basic pattern underlying the short version is retained in the expanded version and remains operative there in most of its essentials. This is especially fortunate, for, whereas the pattern underlying the final version is obscured by the length, repetitiveness, and apparent complexity of that version, that underlying the original version is rendered conspicuous by the very brevity of that version, and, consequently, the identification of the pattern underlying the short version facilitates the isolation of that underlying the final version and the definition of its meaning.

The pattern underlying the short version may, in summary form, be reconstructed as follows:

(1) The first part, which is composed of three incantations, centers on the judgment and execution of the witch. The plaintiff addresses Šamaš, identifies the witches, who are represented by statues, as the culprits who have harmed him, and asks Šamaš to order their execution by fire. He then turns to Nusku, who, as watchman, has guarded him against that witchcraft which was sent during the night,

and asks him to cause that witchcraft to turn back and attack those who originally sent it.

(2) The second part, which is somewhat more difficult to reconstruct because of the damaged state of all three of its incantations and rituals, seems to center on the release of witchcraft through the untying of knots, on protection against future attack, and on purification. The ritual of the third incantation prescribes the placing of a cornel branch in the heart of the witch, which action represents a further stage in her execution.

(3) The third part centers on the transformation of the witch into a ghost and on its expulsion. After having been burned and impaled, the smoldering statue is drenched with water. The drenching serves to extinguish any remaining spark of life and malicious impulse in the witch, who is, thereby, finally and irrevocably killed, divested of all corporeal form, and turned into a ghost. After the ghost has been pacified, the speaker expresses the wish that the mountain, which, in some way, represents death, confine it. He then commands the witch's ghost to be gone and never return, thus expelling it from the world of the living. On this note the original ritual ended.

The expulsion of the witch's ghost, a theme which is crucial for an understanding of *Maqlû*, is bound up with the calendrical setting of the series. It is virtually certain that at least the final version of *Maqlû* was performed in the month of *Abu*, probably during the period of the disappearance of the moon at the end of that month. *Maqlû* was performed in *Abu* because of the cultic-calendrical association of that month with Gilgamesh in his netherworld capacity and with the appearance of ghosts and their return to the netherworld.

It is, however, neither to our general edition and treatment of the body of texts which constitute the witchcraft corpus nor to our study of the nature, history, structure, ritual, and calendrical setting of *Maqlû* that the studies in this volume are devoted. It seems to us that a somewhat more immediate and pressing need would perhaps be served by an exposition in case-study form of what we believe to be a productive approach to the materials.

Students of Mesopotamian magical literature will surely agree that this branch of cuneiform studies, perhaps more than any other, is in a chaotic state and is, in a profound sense, *terra incognita.*

While it cannot be denied that the difficulties inherent in this type of literature, the imposing mass and complexity of these materials, the nature of their organization in antiquity, and their state of preservation and publication in modern times have been contributing factors, it seems to us that the main cause of this situation is to be sought elsewhere. The study of this literature has suffered from the absence of sympathy for and the presence of antipathy to the magical literature. These sentiments are due, in large measure, to the belief that these texts are not internally coherent and do not express a logical and meaningful pattern of thought. This belief, especially when operating in the study of the very genres most alien to the modern scholar and most prone to expansion, revision, and corruption, can have only one outcome: as a self-fulfilling prophecy, it sounds the death knell of the philological enterprise. The only way in which we fulfill our responsibility as philologists is by assuming that the magical texts do make sense. However, we shall find that sense neither by demanding that the texts speak for themselves nor by according them a false respect cast in the mold of literalism, but rather by approaching them with sympathetic imagination and educated common sense, on the one hand, and strict logic and rigorous criticism, on the other.

The studies herewith presented are predicated on the assumption that the magical texts do make sense, and they have as their main purpose the transformation of that assumption into a self-evident truth. The first study is devoted to an examination of several incantations and prayers which presently display an inordinate number of illogicalities. By the application of several different modes of critical analysis, an attempt is made to demonstrate that these compositions were originally coherent and that their illogicalities first emerged as a result of changes introduced into these compositions in the course of their development. The second study, by way of contrast, is primarily concerned with one incantation and is essentially interpretive. By the probing of the details of this incantation, an attempt is made to discern and to understand the internal logic and the full range of meaning of the incantation.

Although the author is all too certain that some of his arguments and conclusions will turn out to be mistaken, he presents these studies in the hope of having shown that where we do not understand the texts, the failing lies with us and not with the ancients.

PART ONE

Secondary Developments and Synthetic Growth in Akkadian Incantations and Prayers: Some Case Studies in Literary and Textual History

Chapter One

Problem, Hypothesis and Illustration

A study of all published and many unpublished Akkadian prayers and incantations containing witchcraft-related terminology reveals that most of the texts deal primarily with witchcraft and can be typed and assigned to distinct categories on structural and thematic grounds. In a number of texts, however, these terms occur as members of a much larger group of evils and stand in no causal relationship to the non-witchcraft terms. While this creates no essential difficulty for the interpreter in those instances where the text has as its object the combatting of evils of all types (as, for example, in the General Namburbi group represented by *JAOS* 59 11ff. (13:6-8) and parallels: *LKA* 128 (obv. 10f.) // (?) *KAR* 120 and *KAR* 282 (Frag. 1:3) and the related *KAR* 286 (15)[1]), it does pose problems of an internal and/or contextual nature in a number of texts belonging to a wide range of prayer and incantation types.

It is the purpose of this study to demonstrate that many of these texts are not made of whole cloth, but have undergone a series of changes, that these texts are often best understood as recensional stages in the development of a composition and that an understanding of these texts, be it for purposes of interpretation, literary or religious history or translation, requires the application of "higher critical" methods. We propose to examine examples drawn from two text groups. These text groups were chosen because they are characterized by structurally different types of enumeration. The examples drawn from these groups were chosen because they exemplify different processes of development and require different types of analysis.

However, before turning to these texts, it will be of some benefit to illustrate the differences between "manuscripts" of one com-

[1] Cf. *JNES* 19 153, where all these texts, save for the last one, are listed. A witchcraft entry occurs in all General Namburbi incantations of the *JAOS* 59 13 group sufficiently preserved to permit judgment and in almost all the texts influenced by it. See below Chapter 2, Sec. D, 4, Position of Witchcraft Entry, 1), and notes 3, 53 and 54. The appropriateness of the inclusion of this entry in this General Namburbi type will be discussed elsewhere.

position, each of which must be classified as a different recension. K 2467 + 80-7-19, 116 obv. r. col. 12′ - rev. r. col. 2, *KAR* 78:1′-5′ and *KAR* 226 IV 3-13[2] provide us with an excellent example; for the genetic relationship between these texts is undeniable and their differences probably exemplify the simplest form of expansion of a short list of evils. These incantations are particularly relevant to our study because they relate to the General Namburbi,[3] demonstrate the secondary nature of the witchcraft theme and occur in witchcraft contexts.[4]

[2]These texts have been identified as duplicates by Reiner, *Šurpu* (*AfO* Beiheft 11) [Henceforth: *Šurpu*], p. 54, and the first two lines of our incantation have already been transliterated and translated there. For *KAR* 78:4′-5′, cf. *RA* 36 31 n. 4. In K 2467 + and *KAR* 78, as well as in *Šurpu*, p. 12 II 9f., the incantation *aktabsakka* is followed by the incantation *īpuš* [d]*Ea ipšur* [d]*Ea* (cf. *Šurpu*, p. 54). In KAR 226 IV, however, the incantation *aktabsakka* is followed not by *īpuš* [d]*Ea* but by two fragmentary lines (14-15), the first of which ([xx(x) Ú.IN].NU.UŠ GIŠ.[...]; cf. possibly *JCS* 21 10:6+a and references there) probably contains a ritual. Therefore, although it still remains possible that the incantation *īpuš* [d]*Ea* occurs also in *KAR* 226, there is no evidence for this (modify accordingly the statement in *Šurpu*, p. 54). (For lists of occurrences of the incantation *īpuš* [d]*Ea*, cf. *RA* 36 31f., *Or*NS 8 306f. and especially 307 n. 3, *Šurpu*, p. 54, and Caplice, *The Akkadian Text Genre Namburbi* [Diss., University of Chicago, 1963] pp. 172f.)

[3]*KAR* 78 has been classed in *RA* 48 7 as a Namburbi text written on an amulet. It is interesting to note the connections between the incantation found in K 2467 +, *KAR* 78 and *KAR* 226 and the General Namburbis. Three essential elements in this incantation have parallels in that group: (a) the request that the exiting periods carry off evils and the entering ones bring goodness is found in *KAR* 37 rev.(!) 2f. (cf. *RA* 36 31 n. 4) and *JAOS* 59 14:27f.; (b) plants, in their releasing and purifying role, are mentioned in contiguity to the aforementioned motif in *KAR* 37 rev.(!) 1 and *JAOS* 59 14:24-26; and (c) the evils listed in *KAR* 226 IV 8-10 recur in *JAOS* 59 13:3-10, *LKA* 128:5-10 // *KAR* 120:5-8, *KAR* 282 frag. 2:6-8, *AnBi* 12 284:56f., *KAR* 286:10-13 and in texts influenced by this genre (*KAR* 26 obv. 41 f., *Maqlû* VII 123ff., *KAR* 269 rev. 2′-4′ and *JNES* 15 142:60′f.). [Note that a witchcraft sequence almost always occurs in these texts in the larger list of which these lines form part; the only exceptions are *AnBi* 12 and *JNES* 15. See above note 1 and below Chapter 2, Sec. D, 4, Position of Witchcraft Entry, 1), and notes 53 and 54.]

[4]See below note 10.

K 2467 + 80-7-19, 116

obv. r. col.
12′ [ÉN *ak-tab-sa*]-*ka šá-ad-da-ak-ka* GIŠ.Š[INIG]
13′ [GIŠ.SIKIL.LA Ú].⌈IN⌉.NU.UŠ GIŠ.ŠÀ.GIŠ[IMMAR]
14′ [*im-ṭu-ia ta-n*]*i-hi-ia ta-di-ra-ti*-[*ia*]
rev. r. col.
1 U$_4$-*mu* ⌈ITU⌉ [MU.AN.NA *šá it-tal-ku lum-ni lit-ba-lu*]
2 KIMIN *šá* ⌈*ir*⌉-[*ru-bu-ni* TI.LA *li/lu-bi/bil-lu-ni* ÉN]

KAR 78

[ÉN *ak-tab-sa-ka ša-ad-da-ak-ka* GIŠ.ŠINIG]
1′ [GIŠ.SIKIL.L]A!? Ú.IN.NU.UŠ ŠÀ-*bi gi*-[*šim-ma-ri*]
2′ [*im-ṭu-iá*] *ta-ni-hu-iá ta-dir*[5]-⌈*ti*?⌉-[*iá*]
3′ [(x x)] ⌈*ù*⌉-<*a*> *a-a hu-uṣ-ṣu* GAZ ŠÀ-*bi ta*-⌈x⌉ [x x]
4′ [U$_4$-*mu* ITU] MU.AN.NA *ša it-tal-ku lum-ni lit*-⌈*ba*⌉-[*lu*]
5′ [U$_4$-*mu* ITU] MU.AN.NA *ša ir-ru-bu-nu* TIN *lu-bil-lu-ni* É[N]

KAR 226 IV

3 ÉN *ak-tab-sa-k*[*a ša-ad-da-ak-ka* GIŠ.ŠINIG]
4 GIŠ.SIKIL.LA Ú.I[N.NU.UŠ GIŠ.ŠÀ.GIŠIMMAR (...)]
5 *im-ṭu-ia ta-ni-hu-ia ta*-[*di-ra-ti-ia*[6]
6 ⌈*la*⌉-*a ṭu-ub* ŠÀ-*bi-ia* [*la-a ṭu-ub* UZU.MEŠ-*ia*[7] (HUL?)]
7 [*kiš*]-⌈*pi*⌉ *ru-he-e ru-se-e up-ša-še-e* [HUL.MEŠ-*te ša* LÚ.MEŠ-*te*]
8 [HUL MÁŠ].⌈GI$_6$!?⌉.MEŠ Á.MEŠ-*te* GISKIM.MEŠ-*te* HUL.[MEŠ-*te* NU DÙG.GA.MEŠ]
9 [UZU.MEŠ *ha*]-⌈*ṭu*⌉-[*ú-te*[8] H]UL.MEŠ-*te pár-du-ú*-[*te*

[5]Can DIR have the value *dira*? Note Renger's objection (*ZA* 61 37f.) to the assignment of CVCV values to CVC signs.

[6]Perhaps this line is to be further restored according to *KAR* 78:3′.

[7]For our restoration cf., e.g., *LKA* 128 obv. 14 and Laessøe, *Bît rimki*, p. 39:28 (for which cf. p. 42) // *STT* 76:29 // 77:29, and so emend *KAR* 80 rev. 10: NU DÙG ŠÀ-*bi* N[U DÙG.G]A <UZU>.

[8]Similar lists seem to require this restoration of 9a. The major difficulty is that the normal form of this line in these lists is (HUL) UZU(.MEŠ/ME) *ha/haṭ-ṭu-ti/te*/⌈LAL?⌉.MEŠ *par/pár-du-ti/te lem-nu-ti*/HUL.MEŠ NU

(HUL.MEŠ-*te*) NU DÙG.GA.MEŠ]
10 [*hi-niq* UDU.NITÁ SIZKUR SIZ]KUR *li-pit qa-te* KA UK[Ù!.MEŠ[9]
11 [*mim-ma lem-nu ša i*]-⸢*na* SU⸣-*ia ù* É-*ia* ⸢GÁL⸣-[*u*
12 [U$_4$-*mu* ITU MU.AN.NA *ša it*]-⸢*tal*⸣-*ku lum-ni l*[*it-ba-lu*]
13 [KIMIN *ša ir-ru-bu*]-⸢*ni!?*⸣ TI.LA [*lu-bil-lu-ni* ÉN]

A simple comparison of these texts reveals that the group of evils which is limited to one line in K 2467 + 80-7-19, 116 has been expanded by a further line in *KAR* 78 and by six lines in *KAR* 226.[10]

DÙG.GA(.MEŠ) (cf. *KAR* 26:41, *KAR* 269 rev. 2′, *KAR* 286:12, *LKA* 128 obv. 7f. // *KAR* 120:6f., *JAOS* 59 13:5f., *Maqlû* VII 124 and K 5409:4 [which has a shortened formulation to match the nature of the list there]), and our line would be the only one, if our restoration is correct, in which *lemnūte* precedes *pardūti*. Note that only one wedge of -⸢*ṭu*⸣- is preserved and that this wedge might belong to the preceding sign.

[9]Restored and emended according to *KAR* 282 frag. 1:9.

[10]While it is almost certainly true that from a literary and typological point of view the development of the incantation was one of expansion, we are unable to specify the exact motives for the development or to reconstruct the exact chain of events. Our inability is due to the difficulty involved in assuming a direct development of the incantation from the context in which the short version is found (K 2467 +) to that in which the expanded version is found (*KAR* 226). Since the content of the first three columns of *KAR* 226 (cf. Excursus) indicates that that tablet contained either a collection of witchcraft incantations and rituals or a complex witchcraft ritual, it seems reasonable to assume either that the incantation was adapted for use in this witchcraft ritual by the insertion of the line mentioning witchcraft into an already expanded list of evils, or that the incantation, even before it was introduced into this ritual, had already taken on the form known from *KAR* 226 and, therefore, already contained the line mentioning witchcraft. However, since the short version of the incantation (K 2467 +) seems also to be found in a witchcraft context in K 2467 + (obv. r. col. 7′f.: LÚ].UŠ$_{12}$.ZU.MU MÍ.UŠ$_{12}$.ZU.⸢MU⸣ [...] *ru-hi-šú-nu* HUL.⸢MEŠ⸣), the assumption that the incantation was expanded in a direct line of movement from its context in K 2467 + to that in *KAR* 226, while it would account for the addition of the line referring to witchcraft, would not account for the addition of the lines containing the non-witchcraft evils. A detailed reconstruction of the history of the incantation must await either the discovery of more examplars of the incantation or a more precise definition of the overall context of our three tablets, which is presently rendered impossible by their fragmentary state.

Chapter Two

Maqlû VII 119-146 and Related Texts

A. Problem and Explanation

We may now proceed with our detailed examination. In the first text group to be examined, the basic enumeration of evils, which is in list form, seems to have universal use. However, since texts of this group were used primarily against witchcraft, the universal nature of the list of evils does not agree with the use to which these texts were put. How are we to explain this apparent note of discord?

By examining *Maqlû*[11] VII 119-146 we shall see that texts of this group do not possess literary integrity. Rather, they have a long literary history behind them which reflects, at least in part, the process of adaptation from a universal to a particular use.

A reading of M VII 119-146 reveals the following elements: In lines 119-137, the speaker states that he is washing himself in the pure water of Eridu and expresses the hope that all types of evil, which he proceeds to enumerate in list form, may be rinsed off his body together with the wash water and may flow onto a figurine of a substitute. In the following lines, 138-146, he articulates a number of additional wishes, namely, that the substitute bear his sin, that the street release his sin, that another serve as a substitute and receive the evil consequences of an unlucky encounter, that the day, month, and year bring goodness, that Ea, Šamaš and Marduk assist him and, finally, that the witchcraft be released and the *māmīt* take leave of his body.

We are confronted by a text which had universal applicability (121-135), but which seems to have been used for the specific purpose of combatting witchcraft. This use is immediately evident from the following facts: the inclusion of the text in *Maqlû*; the centrality

[11] See Meier, *Maqlû* (*AfO* Beiheft 2), p. 51; for additions and corrections, see Meier, *AfO* 21 79. Henceforth, we shall refer to the series in several different ways: *Maqlû*; Meier, *Maqlû*, (when followed by page number); M (when followed by tablet and line number).

of witchcraft in the last three lines of the text; and the position of the witchcraft entry (135) at the end of the list of evils and in contiguity to the description of the central rite. The text has a disjointed appearance and contains both secondary elaborations which, in part, run counter to the original aim, sense and structure of 119-137, on the one hand, and a number of motifs alien to the witchcraft corpus, such as sin and the substitute, on the other. These observations lead us to assume that M VII 119-146 evolved from a simpler incantation which had universal use and that a long development stands behind the present state of the composition, which in its final form has a synthetic core, namely, 119-137, to which has been added a lengthy appendix, namely 138-146.

B. Texts

The essential correctness of this approach is confirmed by an examination of a number of texts. That our incantation is dependent on, or related to, these or similar texts[12] is clear from the fact that sections of M VII 119-146 constitute part or the whole of these texts. Thus, K 7594:1′ff. // *KAR* 165 rev. 1′ff.[13] contain the core text minus the long list of evils; *JAOS* 59 13, a General Namburbi, contains the basic list of evils;[14] *Or*NS 39 148f., a Namburbi, contains an almost exact version of a number of lines in the appendix;[15] and, most important, *KAR* 269 rev. is a previously unrecognized parallel of our *Maqlû* composition. *KAR* 269 rev. has the same elaborated nucleus as M VII 119ff. However, it has significantly transformed two of the motifs, has introduced minor but significant structural changes and, of greatest importance, does not contain the rather lengthy appendix found in *Maqlû*.

---

[12]That is, their ancestors, descendants or collateral relatives which, for our purposes, amounts to the same thing.

[13]M VII 140, K 7594: 7′, *KAR* 165 rev. 3 and *BMS* 59:16 were already cited together in *CAD* E 180.

[14]Goetze, *JAOS* 59 13, already noted that ll. 3ff. of the text edited there and M VII 123ff. are parallel passages. Cf. now *AfO* 21 79.

[15]Caplice, the editor of the text, already noted the virtual identity of *Or*NS 39 149:23′ff. with M VII 140ff. See below Sec. D, 3.

For the convenience of the reader, to facilitate comparison and because K 7594:1′ff. // *KAR* 165 rev. 1′ff., *KAR* 269 rev., *KAR* 286 and *LKA* 128 have never been edited, we include here transliterations of the relevant parts of these texts.

1.

K 7594:1′-8′ // *KAR* 165 rev.:1′-4′

1′ [*am-si* ŠU^{II}.MU *ub-bi-ib/ba*] SU!.MU
2′ [*ina* A.MEŠ IDIM KÙ.MEŠ *šá ina eri-du*$_{10}$] ⸢*ib!*⸣-*ba-nu-ú*
3′ [*mim-ma lem-nu mim-ma* NU DÙG.GA *šá ina*] SU.MU
UZU.MEŠ.<MU>
4′ [SA.MEŠ.MU] ⸢GÁL-*ú*?⸣ ⸢KI⸣ A.MEŠ *šá* SU!.MU
5′ [*u mu-sa-a-ti*] *šá* ŠU^{II}.MU *liš-šá-hi-iṭ-ma*
6′ *ana* U[GU-*ki*] ⸢*ù*⸣ *la-ni-ki lil-lik*!
7′ *e-ni-tu li-*⸢*na*⸣*-an-ni ma-hir-tú lim-hur-an-*⸢*ni*⸣[16]
8′ *am-hur mi-ih-r*[*a lim*]*-hu-ru-ʾ-in-ni* ⸢ÉN?⸣

2.

JAOS 59 13:3ff.[17]

3 [NAM].⸢BÚR⸣.[BI][18] *lumun šunāte*
4 *idāte ittāte lemnēte lā ṭābāte*
5 *lumun šīrē*! *haṭûte pár-du-te*
6 *lemnūte lā ṭābūte lumun kiš-pi*
7 *ru-he-e ru-se-e up-šá-še-e*
8 *lemnūte šá amēlūte*
9 *li-pit qātē hi-niq immeri*
10 *nīq alpi mim-ma šum-šú nēpeštu bārûte*
11 *ša at-ta-ṭa-lu u*$_4$*-me-šam*

---

[16]*-tu* and *tú* are in *KAR* 165 and K 7594 respectively.

[17]Some changes have been introduced in adapting Goetze's, Caplice's and Meier's transliterations.

[18]Restored on the basis of *LKA* 128 obv. 5.

12 *a-tam-*<*ma*>*-ru ina sūqi ú-kab-*<*bi*>*-su*? *ina a-ha-ti*
13 [^{d}ALÁD/ALÀD H]UL ^{d}UDUG HUL GIG!?
14 [(x) H]UL *di-'*....[19]

LKA 128 obv.

5 NAM.BÚR.BI HUL MÁŠ.GI$_6$.MEŠ
6 Á.MEŠ GISKIM ⸢HUL⸣.MEŠ NU DÙG.GA.MEŠ
7 HUL UZU.MEŠ *haṭ-ṭu-te pár-du-te*
8 HUL.MEŠ NU DÙG.GA *šá li-pit*! ŠU^{II}
9 *hi-niq* UDU.NITÁ SIZKUR SIZKUR-*e*
10 DÙ-*ti* HAL-*te* HUL!.MEŠ UŠ$_{12}$ UŠ$_{12}$
11 UŠ$_{12}$ NÍG!.AG.A.MEŠ HUL.MEŠ *ša* LÚ-*te*
12 GÌR^{II} HUL-*tim* ⸢*gi*⸣*-lit*!*-tú pi-rit-tú*
13 *qu-lu ku-u-ru* SAG.PA.RIM *di-lip-tú*
14 NU DÙG.GA ŠÀ-⸢*bi*⸣ NU DÙG.GA UZU.MEŠ
15 *ár-*[*rat* DINGIR.MEŠ] *ta-zi-im-tú*
16 ⸢x⸣ [xxx] ⸢xx⸣ NAM.TAG.GA
17 [.ME]Š *ma-mit* DINGIR.MEŠ
18 [.ME]Š *la še-ru-te*
19 traces
Break.

KAR 286:10ff.

10 HUL] ⸢Á⸣.MEŠ GISKIM.MEŠ *ha-ṭa-a-ti lem-n*[*a-ti* NU *ṭābāti*
11 (HUL) MÁŠ.GI$_6$].MEŠ *haṭ-ṭa-a-ti pár-da-a-ti lem-na-ti* ⸢NU⸣ [*ṭābāti*

[19]We restore and emend 13-14a on the basis of M VII 128f. Accordingly, HUL at least in 13 (and possibly also in 14) is not the first nominal element in a construct (*lumun*), as previously understood, but an attributive adjective. We suspect, though we are not certain, that a restoration is required at the beginning of 14. If so, the HUL there might also be an attributive adjective, and we would read *di-'u* instead of *di-'i*. For a reading of 14b, cf. *JNES* 19 153.

12 UZU.MEŠ] ⸢*ha*⸣-*ṭu-ti par-du-ti lem-nu-ti* NU [*ṭābūti*
13 *hi*]-⸢*in*⸣-*qi* UDU!.NITÁ! B[AL! SIZKUR?] S[IZ]KUR *li-pit* ŠU^{II} DÙ-*ti* M[ÁŠ.ŠU.GÍD.GÍD (or perhaps N[AM!.UZÚ)
14 Z]É(*martu*) *ha-liq-*⸢*tu*!?⸣ ŠU.SI *ha-liq-*[*tu*
15 HUL *kiš*]-*pi ru-he-e ru-se-e up-šá-še-e* HUL.MEŠ *šá* ⸢LÚ⸣.[MEŠ-*ti*

3.

*Or*NS 39 149:22′-25′[17,20]

22′ *lumna*(HUL) *šu-a-tu*$_4$ *šá iš-šak-na at-ti* ÍD *tab-li ina zu-um-ri-ia*
23′ *e-ni-tu*$_4$ *li-na-an-ni ma-hir-tu*$_4$ *lim-hur-an-ni ma-hi-ru šá lum-ni lim-hur-an-ni*
24′ *u*$_4$*-mu šul-mu arhu hi-du-tú šattu hegalla-šá li-bil-la*
25′ ⸢^{d}*É-a* ^{d}*Šamaš*⸣ *u* ^{d}*Marduk ia-a-ši ru-ṣa-nim-ma*

4.

KAR 269 rev. 1′-13′

Break
1′].ME ⸢x⸣ [
2′ HUL UZU].ME *ha-ṭu-*[*ti par-du-ti* HUL.MEŠ NU DÙG.GA.MEŠ]
(cf. M VII 124)
3′ *li-pit* ŠU^{II} *hi*]-⸢*ni*⸣-*iq* UDU.[NITÁ *ni-iq ni-qi*
4′ *mim-ma šum-šú*] *ni-piš-*⸢*ti*⸣ [LÚ.HAL-*ti*]⸢x⸣ [
(cf. M VII 125)
5′ *ú*]-⸢*kab*!-*bi*⸣-[*su ina* SI]LA *a-*[*tam-ma*]-⸢*ru*⸣ [*ina a-ha*]-*a-*⸢*ti*⸣
(cf. M VII 126f.)

[20] For variants, see the edition.

6′]) ⌈x⌉ *e* ⌈x⌉ [*qu-lu ku-r*]*u ni-*[*is*]*-sa-*⌈*tú!*⌉ [...] ⌈*ni*⌉*-zíq!?-*[*tú*]
(cf. M VII 130)

7′ *mim*]*-*⌈*ma!*⌉ *li-*[*i*]*m-*[*nu mim-ma* NU] DÙG.GA [*šá ina*
<SU.MEŠ-*ia*> UZ]U.MEŠ-⌈*ia*⌉ [...] x ⌈x⌉
(cf. M VII 121f.)

8′ HUL *kiš-pu ru-hu-ú*] *ru-šu-ú*[21] *up-šá-šu-*⌜*ú*⌝ HUL.MEŠ

9′ [*šá* LÚ.MEŠ *šá ina*] ⌜SU⌝*-ia* U[ZU!].MEŠ-*ia* ⌈SA!⌉.[MEŠ]-*ia*

10′ [*ba-šu-ú* KI A].⌜MEŠ⌝ *šá* ⌜SU!⌝*-ia* ⌜*ú*⌝ ⌈*mu*⌉*-sa-*x*-*⌜*ti*⌝

11′ [*šá* ŠU.MEŠ-*ia liš-šá-hi*]*-*⌈*iṭ*⌉*-ma a-na* UGU-⌈*ki?*⌉
[*u la-n*]*i-*⌈*ki?*⌉

12′ [*lil-lik*(*-ma anāku lubluṭ*) LÚ.UŠ$_{12}$].⌈MU⌉ *u* MÍ.UŠ$_{12}$.⌜MU⌝ [...
(cf. M VII 135ff.)

13′ [INIM.INIM.MA *ana* UGU NU MÍ.UŠ$_{12}$.Z]U ŠU.MEŠ LUH-*s*[*i* (or perhaps [*ana* UGU NU LÚ.UŠ$_{12}$.ZU *u* MÍ.UŠ$_{12}$.Z]U ŠU.MEŠ LUH-*s*[*i*)

Maqlû VII 119-146[17,22]

119 ÉN *am-si qa-ti-ia ub-bi-ib zu-um-ri*

120 *ina mê naqbi ellūti šá ina eri-du$_{10}$ ib-ba-nu-u*

121 *mim-ma lem-nu mim-ma lā ṭābu*

122 *šá ina zumri-ia$_5$ šīrē-ia$_5$ šir'ānē-ia$_5$ bašû*

123 *lumun šunāti idāti ittāti lemnēti lā ṭābāti*

124 *lumun šīrī ha-*[*ṭu-ti*] *par-du-ti lemnūti lā ṭābūti*

125 *lipit qātē hi-niq immeri ni-iq ni-qi* (*mimma šum-šú*) *nēpešti bārûti* Core

126 *ša at-ta-ṭa-lu u$_4$-me-šam*

127 *ú-kab-bi-su ina sūqi e-tam-ma-ru ina a-ha-a-ti*

128 *še-ed lem*[*utti*] *ú-tuk-ku lem-nu*

129 *murṣu* [*di*]-' *di-lip-ta*

130 *qu-lu ku-*[*ru ni-is*]*-sa-tú ni-ziq-tú im-ṭu-u ta-ni-hu*

---

[21] Note well this spelling.

[22] See Meier, *Maqlû*, p. 51 and *AfO* 21.

131 *'ú-a a-*[*a*] *hu-uṣ-ṣu hip lìb-bi*
132 *gi-lit-tu$_4$ pi-rit-tu$_4$ a-dir-tu$_4$*
133 *ár-rat ilī* [*m*]*i-hir-ti ilī ta-zi-im-ti*
134 [*n*]*i-iš ilī* [x *n*]*i-iš ilī ni-iš qātē ma-mit* — Core
135 *lum-nu kiš-pi r*[*u-he*]*-e ru-se-e up-šá-še-e lem-nu-ti šá amēlūti*
136 *it-ti mê šá* [*zumri*]*-ia$_5$ u mu-sa-a-ti šá qātē-ia$_5$*
137 *liš-šá-hi-iṭ-m*[*a ana mu*]*hhi ṣalam nigsagilê lil-lik*
138 *ṣalam nigsagi*[*lê* x] x *ár-ni di-na-ni li-iz-bil*
139 *su-ú-qu ù su-lu-ú li-paṭ-ṭi-ru ár-ni-ia*

*** *** *** ***

140 *e-ni-tu$_4$ li-na-an-ni ma-hir-tu$_4$ lim-hur-an-ni*
141 *am-hur mi-ih-ru lim-hu-ru-in-ni*
142 *u$_4$-mu šul-ma arhu hi-du-ti šattu hegalla-šá li-bil-la* — Appendix
143 *^{d}É-a ^{d}Šamaš u ^{d}Marduk ia-a-ši ru-ṣa-nim-ma*

*** *** *** ***

144 *lip-pa-áš-ru kiš-pu ru-hu-u ru-su-u*
145 *up-šá-šu-ú lem-nu-ti šá a-me-lu-ti*
146 *ù ma-mit lit-ta-ṣi šá zumri-ia$_5$*

— — — — — —

Ritual: M IX 164:
[*ana muhh*]*i ṣalam nigsagilê qātēšu imessi*

C. Historical Reconstruction[23]

These texts allow us to reconstruct the history of M VII 119-146. *KAR* 269 rev. and the core text of M VII 119-146, viz. 119-137, derive from a text which had been constructed by means of the insertion of a list of evils taken from a General Namburbi, such as *JAOS* 59 13, into an incantation identical with K 7594 (// *KAR* 165):1′-6′. By

[23] The argumentation and documentation upon which depend a number of the statements made in this section will be found below in Sec. D.

this insertion, the author of the common ancestor of M VII 119ff. and *KAR* 269 rev. specified the generic statement in K 7594:3′f., *mimma lemnu mimma lā ṭābu ša ina zumriya šērēya šērānēya bašû*, by means of a list of evils. This common ancestor was of a general nature and was not primarily concerned with witchcraft.

In the source of the original list of evils and in the common ancestor of M VII 119ff. and *KAR* 269 rev., the witchcraft entry was to be found in proximity to the sequence "evil portended by dreams, by signs and by acts of extispicy," thus in the very heart of the list. In contrast to its position in these texts, the witchcraft entry in M VII 119ff. is situated at the very end of the list (M VII 135), while in *KAR* 269 rev. it is outside the list (*KAR* 269 rev. 8′ff.). In these two texts, the witchcraft entry has been moved from its original position in order to accord it special importance in line with the intention of adapting these texts for primary use against witchcraft.

The differences between these two parallel texts are most instructive. Their chief significance for our analysis lies in the fact that they are indicators of relative chronology and thus enable us to reconstruct the stages of composition.

One of the most important differences is evident in the treatment accorded the witchcraft entry. Although the witchcraft entry in M VII 119ff. has been moved for purposes of emphasis to the final position in the list of evils (135), it remains an integral part of that list. In *KAR* 269 rev., on the other hand, the witchcraft entry (8′ff.) has been removed from the list and set apart from the other evils by being placed after the catch phrase *mimma lemnu mimma lā tābu ša ina zumriya ... bašû* (7′), which appears in this text at the end of the main list in contrast to its position in M VII 119ff. at the beginning of the list (121f.). Moreover, the author of *KAR* 269 rev. has further emphasized the witchcraft entry by repeating the catch phrase in truncated form (*ša ina zumriya ... bašû*) after it.

It is possible that the superior treatment of the witchcraft entry in *KAR* 269 rev. reflects a greater mastery of the techniques of composition and a more critical use of traditional material and, therefore, that the different treatments of the witchcraft entry in the two texts only reflect unequal artistic ability. However, it would be wrong to treat this difference as an isolated phenomenon. The different treatments of the witchcraft entry must be examined and evaluated in conjunction with several other differences and with the respective configurations of the two texts produced by these differences. These other differences are: the fuller form and more heterogeneous character of the list of evils in the core text of M VII 119ff. in contrast to its simple form in *KAR* 269 rev.; the washing over a general substitute in M VII 119ff. (136ff.) in contrast to the washing over a witch in *KAR* 269 rev. (10′ff.); and the development of the appendix in M VII 119ff. (up to 143) along non-witchcraft lines and the complete absence of an appendix in *KAR* 269 rev. The non-witchcraft character of M VII 136-143 must be correlated with the further observations that, apart from line 135 (which belongs to the basic repertoire of the Namburbi type of "Universal Beschwörung" cited earlier), witchcraft is mentioned in M VII 119ff. only in the very last three lines of the text, 144-146, and that a version of 140-143 occurs elsewhere independent of these very last lines.

If the texts are examined from this fuller perspective, it becomes clear that, while *KAR* 269 rev. was adapted for the specialized purpose of combatting witchcraft at a very early stage of the development of the "Universal" core text—prior to the addition of the appendix—, M VII 119ff. was so adapted only after this core text had been stabilized and the appendix up to 143 added, that is, after the text had a long development behind it as a "Universal Beschwörung" type composition. It is further clear that the adaptation of M VII 119ff. for primary use against witchcraft was accomplished by adding the last three lines of the text (144-146), which center on witchcraft, and by shifting the witchcraft entry from its original position in the list of evils to the end of the list.

Accordingly, the differences between M VII 119ff. and *KAR* 269 rev. must first be explained in historical terms before they can serve as criteria for an artistic evaluation. This historical reconstruction of *KAR* 269 rev. and M VII 119ff. indicates that the adaptors of these two texts worked under different conditions and that these conditions imposed different limitations on each. Since *KAR* 269 rev. was adapted at a time when the composition contained only the list of evils and the central rite of washing and since M VII 119ff. was adapted after most of the appendix had already been added to the list and to the central rite, it is clear that the freedom of the adaptor of *KAR* 269 rev. was less narrowly circumscribed than that of the adaptor of M VII 119ff. Therefore, while the adaptor of *KAR* 269 rev. was free to restructure the end of the list and to specify the witch as the object of the transference because these sections came at the end of the text and because the object of the transference had not yet been specified, the adaptor of M VII 119ff. was unable to do so, because, in the period intervening between the adaptation of the text in *KAR* 269 rev. and his own adaptation, a number of lines had already been added to the text, and, therefore, the end of the list and the rite no longer formed the end of the text, and because the general substitute had already been specified as the object of the transference. The adaptor of M VII 119ff. was forced to confine his activities to minor revisions and had to make do with adding a section dealing with witchcraft (i.e., 144-146) to the end of the text as he knew it (143) and with moving the witchcraft entry to the end of the list (135).

It is virtually unthinkable, and, therefore, unfair to expect, that the adaptor of M VII 119ff. could have eliminated the appendix up to 143 (or, for that matter, that either adaptor could have eliminated the various non-witchcraft evils mentioned in the texts), although this section was no longer germane to the central interest of the adapted text. For Akkadian incantations and prayers almost never underwent contraction through the conscious elimination of sections, and, if anything, the most frequent type of change in these texts is that of expansion through the insertion or addition of material.

However, freedom to act does not imply compulsion to act, and while freedom to innovate is a necessary condition for creativity, it surely is not a sufficient explanation of it. Thus, while our historical reconstruction explains why the adaptor of *KAR* 269 rev. was free to restructure the text and why the adaptor of M VII 119ff. did not restructure it, it does not and cannot explain why the adaptor of *KAR* 269 rev. did, in fact, do so. Therefore, while the differences between the two texts can tell us very little about the literary ability of the final adaptor of M VII 119-146, they do point to the conclusion that the adaptor of *KAR* 269 rev. was a master of the techniques of composition and was able to use traditional material critically. To all intents and purposes, we may treat the adaptor responsible for *KAR* 269 rev. as an author who composed an essentially new composition and the adaptor responsible for the present text of M VII 119-146 as a redactor who prepared a final recension.

D. Argumentation

Several of the observations made in the previous section must be more fully documented and expounded. They relate to:

1. the position of the witchcraft entry in relation to the catch phrase and to the list of evils in M VII 121-135 and *KAR* 269 rev. 1′-10′;
2. the recipient and formulation of the rite of transference of evil in M VII 136-139 and *KAR* 269 rev. 10′-12′;
3. the literary source of M VII 140-143;
4. the addition of M VII 144-146 and the shift of the witchcraft entry from its original position to M VII 135.

1. Position of Witchcraft Entry

The division of the basic incantation K 7594 (// *KAR* 165 rev.):1′-6′ (see below Sec. D, 3.) in M VII 119ff. is different from its division in *KAR* 269 rev. While in M VII 119ff. the list of evils follows the catch phrase *mimma lemnu ... ša ina zumriya ... bašû*, in *KAR* 269 rev. the list precedes it. Furthermore, while in M VII 119ff. the witchcraft entry is a member of the list, in *KAR* 269 rev. it is the only entry which stands outside the list. For in this text this entry follows the catch phrase and is independently qualified by a truncated version of it (*ša ina zumriya ... bašû*).

To appreciate these differences and to draw chronological inferences therefrom, we must recognize that, at least in these texts, structure is an expression of purpose and reflects the intentions of the composers. In M VII 119ff. the list of evils is simply inserted after the catch phrase, and the function of the list is to define the generic statement *mimma lemnu ... bašû* in terms of a number of evils one of which is witchcraft. This method of composition, while perhaps somewhat clumsy,[24] is to be expected and is understandable in a text whose concern is "universal." The structure of *KAR* 269 rev., on the other hand, gives clear expression to the centrality of witchcraft and, therefore, must reflect the intention of transforming a "universal" text into one which is primarily concerned with combatting witchcraft. By placing *mimma lemnu mimma lā ṭābu ša ina zumriya ... bašû* (7′), which sums up the list of evils (1′-6′), in clear parallelism with HUL *kišpū ruhû ... ša ina zumriya ... bašû* (8′ff.), the composer of *KAR* 269 rev. has produced an organic and balanced whole in which witchcraft plays a central role. More than just according equal weight to the two components (1′-7′; 8′ff.), this parallelistic structure, which may be classified as that of parallelism of definition or specification, defines all previous evils as witchcraft and thus integrates the two and raises the witchcraft entry to a level of supreme importance.

The very nature of the list of evils found in M VII 119ff. and *KAR* 269 rev. and the fact that similar lists are found in the General Namburbis indicate that originally the lists found in M VII 119ff. and in *KAR* 269 rev. had a "general" purpose. Since the structure of the list in M VII 119ff. reflects such a purpose, while the structure of the one in *KAR* 269 rev. does not, it follows that the structure of the list in M VII 119ff. is the more original and was already to be found in the common ancestor of both these texts. Therefore, while M VII 119ff. developed as a general text continuing the tradition and preserving the structure of this ancestor and adding the appendix up to 143 in line with the "general" purpose, *KAR* 269 rev. deviated from this purpose and broke off from the tradition before

[24] The phrase *mimma lemnu mimma lā ṭābu ša ... bašû* may either occur by itself, as in K 7594:3′f. // *KAR* 165 rev. 1′, in which case it fulfills a generic function, or it may be joined to a list of evils, as in our two parallels. In the latter instance it functions as a catch phrase which sums up all the evils mentioned and includes any left unmentioned. It seems to us that in this latter function it should properly appear at the end of the list. However, since this phrase and its short version *mimma lemnu mimma lā ṭābu* do often occur before the enumeration of specific evils (Cf., e.g., M VII 174-176 and *MVAG* 23/2 23:61ff.), is it possible that its occurrence before an enumeration points to the mechanical (and [sometimes] secondary) insertion of the enumeration? This problem requires a thorough investigation.

the text had been expanded in such a way as to hinder a radical restructuring. While it is true that the composer of *KAR* 269 rev. did not eliminate the general list of evils, he did restructure it in such a way as to create a new composition with a new purpose.

2. Rite of Transference

K 7594 (// *KAR* 165 rev.):1′-8′, *KAR* 269 rev. and M VII 119ff. are built around the rite of washing over an object. The purpose of this rite is to transfer (impending) evil to the aforementioned object. This rite comprises, as it were, two "separate" acts. The evil must first be removed from the body of the patient through the medium of water. This removal is uniformly expressed in the aforementioned texts in the form: *itti mê ša zumriya u musâti ša qātēya liššahiṭma*, and it may, therefore, be taken for granted that this line was present in the common ancestor of *KAR* 269 rev. and M VII 119ff.

The evil removed must then be transferred to another object. This object may be variously specified[25] according to the use to which an incantation is put. In the witchcraft corpus generally the object is the witch represented in effigy.[26] The use of a representation of the witch as the object of the transference differs essentially from the use of a simple substitute; for, while the basic act is neutral and simply serves to transfer the evil, washing over the witch carries the added and essential nuances of reversion, inhibition and revenge. It is in regard to the identity of this object that *KAR* 269 rev. and M VII 119ff. disagree. Following the line quoted above, the several texts read:

K 7594 (// *KAR* 165 rev.): 6′:
6′ *ana* U[GU-*ki*] ⌈*ù*⌉ *la-ni-ki lil-lik*!

---

[25] For example: the River: *mim-ma lem-nu mim-ma* NU DÙG.GA *šá ina* S[U NENNI] A NENNI GÁL-*ú* KI A.MEŠ *šá zu-um-ri-šu u mu-sa-a-ti šá* ŠU^{II}-*šú liš-šá-hi-iṭ-ma* ÍD *a-na šap-lu-šá lit-bal* (*JNES* 15 138:100-102); the ground, see below note 33; the *nigsagilû*, see below note 32; the witch, see below note 26.

[26] See Laessøe, *Bît rimki*, p. 39:37ff., and *passim* in the witchcraft corpus.

KAR 269 rev. 11′f.:
11′ *a-na* UGU-⌈*ki*(?)⌉ [*u la-n*]*i*-⌈*ki*(?)⌉
12′ [*lil-lik*(-*ma anāku lubluṭ*) LÚ.UŠ$_{12}$].⌈MU⌉ *u* MÍ.UŠ$_{12}$.⌈MU⌉ [...

M VII 137-139:
137 ... [... *ana mu*]*hhi ṣalam nigsagilê lillik*
138 *ṣalam nigsagi*[*lê* x] x *arnī dinānī lizbil*
139 *sūqu u sulû lipaṭṭirū arnīya*

It is our contention:

(1) that a text identical with K 7594 (// *KAR* 165 rev.):1′-6′ served as the framework for the common ancestor of M VII 119ff. and *KAR* 269 rev.;

(2) that when this incantation, which had a "universal" purpose, was transformed in *KAR* 269 rev. into one which was primarily concerned with combatting witchcraft, the formulation *ana muhhiki u lāniki lillik* of the common ancestor was retained, and the witch was specified as the object of the rite of transference by the addition of 12′b, the last line in this incantation, in conformity to the normal usage of the witchcraft corpus and as an expression of the clear anti-witchcraft purpose of the transformed text;

(3) that after M VII 119ff. (or, more precisely, its direct ancestor) and *KAR* 269 rev. had branched off from their common ancestor, but before M VII 119ff. was transformed into an incantation primarily concerned with combatting witchcraft, the *ṣalam nigsagilê* (i.e., the general substitute) was specified as the object of the rite of transference in M VII 119ff. by the modification of *ana muhhiki u lāniki lillik* to *ana muhhi ṣalam nigsagilê lillik* (137), and the theme of sin as the burden to be borne by this substitute was introduced by the addition to this text of 138-139.

These contentions depend on a number of individual points, and several of these points must now be established.

M VII 137. M VII 137 reads: *ana muhhi ṣalam nigsagilê lillik.* K 7594 (// *KAR* 165 rev.), the forerunner to the common ancestor of M VII 119ff. and *KAR* 269 rev., and *KAR* 269 rev., one of the two known descendants of that ancestor, agree together against M VII

119ff. in not having this line and in reading instead: *ana muhhiki u lāniki lillik*. From this agreement it must be inferred that: *ana muhhi ṣalam nigsagilê lillik* was not in the common ancestor of M VII 119ff. and *KAR* 269 rev.; the common ancestor had instead *ana muhhiki u lāniki lillik*; *KAR* 269 rev. preserves the reading of the common ancestor; and the *ṣalam nigsagilê* was specified as the object of the rite and *ana muhhiki u lāniki lillik* was changed to *ana muhhi ṣalam nigsagilê lillik*, presently found in M VII 137, only after M VII 119ff. and *KAR* 269 rev. had branched off from their common ancestor.[27]

M VII 138-139. M VII 138-139 center on sin, and 138 develops the theme of the *ṣalam nigsagilê* introduced already in 137. M VII 138-139 are absent in K 7594 (// *KAR* 165 rev.), the forerunner to the common ancestor of M VII 119ff. and *KAR* 269 rev., and in *KAR* 269 rev., one of the two known descendants of that ancestor. From this absence it must be inferred that M VII 138-139 were not present in the common ancestor and that they were only added to the text[28] after M VII 119ff. and *KAR* 269 rev. branched off from their common ancestor. These inferences are supported by the absence of any mention of sin in the basic list of evils found in M VII 123-135 and *KAR* 269 rev. 1′-6′. Furthermore, the demonstrable (see above) absence in the common ancestor of M VII 137, in which line the theme of the *ṣalam nigsagilê* is first mentioned in the text and from which line, therefore, 138 cannot be disassociated, supports the aforementioned inferences insofar as they relate to 138.[29]

We have seen that M VII 137 took on its present form and that 138-139 were added to the text after M VII 119ff. and *KAR* 269 rev. had branched off from their common ancestor. It is possible to delimit even further the (relative) time of these changes. Several considerations render it virtually certain that these changes took place before M VII 119ff. was transformed into an anti-witchcraft text (by the addition of 144-146 and by the shift of 135 to its present position) and, therefore, before the incantation took on the textual

[27] These inferences may find some support in the not infrequent occurrence of *ana muhhiki/ša u lāniki/ša lillik* (in contrast to the general absence of M VII 137) in incantations centering on a washing rite. Also see below note 29.

[28] We are unable to specify the textual or generic source of these lines.

[29] This argument can probably be reversed and used, though with less force, as further support for the absence of M VII 137 in the common ancestor.

form known from the series. These considerations are: (1) in the witchcraft corpus a representation of a witch, rather than that of an undefined substitute, is commonly used in washing rites; [30,31] (2) in any case, a *nigsagilû* appears nowhere else in that corpus;[31,32] and (3) sin plays a neglible role in the witchcraft corpus and is, in our opinion, alien to it.

(While it can be regarded as certain that these changes took place after M VII 119ff. and *KAR* 269 rev. had branched off from their common ancestor and before M VII 119ff. was transformed into an

[30] Contrast M VII 119ff. with *KAR* 269 rev.; and see above note 26.

[31] It is true that the ritual tablet of *Maqlû* prescribes the use of a *ṣalam nigsagilê* in the ritual for VII 119ff. (IX 164: [*ana muh*]*hi ṣalam nigsagilê qātēšu imessi*). It must be emphasized, therefore, that the statements in **M VII 137** and **M VII 138-139** are in no way affected by this usage; for IX 164 is not the original reading of the line, and it was simply modelled on VII 137 and not on the actual ritual or on the (otherwise non-existent [see note 32]) use of the *nigsagilû* elsewhere in the witchcraft corpus. The original text of the ritual is preserved in the Sultantepe recension of the ritual tablet (*STT* 83:72′: [ÉN *am-si* ŠU^{II}].MU *u*[*b*]-*ba*-⌈*ab*⌉ SU LUH ŠU^{II}), and it was replaced by the present IX 164 as part of an overall Kuyunjik expansion of the ritual tablet. We discuss the history of the ritual tablet and its implications for the history of *Maqlû* elsewhere, and the reader is referred to our paper on this topic which was delivered before the American Oriental Society in 1969.

It is interesting to notice that the translation of M VII 137 in *CAD* A/1 310 (" ... the substitue figurine (of my enemy) ... ") reveals that *CAD* is also disturbed by the use of a simple substitute in a witchcraft text. It is possible that when our text was adapted for anti-witchcraft purposes, the figurine of the *nigsagilû* would have been reinterpreted by the reciter as representing the enemy = the witch.

[32] The introduction of the *nigsagilû* into M VII 137f. is perhaps all the more striking in view of the very few appearances of *nigsagilû* in Akkadian contexts; cf. *AHw* s.v. Note that of the three incantation texts cited there, one is our text (VII 137f. [and IX 164]) and the other two are bilinguals: *CT* 17 37 and *LKA* 75 rev. While the former evidences no other similarity to our text, the latter should certainly be compared with it. It is MS Q of Borger's recent edition of the third house of *Bît rimki* in *JCS* 21 1ff. (see 6:46ff. [washing over a substitute; cf. 8:75ff.]), and it is the only MS of this text to have *nigsagilû* ; all the others have *andunānu*. (A few additions to Borger's edition of K 5013 [*JCS* 21 6] can be made on the basis of a copy prepared by Weissbach now in the possession of the Oriental Institute: between obv. 2′ and 3′ W. copied traces of two signs at the beginning of the line and, therefore, obv. 3′ff. should be changed to 4′ff.; W. saw traces of a sign after *le-mut-ti* in rev. 3 and copied traces of a further line after rev. 5.)

anti-witchcraft text, it remains difficult to determine with certainty whether 138 and 139 were added together to the text and whether 138(-139) was (/were) added at the same time as 137 was given its present form. Yet in view of the mention of the *ṣalam nigsagilê* in both 137 and 138, it may be regarded as probable that 138 was added to the text at the same time as 137 took on its present form. Moreover, in view of the mention of sin in both 138 and 139, it might be permissible to assume for schematic purposes that these two lines were added to the text at the same time. However, it must be emphasized that this assumption is questionable. For, in spite of the fact that 138 and 139 are jointly concerned with sin, 139 appears not to have an organic connection with the two preceding lines, since its ritual *Sitz im Leben* is an act of washing over the ground[33] and not over a representation; and 137-139 must be regarded as a literary ((?) and textual) conflation of two similar but distinct motifs.)

Specification of Witch. Although it is sufficiently obvious, it should be noted for the sake of completeness that the specification of the witch as the object of the rite of transference in *KAR* 269 rev. (cf. 12′b-13′) and the addition of 12′b to that text took place after *KAR* 269 rev. and M VII 119ff. branched off from their common ancestor and at the time that the text was transformed in *KAR* 269 rev. into an anti-witchcraft text. That this is the case is evident from the following considerations: (1) the common ancestor of M VII 119ff. and *KAR* 269 rev. was a general text and was not primarily concerned with witchcraft, and the specification of the witch as the object of the ritual is neither normal for nor original to this type of text; (2) neither is the witch mentioned nor is *KAR* 269 rev. 12′b found either in K 7594 (// *KAR* 165 rev.), the forerunner to the common ancestor of M VII 119ff. and *KAR* 269 rev., or in M VII 119ff., one of the two known descendants of that ancestor; and (3) the specification of the witch as the object of a ritual is characteristic of texts primarily concerned with witchcraft.

[33] Cf., e.g., M VII 147f. and *Šurpu* VIII 83-90, especially 89f.: *it-ti* A.MEŠ *šá* SU-*ka u mu-sa-a-ti šá* ŠU^{II}-*k*[*a*] *liš-šá-hi- iṭ-ma* KI-*tum lit-bal* ^{d}*gam-lum a-ra-an-ka lip-ṭ*[*ur*].

3. Source of M VII 140-143

We have repeatedly asserted in the preceding sections that an incantation identical with K 7594 (// *KAR* 165 rev.): 1′-6′ served as the framework for the common ancestor of M VII 119ff. and *KAR* 269 rev. This assertion may appear objectionable to our reader; for he will have surely noticed that lines virtually identical with M VII 140-141 (*ēnītu līnânni māhirtu limhuranni amhur mihru limhurū'inni*) appear in K 7594:7′-8′ // *KAR* 165 rev.3′-4′ (*e-ni-tu li-*⌈*na*⌉*-an-ni ma-hir-tú lim-hur-an-*⌈*ni*⌉ *am-hur mi-ih-r*[*a lim*]*-hu-ru-ʾ-in-ni* ⌈ÉN?⌉). It therefore may appear preferable to our reader to reason as follows: Since M VII 140-141 occur in the very incantation (K 7594:7′-8′ // *KAR* 165 rev. 3′-4′) from which the framework of *KAR* 269 rev. and of the core text of M VII 119ff. ultimately derives, M VII 140-141 must also derive from there and must have been present in the common ancestor of M VII 119ff. and *KAR* 269 rev. This conclusion would, of course, imply that a redactor of M VII 119ff. separated K 7594:6′ (> M VII 137) and 7′-8′ (= M VII 140-141) and inserted 138-139 between them and that the writer of *KAR* 269 rev. purposely omitted K 7594:7′-8′. However, in spite of appearances this is not the case. The identity of M VII 140-141 with K 7594:7′-8′ notwithstanding, these lines were not in the common ancestor of M VII 119ff. and *KAR* 269 rev.

M VII 140-141 cannot be considered apart from 142-143, since – as was already recognized by Caplice[34] – an almost identical version of M VII 140-143 is found in *Or*NS 39 149:23′-25′, which is the middle section of a Namburbi incantation addressed to the River. The absence of M VII 142-143 in K 7594 (// *KAR* 165 rev.), the forerunner to the common ancestor of M VII 119ff. and *KAR* 269 rev., and in *KAR* 269 rev., one of the two descendants of that common ancestor, indicates that M VII 142-143 were not present in the common ancestor. This is supported by the absence elsewhere in the incantation of the gods mentioned in 143 (^{d}*Ea* ^{d}*Šamaš u* ^{d}*Marduk yâši rūṣānimma*). The occurrence of M VII 140-143 as a unit both in our incantation and in *Or*NS 39 149, therefore, raises the possibility that M VII 140-143 form a well established sequence, that all four

[34] *Or*NS 39 151; cf. *CAD* A/2 261.

lines were together in the source from which M VII 142-143 derive and that 140-141 also derive from that same source and were not present in the common ancestor of M VII 119ff. and *KAR* 269 rev.

The task of determining whether this possibility is, in fact, true is complicated by Caplice's assertion that *Or*NS 39 149:23′-25′ "are a quotation from Maqlû VII:140-143 with the substitution of *māhiru ša lumni* (a 'receiver of evil') *limhuranni* for Maqlû's *amhur mihru limhuru'inni.*"[35,36] For if this assertion is correct, the question would be thrown back upon our *Maqlû* incantation, and, assuming that no new evidence were forthcoming, we would be required to conclude that M VII 140-141 were probably present in the common ancestor.

This complication requires that the scope of our inquiry be widened to include the following two separate but related questions:

1) What is the most probable point of origin of M VII 140-143, and does that point of origin support the claim that *Or*NS 39 149:23′-25′ are a quotation from M VII 140-143?

2) If it can be shown that M VII 119ff. is probably neither the point of origin of M VII 140-143 nor the direct source for *Or*NS 39 149:23′-25′, were M VII 140-141 present in the common ancestor of M VII 119ff. and *KAR* 269 rev., or were they added to our text together with 142-143?

1) The probable point of origin of the sequence found in *Or*NS 39 149:23′-25′ and in M VII 140-143 is the Namburbi tradition of the Ea-Šamaš-Marduk and River incantation groups. These lines, as a unit, probably originated either in an Ea-Šamaš-Marduk incantation or in an incantation addressed to the River which was composed under the influence of the Ea-Šamaš-Marduk group and was recited together with it. The occurrence of the sequence in the Namburbi address to the River in *Or*NS 39 149 is probably due, directly or indirectly, to the contact of these two groups, and the immediate source of *Or*NS 39 149:23′-25′ is probably either an Ea-Šamaš-Marduk incantation or another address to the River.

---

35 *Or*NS 39 151. The assertion is not accompanied by supporting evidence or argumentation.

36 *lim-hu-ru-ʾ-in-ni*/*lim-hu-ru-in-ni* is a plural verb and should be normalized *limhurū'inni.*

These conclusions may be inferred from the following considerations (note that almost all the passages quoted below are from Namburbis):

a) In M VII 143 we read: ^{d}*Ea* ^{d}*Šamaš u* ^{d}*Marduk yâši rūṣānimma.* This line clearly reflects the setting of the Ea-Šamaš-Marduk incantations frequently found in the Namburbis and therefore may be regarded as having ultimately originated in that group of incantations.[37] This is confirmed by the actual presence of this line there. In fact, not only this line, but all the lines in M VII 140-143 are present in Ea-Šamas-Marduk incantations. More specifically, we note that each of the three elements in M VII 140-143 (140-141, 142, 143) occurs individually there and that two of them (140-141, 143) occur together:

(i) **M VII 140-141**

*Or*NS 36 31 rev. 4′-6′[38] (Namb.):
... [... *ēnītu*] *līnânni mā*[*hirtu* [39] *limhuranni*] *amhur mihra* [*limhurū'inni*]

KAR 28 obv. 1′f. (Namb.): See below s. (iv).

(*Or*NS 36 10 rev. 10′ [Namb.]:
māhiru limhuranni pē/*ādû lipdânni.*)

---

[37]For lists of the Ea-Šamaš-Marduk incantations, see Kunstmann, *LSS* nf 2, 86ff. and Caplice, *The Akkadian Text Genre Namburbi*, p. 98.

[38]Our citation of this text as an example of the usage of these lines in an Ea-Šamaš-Marduk incantation is predicated on the assumption that the reverse continues the prayer begun in obverse 8′.

[39]The edition reads: *li-na-an-ni-ma* [*ma-hir-tu₄*. However, since the enclitic *-ma* never occurs in the many examples of this sequence known to us, we have attached the *ma* to *māhirtu.* While we follow the edition in restoring feminine nouns, it is just as possible to restore *ēnû* and *māhiru*; cf. *Or*NS 36 10 rev. 10′, *KAR* 28 obv. 1′f. and King, *STC* I, 201: Sm 1704:15f., all of which are quoted below.

(ii) M VII 142[40]

STT 72:74[41] // *STT* 251:38′ (Namb.):
STT 72: U$_4$-*mu šul-*[*mu*] [...]-⌜*šá*⌝ *lib*!?-*b*[*il* !?- ...,
STT 251: ... U$_4$-*mu š*[*u*]*l-mu* ITU *u* MU.AN.N[A!? .... [42]

(iii) M VII 143

KAR 28 obv. 3′ (Namb.): See below s. (iv):

BMS 53 obv. 4 // *KAR* 267 rev. 3:
^{d}*É-a* ^{d}UTU *u* ^{d}AMAR.UD *ia-a-ši* (*KAR*: *ana iá-a-ši*)
ru-ṣa-nim-ma

KAR 267[43] rev. 22:
[^{d}*É-a* <^{d}UTU?>] *u* ^{d}AMAR.UD *ana iá-a-ši ru-ṣa-nim-ma*

PBS 1/1 14 obv. 21-22:
^{d}*É-a u* ^{d}UTU *u* ^{d}AMAR.UD *ia-a-ši ru-*⌜*ṣa*!⌝-*nim-ma*

---

[40] Note that a line similar to M VII 142 may be present after M VII 83 (= M VII 140) in a variant Assur MS of tablet VII. Thus while the end of the incantation M VII 58-83 in the published Kuyunjik MS K 2950 + (Tallqvist, *Maqlû*, II, p. 44) is in the form given in Meier's edition (*ēnītu līnânni māhirtu limhuranni*), the end of this incantation in the Assur MS *KAR* 268 reads: *m*]*a-*^{hi}*hir-tú lim*!?-*hur-an-ni* U$_4$-[...] (obv. 37) [add this to Meier's variorum], and it seems reasonable–especially since there is enough room–to restore M VII 142. In any case, the ending of the incantation in the Assur MS is different from its ending in the Kuyunjik MS.

[41] *STT* 72 was already cited in this connection by Caplice, *Or*NS 39 151.

[42] *STT* 72:75 // *STT* 251:39′ is not intelligible to us.

[43] While *KAR* 267 is not a Namburbi, it does contain a sequence of lines (rev. 17-21) characteristic of that genre.

(iv) **M VII 140-141. 143**

KAR 28 obv. 1′-3′ (Namb.):
[ ] ⌈x⌉ [*ēnû līnânni*]
[*ma*]-⌈*hi*!?-*ru*!? *lim-hur*⌉-*an-ni m*[*i*?-*ihru*? ...]

---

^{d}*É-a* ^{d}UTU ^{d}AMAR.UD *ana iá-ši ru-ṣa-nim-*[*ma*][44]

b) The incantations addressed to the River, of which *Or*NS 39 149 is an example, are open to the influence of the incantations of the Ea-Šamaš-Marduk group. This may be inferred from the joint recitation of incantations belonging to these two groups (cf. *STT* 72:61-87 [Namb.]) and from the appearance of the request to the River to take over the evil as part of the Ea-Šamaš-Marduk incantations (cf. *STT* 251:37′ // 72:73 [Namb.]: [ÍD *lim-hur*]-*an-ni* ÍD *lip-dan*!-[45]-*ni* and *PBS* 1/1 14 obv. 20: ÍD *lim-hu-ra ár*!?-⌈*ni*⌉.[46])

c) Central to M VII 140-141 is the theme of receiving (*mahāru*) evil. It is significant, therefore, that this is one of the major functions of the River. This function is evident from the frequent occurrence of the request to the River to take over (*mahāru*) the evil in incantations addressed to the River and in other incantations.

(i) **Incantations to the River**

*Or*NS 39 135:23 (Namb.):
muh-ri-in-ni HUL *kiš-pe-e* KI.A.MEŠ-*ki lim-hu-ru ka*!-*lu hi-ṭi*!-*ia*

STT 72:82ff. (Namb.):
muh-ri-<*i*>*n*(text: *ir*)-*ni*!(text: *giš*)[47] HUL ... [Í]D *lim-hur-an-ni*

---

[44]Note the interesting scribal error in line 6′ of this text: the first two signs in the line, *lud-lul*, must be transposed and read *lub-luṭ*. The scribe was probably influenced by *lud-l*[*ul*] and *lud-lu*[*l*] at the end of lines 6′ and 7′ respectively.

[45]Both texts have -*kid*- instead of -*dan*-.

[46]This reading follows von Soden's translation of the line (*SAHG*, p. 338). If *lim-hu-ra-an-ni* is to be read instead (so *PSBA* 34 76), is it possible that *ár-ni* at the end of 19 is the object of *limhuranni* (20) and not the subject of the preceding *lirīq* (19)?

[47]Or, *muh-ri-*<*in*>-*ni*!(text: *ir*)-*ma*!(text: *giš*).

ÍD *lip-dan-<<a>>-ni lim-hur* ...

LKA 125 rev. 7f. (Namb.):
H]UL! *šá-a-<tu(?)> muh-ri-in-ni-ma* [...] ... *tab-li.*

(ii) **Other Incantations**

*Or*NS 39 135:16 (Namb.):
[HUL *šú-n*]*u-ti* ÍD *lim-hur-an-ni* ÍD *lip-dan-ni*

Wevers and Redford (ed.), *Essays on the Ancient Semitic World* (Toronto, 1970), p. 7 rev. 12 (Namb.):
⸢HUL⸣ [ÍD] *lim-hur-ma* IGI-*ka lu-bi-i*[*b*]

STT 251:37′ // 72:73 (Namb.): See above s. b)

PBS 1/1 14 obv. 20: See above s. b)

d) Not only do M VII 140-141 appear as a unit in a Namburbi incantation addressed to the River, but even the full sequence of lines found in M VII 140-143 appears as a unit in a Namburbi incantation of this type.

(i) **M VII 140-141**

King, *STC* I, 201: Sm 1704:15-17 (Namb.):[48]
... *e-nu-*[*ú*]
[*līnânni ma-hi*]-⸢*ru*⸣ *lim-hu-ra-*⸢*an*⸣-[*ni*]
[*amhur mihru*] *lim-hu-ru-*[*in*]*-ni*

(ii) **M VII 140-143**

*Or*NS 39 149:23′-25′: See above Sec. B, 3.

[48] Ebeling, *RA* 48 82 n. 3, referred to Sm 1704:15-16 (without transliteration) for his restoration of l. 16 (top) of the text edited there. Perhaps *amhur mihru limhurū'inni* should also be restored there.

e) Neither general nor specific considerations favor the view that M VII 119ff. is either the ultimate point of origin of the sequence found in M VII 140-143 and in *Or*NS 39 149:23′-25′ or the direct source from which *Or*NS 39 149:23′-25′ were quoted.

(i) It is not permissible to appeal to the dating of *Maqlû* in the Cassite period (Schott, *ZDMG* 81 p. XLVII and von Soden, *MDOG* 85 24) in contrast to the dating of the Namburbis in the first millennium (Caplice, *Or*NS 34 105) in support of the dependence of *Or*NS 39 149:23′-25′ upon M VII 140-143. The allegation that the series was composed in the Cassite period remains unproved and is probably wrong. Furthermore, even if that allegation is correct, it may be regarded as certain that M VII 119-146 was not part of the series at that time.[49]

(ii) M VII 142-143 were not present in the common ancestor of M VII 119ff. and *KAR* 269 rev., and, in any case, M VII 143 reflects clearly the setting of the Ea-Šamaš-Marduk incantations and must have originated in that group.

2) If, then, we are agreed that M VII 119ff. is probably neither the point of origin of M VII 140-143 nor the direct source for *Or*NS 39 149:23′-25′, we are ready to turn to our second question: were K 7594:7′-8′ = M VII 140-141 present in the common ancestor of M VII 119ff. and *KAR* 269 rev.? We note that K 7594:7′-8′ (=M VII 140-141) are not present in *KAR* 269 rev. and that M VII 138-139 intrude between K 7594:6′ (>M VII 137; = *KAR* 269 rev. 11′-12′) and K 7594: 7′-8′ (= M VII 140-141). Thus, the occurrence of K 7594:7′-8′(= M VII 140-141) in immediate connection with K 7594:6′ (>M VII 137; = KAR 269 rev. 11′-12′) is supported by neither M VII 119ff. nor *KAR* 269 rev.[50] Since M VII 140-141

[49] The dating of *Maqlû*, as we know it, must be based, in part, on individual studies of the incantations. If anything, a dependence on the General Namburbis and, therefore, a late date for M VII 119ff. is indicated by our study. It may be mentioned here that also on other grounds we think a first millennium date for *Maqlû* more probable. This will be discussed elsewhere.

[50] This is a classic textual situation. Just to cite one other example, "there are instances in which either Matthew or Luke has a different order from that of Mark, while the other omits ... Thus we see that, while it is generally true that either Matthew or Luke supports Mark's order, there are important exceptions when

occur together with 142-143 outside of *Maqlû* in what may well be a well established sequence in the Namburbi genre, it is far more likely that M VII 140-141 were introduced into M VII 119ff. along with M VII 142-143 than that they were in the common ancestor of M VII 119ff. and *KAR* 269 rev., were omitted in *KAR* 269 rev., were separated in M VII 119ff. from M VII 137 by the introduction of 138-139 and were then responsible for attracting 142-143. To sum up: M VII 140-141 were not present in the common ancestor of M VII 119ff. and *KAR* 269 rev., and M VII 140-143 were borrowed from a Namburbi related to, or standing in the same tradition as, *Or*NS 39 148:22′-26′ and added as a unit to M VII 119ff. after this text and *KAR* 269 had branched off from their common ancestor. Since M VII 119ff. had not yet been transformed into an anti-witchcraft text at the time of the addition of 140-143, it may be surmised that its General Namburbi character was probably responsible for attracting these lines.

4. Addition of M VII 144-146 and Shift of Witchcraft Entry

We have seen that M VII 119ff. was originally of a general character and that this character is maintained through 143. This incantation was transformed into an incantation primarily concerned with combatting witchcraft by the shift of the witchcraft entry from its original position either between 124 and 125 or following 127 to 135 and by the addition of 144-146. These changes represent the final redaction of the incantation. These assertions are based on the following arguments:

M VII 144-146. 1) 144-146 are an addition to the text. The addition of these lines is separate from and later than the addition of 140-143.

a) 144-146 are absent in K 7594 (// *KAR* 165 rev.), the forerunner to the common ancestor of M VII 119ff. and *KAR* 269 rev., and in *KAR* 269 rev., one of the two known descendants of that

neither does." (E.P. Sanders, "The Argument from Order and the Relationship between Matthew and Luke," *New Test. Stud.* 15 257.)

ancestor. From this absence it must be inferred that 144-146 were not present in the common ancestor and that they are an addition. This inference is supported by the contrast offered by the centrality of witchcraft in 144-146 and its minor importance in the rest of the text. For elsewhere in the text witchcraft is only mentioned in 135; and, since that entry was already part of the list of evils in the General Namburbis (and therefore also in the common ancestor of *KAR* 269 rev. and M VII 119ff.), witchcraft was simply regarded as one evil among many.[51]

b) The absence of an organic connection between 140-143 and 144-146 and the occurrence elsewhere of 140-143 as a unit independent of 144-146 indicate that the addition of 144-146 is separate from that of 140-143.

c) That the addition of 144-146 is later than that of 140-143 is evident from the fact that while 140-143 continue the tenor of 119-

[51]Only one entry in M VII 121-135 and in the lists in the General Namburbis of the *JAOS* 59 13 group deals with witchcraft or black magic; namely, *lumun kišpī ruhî rusî upšāšê lemnūte ša amēlūti*. None of the entries in M VII 125, *KAR* 269 rev. 3′, *JAOS* 59 13:9f., *KAR* 286:13 and *LKA* 128:8f. (cf. further *AnBi* 12 284:56f., *KAR* 120:4, *KAR* 282 frag. 2:7, *KAR* 226 IV 10, *KAR* 26 obv. 42, *JNES* 15 142:61′, *RA* 50 22 rev. 3) refers, as has sometimes been thought (*JAOS* 59 16, *JNES* 15 143:61′ and note on p. 149 [cf. *CAD* E 245], *AnBi* 12 288 [translation of 284:56], *CAD* H 195), to acts of black magic. Rather, they all refer to evil portents deriving from divinatory activities of the diviner. Within the context of this type of literature this is most clear from *KAR* 286, cited above (note especially *KAR* 286:14 [for *martu halqat* and *ubānu halqat*, cf. recently Labat, *Un Calendrier Babylonien*, pp. 138f. n.4]), from *STT* 63:47′ff., a General Namburbi, for which we have identified the duplicate K 5409a:1ff. (a composite of the relevant lines, K 5409a:2ff. (A) // *STT* 63:47′ff. (B), reads: ⌈KI⌉ LÚ.HAL (B:⌈x⌉) *u* (B: omits) LÚ.ENSI DI-*šú* NU SI.S[Á] *lu ina* SIZKUR SIZKUR *lu ina* NÍG.ŠU.TAG.GA *lu ina*!? DÙ-*ti* LÚ.HAL-*ú-ti lu-u* (B: omits -*u*) ZÉ *hal-qat lu-u* (B: omits -*u*) ŠU.SI *hal-qat lu-u* UZU.MEŠ *ha-ṭu-ti* ...), and especially from *STT* 231 (*JNES* 26 186ff.) [we are indebted to Miss Reiner for the knowledge of this last text.]. For the individual terms see especially *JCS* 11 94, *ZA* 59 210, *AHw* s. *hinqu* and *CAD* B 132:1a. [Miss Reiner suggested to us that *lipit qāti* might refer specifically to the act of touching the forehead of the animal before sacrifice. It is possible that Ebeling had this in mind when he translated that term as "Handanlegung(?)" (*RA* 50 23 rev. 3). Cf., also, *lāpit pūt immeri*, which is translated by *CAD* I 131 as "(the owner) who placed his hand on the forehead of the sheep (before the extispicy) ...." (Gurney, *AnSt* 5 108, in comparing *puhāda lapātu* with this phrase [a comparison implicitly abandoned in *AnSt* 6 163], introduces the "laying on of hands" in Leviticus as a parallel.)]

140, 144-146 through the emphasis on witchcraft deviate from that tenor and agree with the tenor of the environment (i.e., *Maqlû*) in which the incantation is presently found.

2) 144-146 must have been added to the text for a reason. Since these lines center on witchcraft, since they contrast in this regard with the rest of the text and since the incantation is presently used in an anti-witchcraft context (i.e., *Maqlû*), these lines must have been added for the purpose of transforming a text of general character into one primarily concerned with combatting witchcraft.[52]

Position of Witchcraft Entry. 1) The present position of the witchcraft entry in 135 is not its original one, for originally it occurred either between 124 and 125 or right after 127.

a) A simple comparison of M VII 119ff. and *KAR* 269 rev. with the General Namburbis of the *JAOS* 59 13 group suffices to demonstrate that the basic list of evils contained in the common ancestor of M VII 119ff. and *KAR* 269 rev. was indigenous to the General Namburbis of the *JAOS* 59 13 group. The presence of the witchcraft entry in the common ancestor may be inferred, therefore, from the consistent occurrence of this entry in texts of the *JAOS* 59 13 group.[53] This inference receives some confirmation from the presence of the entry in both descendants of the common ancestor. However, since the entry is in a slightly different position in each of these descendants, the confirmatory force of its presence in the two descendants is proportionately weakened, and

[52]The mention of *māmīt* in 146 in no way affects our statement that 144-146 center on witchcraft; for here, as in a number of other passages, the *māmīt* seizure is due to the workings of witchcraft. This will be discussed elsewhere.

[53]The sequence HUL(.MEŠ) $UŠ_{12}$/*kiš-pi* $UŠ_{12}$/*ru-he-e* $UŠ_{12}$/*ru-se-e* NÍG.AG.A.MEŠ/*up-šá-še-e* HUL.MEŠ *šá* LÚ-*te*/.MEŠ occurs in all texts of this incantation type sufficiently preserved to permit judgment (see immediately below b) and above Chapter 1 and notes 1 and 3). This consistent occurrence is all the more striking in view of the absolute absence of the witchcraft sequence in other groups of General Namburbis. Thus, with the exception of the anti-witchcraft subtype (*KAR* 35, *KAR* 36 + 261 and, possibly, *KAR* 37 rev. (!)), none of the published General Namburbi prayers of the Ea-Šamaš-Marduk type listed in Caplice, *The Akkadian Text Genre Namburbi*, pp. 98 and 248f. (*OECT* 6 pl. 22 + *BMS* 62, *CT* 41 23f., *KAR* 387 +, *LKA* 109 and *LKA* 129) contains any mention of witchcraft. This is also true of the one other published General Namburbi, *AnBi* 12 282ff.

further confirmation, while not necessary, would be welcome. It is therefore fortunate that the witchcraft entry itself provides this confirmation; for its very formulation (M VII 135: *lum-nu kišpī* ...) clearly reveals the Namburbi character and derivation of the line, since the form of the entry with introductory HUL is almost never found in normal witchcraft texts, but is the normal form in Namburbis of the *JAOS* 59 13 group and in texts dependent upon them.[54]

b) Since the witchcraft entry is always to be found in proximity to the sequence "evil portended by dreams, by signs and by acts of extispicy" in the *JAOS* 59 13 group of Namburbis (*JAOS* 59 13:3ff., *LKA* 128:5ff., *KAR* 286:10ff.) and in related texts (e.g., *KAR* 226 IV 7ff., *KAR* 26 obv. 37ff.) and since the common ancestor of M VII 119ff. and *KAR* 269 rev. had a general (rather than a witchcraft) concern, the witchcraft entry must have been in the same position in this ancestor as in the aforementioned group of General Namburbis, i.e., following or inserted into M VII 123-127 and *KAR* 269 rev. 1′-5′. The marked similarity between M VII 123-129 and *JAOS* 59 13:3b-14a and, especially, between M VII 126-127 and *JAOS* 59 13:11-12 would seem to require the assumption that M VII 135 was between 124 and 125 in the common ancestor. However, this is an aberrant position, and the writer of *JAOS* 59 13:3ff. almost certainly erred in placing the witchcraft entry between 5-6a and 9f., because he thereby broke up a series of entries referring to extispicy activities. (Contrast *KAR* 286 and *LKA* 128 [Sec. B, 2. above], where the witchcraft entry follows the extispicy series.) If it is correct to restore *KAR* 282 frag. 1:1′-3′ as:

[54]See immediately below b) and above Chapter 1 and note 3 for references, and see above note 53 for the form. Originally HUL in this usage represented *lumun*, and HUL *kišpī* ... was "the evil of witchcraft ..." (and not "the evil (and) the witchcraft ..."). The form *lum-nu* in M VII 135, unless it is a plural (does *lumnu* form a plural in -*ū* ?; if so, cf. *LKA* 128:10: HUL.MEŠ UŠ$_{12}$ ...), represents a scribal re-/misinterpretation of HUL (*lumun*) as *lumnu*. A similar re-/misinterpretation is to be found also in the parallel text, *KAR* 269 rev. 8′. This is evident from the nominative forms (*rušû upšāšû*) there, instead of the more original oblique ones.

a-t[*a-am-ma-ru ina ahâti ukabbisu*]
ina su!-[*qi lumun kišpī ruhê rusê*]
NÍG.AG.[A.MEŠ *lemnūti ša awēlūti*],

we would prefer to assume that the common ancestor of M VII 119ff. and *KAR* 269 rev. had the witchcraft entry between M VII 127 and 128: *KAR* 269 rev. 5′ and 6′.

2) Since the position of the witchcraft entry in M VII 119ff. (135) (and in *KAR* 269 rev. [8′f.]) is different from its position in the common ancestor, this entry must have been shifted from its original position and this shift must have taken place for a reason. Since M VII 135 deals only with witchcraft, since its present position at the end of the list and in contiguity to the description of the central rite highlights and emphasizes the entry, since the incantation is presently used in an anti-witchcraft context (i.e., *Maqlû*) and since 144-146 were added for the purpose of transforming the text into an incantation concerned primarily with combatting witchcraft, 135 must have been shifted from its original position to its present one in order to emphasize witchcraft and for the purpose of the aforementioned transformation.

Final Redaction. Although certainty is out of the question, it may be regarded as highly probable that the witchcraft entry was shifted to its present position in 135 at the same time as 144-146 were added to the text. Moreover–and finally–since 144-146, the very lines which center on witchcraft, are the latest (significant) addition to the text and are (therefore) the last lines in the text and since the text is presently found in an anti-witchcraft context (i.e., *Maqlû*), it may be taken for granted that the addition of 144-146 (and the shift of the witchcraft entry to its present position) represent the final redaction of the incantation and that the version known from *Maqlû* is that redaction.

E. Summary

We may review by way of summary the history of *KAR* 269 rev. and M VII 119ff. from the point at which they branch off from their common ancestor.

The author of *KAR* 269 rev. adapted the text for primary use against witchcraft by restructuring the list of evils so as to emphasize witchcraft and by specifying the witch as the object of the washing ritual in accordance with the standard usage of the witchcraft corpus. *KAR* 269 ends on this note. *KAR* 269 rev. is part of an independent Assur collection or complex ritual parallel or antecedent to the standard complex ritual *Maqlû*.[55]

Maqlû VII 119ff., on the other hand, was not immediately adapted for primary use against witchcraft, and the witchcraft entry was retained in its original position either between 124 and 125 or following 127. Prior to the aforementioned adaptation, the *ṣalam nigsagilê* was specified as the object of the rite by the modification of *ana muhhiki u lāniki lillik* to *ana muhhi ṣalam nigsagilê lillik* (137), and 138-143 were added. While it is possible that the modification of 137 and the addition of 138-143 represent as many as four temporally distinct activities (change of 137; addition of 138; addition of 139; addition of 140-143), it is more probable that they represent no more than two stages of redaction: 137-139; 140-143. In any case, 140-143 derive from a non-extant variant of *Or*NS 39 149:23′-25′. Some time subsequent to these changes in the text, the final redactor (perhaps under the influence of a text like *KAR* 269 rev.[56]) adapted the text for

[55] See Excursus.

[56] Although our suggestion that a text similar to or identical with *KAR* 269 rev. may have been the source of the influence is no more than a convenient guess, it may find some support in the probable presence (see below) of M VII 119-146 on the obverse of the same tablet and, therefore, in the association of these two texts in the scribal tradition. Our reconstruction of *KAR* 269 obv. II 1-3 indicates that these lines are virtually identical with M VII 144-146 (see Excursus). Although the absence of the lower part of obverse I does not permit us to exclude the possibility that *KAR* 269 obv. II 1-3 (= M VII 144-146) are the final lines of an otherwise unknown incantation (if so, this might be the source from which M VII 144-146 derive), it is more judicious to presume that these lines are the final part of M VII 119-146 and that M VII 119-143 were to be found in the presently missing lower part of obv. I. It may also be emphasized that the presence of M VII 119-146 and the parallel incantation *KAR* 269 rev. in the same tablet in no way affects our chronological reconstruction, and, if anything, it further delimits the period in which the changes in M VII 119-146 were made and in which M VII 119-146 was transformed into an anti-witchcraft incantation. For this presence simply indicates that the changes were introduced into M VII 119-146 prior to the writing of this tablet.

primary use against witchcraft by adding the last three lines and by shifting the witchcraft entry to its present position (135) at the end of the list of evils. We may surmise that only then was our composition incorporated, or fit to be incorporated, into *Maqlû*. It is to be noted that the major line of growth of M VII 119-146 was along its terminus (i.e., the material was added in the main to the end of the text).

The results of our analysis are embodied in the following chart which presents in genetic form the course of the composition of M VII 119-146 and the influences or traditions which have entered into its construction.

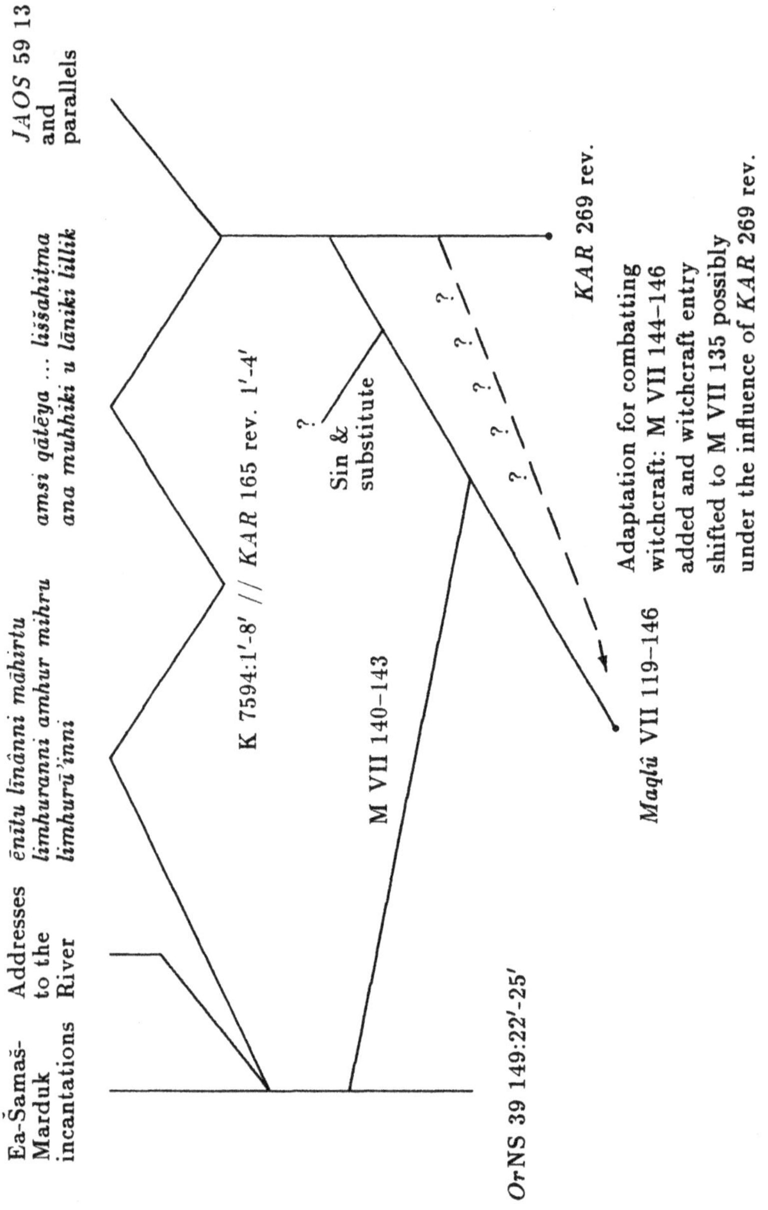
Ea-Šamaš-Marduk incantations
Addresses to the River
ēnītu līnânni māhirtu limhuranni amhur mihru limhurū'inni
amsi qātēya ... liššahitma ana muhhiki u lāniki lillik
JAOS 59 13 and parallels
*Or*NS 39 149:22′-25′
M VII 140–143
K 7594:1′-8′ // *KAR* 165 rev. 1′-4′
? Sin & substitute
KAR 269 rev.
Maqlû VII 119–146
Adaptation for combatting witchcraft: M VII 144–146 added and witchcraft entry shifted to M VII 135 possibly under the influence of *KAR* 269 rev.

Chapter Three

KAR 26 and *BMS* 12

A. Principles and Problems

Before we proceed to the next group of texts, it will be of some value to summarize a few of the more general results which have emerged thus far from our study.

By examining texts related to *KAR* 226 IV and to M VII 119-146, we noticed the existence of actually extant representatives of different stages of development of these two compositions. Our detailed study of the latter group (M VII 119-146) demonstrated that changes introduced into a composition in the course of its development may lead to the emergence of logical, structural and/or contextual anomalies in a specific recension or representative of that composition and that these anomalies are explicable therefore in terms of that development.

This demonstration tends to validate two rather obvious though rarely applied principles: (1) It is to be assumed that every magical text, regardless of its present state , was at one time coherent. While this is perhaps not actually true of every text, the burden of proof is always on the scholar who wishes to deny its applicability to a specific text. (2) Since there is an unfortunate absence of correspondence between texts which contain internal difficulties and texts for which we possess forerunners, parallels and variant manuscripts, it is both proper and necessary to seek a "higher critical" solution of internal textual problems even when, or perhaps especially when, the aforementioned types of witnesses are not extant. This is, of course, not to say that the results reached through a purely internal analysis partake of the same degree of certainty as those reached through a comparison of actually extant texts. But, then, the results of literary criticism, analysis and interpretation never partake of any real certainty, and they can only be evaluated in terms of their likelihood and of their contribution to understanding.

In contrast with the previously examined text group in which the evils were enumerated in list form, the text group to which we now turn comprises prayers in which the evils, including witchcraft, encountered by the sufferer are enumerated and their actions and/or effects described in verbal sentences. These sentences jointly form a lament. These laments present a "scene" in which several "events" take place; and the presentation posits, implicitly or explicitly, a relationship of contemporaneity, identity or causality among its members. However, all too often the presentation appears disjointed and incoherent, and the absence of a clear definition of the relationship existing among all the members, generally, and between witchcraft and the other members, specifically, creates problems of a linguistic, literary and religious nature. How are we to explain the apparent lack of unity and the occasional presence of internal contradiction in these laments?

It seems reasonable to assume that these texts, just as the texts of our earlier group, underwent change and that these changes are responsible for the present appearance of the laments. That this is, in fact, the case and that textual evidence attesting to development and change exists also for this group are evident in varying degrees from a comparison, for example, of *KAR* 23 II 9ff. and *LKA* 40a with *LKA* 57:16ff.; of *BMS* 22:11ff. with *LKA* 56 obv. 11f.; and of *STC* II 75ff. with its Boghazkoi forerunners recently edited by Reiner and Güterbock.[57] These changes may be due to different causes and may serve different purposes. To take just one example: it is clear from the first comparison that witchcraft has been secondarily inserted into the text of a prayer which originally dealt with illness and that this illness has been redefined as having been caused by witchcraft.

While it would be most instructive to compare the variant manuscripts of compositions belonging to this group, very little purpose would be served by this in the context of the present study. For the purpose of this study is to provide examples of several different modes of critical analysis of incantations and prayers (and not to solve all problems of interpretation created by the occurrence of witchcraft terms), and we have already provided an example of the comparative mode. We propose, therefore, to leave an examination of the variant manuscripts of this group for another occasion and

[57]See *JCS* 21 255ff.

to concentrate instead on two well known prayers to Marduk for which, as far as we are aware, manuscript evidence of change does not exist.

Although both *KAR* 26 and *BMS* 12 are known from several examplars, these examplars present, as it were, a united front and are of no real assistance in resolving difficulties found in these compositions. Thus, these compositions can only be analyzed, their history reconstructed and the difficulties found in them resolved by means of a purely internal analysis. These prayers exemplify, as we shall see, diametrically opposed developments: the one, *KAR* 26, a prayer originally concerned with the effects of witchcraft, has been changed into one which has universal applicability and which regards the anger of the gods as the source of the sufferer's difficulty; the other, *BMS* 12, has been reworked so as to have a primarily anti-witchcraft concern. Yet, while each text developed in a direction opposite to that of the other, the configuration in each of internal and contextual phenomena representative of the development parallels that of the other and therefore confirms the analysis of the other.

B. *KAR* 26

1. Lament

KAR 26[58] obv. 35-42 read:

35 [*su*]-[*lim*[59] D]INGIR.MU *ze-ni-i u* ^{d}U.DAR.MU *ze-ni-tú šá kam-lu lìb-ba-šú-nu-ma ze-nu-u* KI-*ia*
36 *ina su-*⸢*hu*⸣*-ur pa-ni u ma-le-e lìb-ba-te* UŠ.MEŠ-*ni*
37 *kiš-pi ru-he-e ru-se-e up-šá-še-e lem-nu-ti šá a-me-lu-ti ip-par*!*-ku-ni-ma*[60] *ina* IGI DINGIR-⸢*ti*⸣-[*ka* GAL]-⸢*ti*⸣
38a *ina pa-an* DINGIR *u* ^{d}U.DAR ⸢*ú*⸣*-šá-áš-*⸢*ki*⸣*-nu-in-ni*
38b AN.TA.ŠUB.BA ^{d}LUGAL.ÙR.RA ŠU.DINGIR.RA ŠU.^{d}INANNA ⸢ŠU.GIDIM⸣.MA
39 ŠU.NAM.ERÍM ⸢ŠU⸣.NAM.<LÚ>.U_x.LU SAG.PA.RIM *u* NU DÙG.GA UZU.MEŠ *iṭ-hu-nim-ma a-na-su-sa* u_4*-me-šam-ma*

[58] An edition of *KAR* 26 was published by Ebeling, *ZDMG* 69 96ff. and improved upon by Meissner, *ZDMG* 69 413f.; von Soden, *SAHG*, pp. 306ff., translated the main prayer to Marduk. For previous discussions of different parts of *KAR* 26, see Kunstmann, *LSS* nf 2 71 and 96f., *SAHG*, pp. 396f. and *AS* 16 294f. *KAR* 26 is duplicated by *AMT* 96/7 (= *KAR* 26 obv. 1-10) // Rm 2, 171 (obv. = *KAR* 26 obv. 1-16; rev. = part of a colophon) (+) Th. 1905-4-9, 117 + K 3268 + 8176 + 6033 (lower part of obv. and upper part of rev. = *KAR* 26 obv. 55 - rev. 25) // K 5937, (= *KAR* 26 obv. 40-55). All the unpublished fragments were already identified as duplicates in the margins of Geers' copies, and some have already been quoted in the dictionaries. For K 6033, see already Kunstmann, *LSS* nf 2 97. Kunstmann, *ibid.*, treated *AMT* 96/7 in conjunction with K 2832 (= *BMS* p. XIX) and concluded that it "ist vielleicht bloss eine Variante" to *KAR* 26. As for the new joins: in the margin of Geers' copy of K 3268 + 8176 (before it was joined to 6033) there is a note (written probably by G. Meier, if we may judge from the handwriting) that it "gehort viell. zur gleich Tafel wie Rm 2, 171." This was confirmed by Mr. C. Walker of the British Museum, to whom we communicated this information. Mr. Walker also confirmed our suggestion that Th. 1905-4-9, 117 joins K 3268 + and informed us that K 3268 + and K 5937 are written in different scripts.

[59] This restoration is based on Meissner's comment, *ZDMG* 69 413, that 35 "muss am Anfange ungefähr ergänzt werden: '(Versöhnt mich mit) meinem zürnenden Gotte' "; cf. also *SAHG* p. 308: "[Versöhne] meinen zürnenden Gott ...." Compare similar passages in *CAD* Z s. *zenû* adj. a2'.

[60] For this emendation, see *CAD* A/1 10 and *AHw* s. *parāku* N1b.

40 DINGIR XX IDIM *u* NUN *ú-šá-as-hi-ru-nin-ni*
41 HUL Á.MEŠ GISKIM.MEŠ HUL.MEŠ NU DÙG.GA.MEŠ
UZU *ha-ṭu-te pár-du-te* HUL.MEŠ NU DÙG.GA.MEŠ
42 TAG ŠU *hi-niq* UDU.NITÁ BAL ⌜ÁB⌝.GUD![61] *ni-piš-ti*
ba-ru-te šá ina IGI-*ia* GIB.[M]EŠ

In its present form, this lament contains the mention of a large number of evils (e.g., anger of the personal gods, witchcraft, the Hand of the god, of the goddess, of the ghost, of the oath and of mankind, evil signs, etc.); and these evils appear to be strung out helter-skelter. To understand this lament we must determine its original form.

Let us begin with 38b-39. Kunstmann, *LSS* nf 2 96f., has already suggested that our prayer had "vielleicht durch Einfügung von Z.38b und 39 aus dem allgemeinen š.-i. Nr. 10 entstanden." Kunstmann's suggestion that 38b-39 are secondary is confirmed by the fact that the long list of evils in these lines breaks up the sequence 37-38a and 40, which seems to belong together. The unity of this sequence is suggested by several texts in which lines comparable to 37-38a and 40 occur in a contiguous and effectual relationship:

AMT 87/1 rev. 1ff. (cf. *BAM* 315 II 42ff.):

DIŠ NA <EN INIM-*šú*>[62] HUL.GIG ZI.KU$_5$.RU.DA DI.BAL.A
KA.DIB.BI.DA *ú-pi-šú* HUL.MEŠ
<<EN INIM-*šú*>>[63] NIGIN-*šu*-[*ma*]
ina IGI DINGIR LUGAL IDIM *u* NUN *šu-uš-kun*-[(*ma*)][64]
UGU IGI-*šú* GIG(= *eli āmirišu maruṣ*)

---

[61] For this emendation, see *JAOS* 59 16.

[62] *AMT* 87/1 rev. 3 incorrectly places EN INIM-*šú* immediately before NIGIN-*šu*-[*ma*]. *BAM* 315 II 42 preserves the correct order, and we have corrected the word order in *AMT* accordingly.

[63] See above note 62.

[64] 4 *R* 55/2:4f. and *AMT* 87/1 rev. 4 suggest a restoration for M IV 64; instead of *ina pâ*[*n* ....]-*zi u bâb bîti ma*-[....] of the present edition, read: *ina* IG[I DINGIR LUGAL/XX IDIM NUN (TIRU) *na-an-za*]-*zi u* KÁ É.GA[L *tušaškininni* ?].

4*R* 55/2 obv. 1ff.:

DIŠ NA EN HUL-*tim* TUK-*ši* ...

....

... UŠ$_{12}$ UŠ$_{12}$ UŠ$_{12}$ NÍG.AG.A.MEŠ HUL.MEŠ
ina NU ZU NIGIN-*šú* DINGIR LUGAL IDIM NUN TIRU
na-an-za-zu ù KÁ É.GAL
KI-*šú ú-šá-áš-ki-nu-ma* [64] ... [65]

The propriety of drawing a comparison between these texts, which center on the activities of an adversary, and ours is indicated not only by the obvious similarities between them, but also by the sequence of entries in 48ff. and 53ff. (See below Sec. B, 2, Prayer.) Moreover, the series of afflictions in 38b-39 and in 54b-55 itself provides internal support for the contention that these lines are secondarily inserted; for ŠU.NAM.LÚ.U$_x$.LU (*qāt amēlūti*), which is part of the series in all its occurrences (obv. 2, 38b, 55, rev. 8, 32) refers to acts of witchcraft initiated by an adversary.[66] Accordingly, this entry is rendered superfluous by l. 37, and therefore both entries may be presumed to have originated from different hands.

Accordingly, 38b and 39 and their repetition in 54b-55 must be regarded as additions to the text of this prayer. Omitting then 38b and 39 as secondary, we would translate 37, 38a and 40 as follows:

[65] Among many additional examples, cf. the following: *AfO* 18 293:66ff.: ^{d}*šamaš šá kiš-pi ru-he-e ru-se-e up-šá-še-e limnūti*[^{meš} ....] / *ilu šarru kabtu*(idim) *u rubû ni-kil-mu-*[*in-n*]*i* / *itti ili u* ^{d}*ištar*(XV) *ú-zi-nu-in-ni ú-lam-me-nu-in-ni* (var. *ú-sah-hi-ru k*[*i-šad-sun*]); M I 4ff.: *aššu kaššaptu ukaššipanni* / ... / *iliya u* ^{d}*ištariya ušessû eliya* / *eli āmeriya amruṣ anāku*; M II 86ff.: *ina kišpī* [*l*]*upputākuma maharka azziz* / *ina pān ili u šarri na*[*n*]*zurākuma* ... / *eli ā*[*meriya mar*]*ṣākuma šapalka akmis*; M I 109: *ila šarra kabta u rubâ ittiya uzannû*; *KAR* 80 rev. 6: [DINGIR LUGAL I]DIM NUN KI-*ia ú-za-an-nu-u*.

[66] That *qāt amēlūti* refers to acts of witchcraft initiated by an adversary is clear, for example, from the overall context of the aetiological diagnosis *STT* 256:11: NA.BI ŠU.NAM.LÚ.U$_x$.LU ⌈UGU⌉-[*šú* GÁL-*ši*]. Note that the description of the patient's misfortunes begins with ⌈DIŠ NA⌉ EN HUL-*ti* ⌈TUKU⌉ (1) (cf. 17: UGU EN KA-*šú* <*ana*> GUB-*zi*) and that the ritual itself is directed against a warlock and a witch (34: ... 2 NU LÚ.UŠ$_{12}$.ZU *u* MÍ.UŠ$_{12}$.ZU *ša* IM DÙ-[*uš*]) who are referred to as kúr.kúr: *nakara* in one of the accompanying incantations (41ff.). See Part Two, notes 35 II 1) and 115.

Witchcraft, charms, spells and evil machinations performed by people[67] have come athwart of me,[68] have caused me to be dismissed[69] from before your great divinity and from before god and

[67] The translation of these terms is conventional and is not meant to be precise. Elsewhere, we will discuss *upšāšû*.

[68] *napruku* refers to a confrontation by ominous happenings which portend and cause a negative chain of events. The ominous force of certain witchcraft phenomena will be discussed elsewhere. Note that *napruku* here and NIGIN in *AMT* 87/1 rev. 3 and 4 *R* 55/2:4 (cf. also *KAR* 80 obv. 6; *AMT* 89/1 II [we have joined this tablet to *AMT* 87/5 - confirmed - and so II = rev. col. V] 11, 16, 19 [duplicate: *KMI* 51, bottom: K 249 + V! 8, 14, 17]; *TCS* II 64 [*LKA* 102] :23) refer to two aspects of the same event: an enemy encircles (NIGIN) his victim with potentially ominous objects/events, and these objects/events then confront (*napruku*) his victim.

[69] Our translation of *ušaškinū'inni* is based on the meaning "to cause to be dismissed" proposed by Jacobsen, *MSL* IV 45* and 48*, for *šuškunu*. Jacobsen (45*) has already cited *AMT* 87/1 rev. 4 in this connection and has translated that line as "he is dismissed from (service) before god, king, magnate and prince." For different translations of *šuškunu* in the passages cited in our text, see *ZDMG* 69 100 and *SAHG*, p. 308 (*KAR* 26); *ArOr* 17/1 188, *CAD* Z 86 and *AS* 16 290 (4 *R* 55/2); *RA* 26 84 (*AMT* 87/1). Note that also in 4 *R* 55/2, "god, king, ..." are probably in the accusative (in spite of *nanzāzu*); and that line should be translated approximately "they (= the witchcraft) have caused god, king, ... to move away from me." While there is a slight difference in perspective between *ila ... ittišu ušaškinūma* (4 *R* 55/2) and *ina pān ili ... ušaškinū'inni* (*KAR* 26), that difference is nonessential and is comparable to the equally nonessential difference between *ila ... ittiya uzannû* (M I 109; *KAR* 80 rev. 6) and *itti ili ... uzennū'inni* (*AfO* 18 293:68). The local force of *šuškunu* is comparable to that of *šussû* (*nesû*) in *iliya u ištariya ušessû eliya* (M I 6) and *ušassi iliya u ištariya ina zumriya* (M III 16). *šuškunu* in this meaning is virtually synonymous with *šushuru* in such a passage as *KAR* 26:40 and with *kišāda suhhuru* in *AfO* 18 293:68 (see above note 65).

It seems to us that the referent of *šuškunu* is not dismissal from service, but rather the dismissal of a petitioner by the powers to whom he turns with a request and from whom he does not receive satisfaction. Such statements in the magical corpus as *STT* 256:10, which is part of a description of a patient's misfortunes beginning with ⌈DIŠ NA⌉ EN HUL-*ti* [TUKU] (1), exemplifies this type of dismissal. *STT* 256:10 reads: *i-na* É.GAL GIN.⌈GIN⌉-*ak* NU IGI-*šú i-qab-bi-ma ul i-šem-*[*mu-šú*], "Whenever he goes to the palace, he is not welcome (?); and when he speaks, no one pays any attention to him." (The reading of IGI-*šú* in this line is either *mahrāšu* or *mahraššu*; this is required by *AfO* 18 298: 16f., *BAM* 315 III 4 // 316 II 7'f., and *STT* 95 III 133 // Bu 91-5-9, 214:6', all of which are quoted below; our translation, however, remains uncertain.) (A further example is *KAR* 26:7, which is a reflex of *KAR* 26:40. Contra *AS* 16 291, *KAR* 26:7, which must be compared to *STT* 256:10, should be translated:

"God, king, magnate and prince treat him contemptuously; he speaks but no one grants him anything.") The opposite of the dismissal described in *STT* 256:10 is found in the statement of purpose of the ritual of this text: Ù.MA-*šú a-na ka-šá-*⸢*di*⸣ *i-na* É.GAL-*šú šal-meš a-na* GIN.GIN-*ki* [...] (16) (cf. *ArOr* 17/1 186f.:6f., 10f., 13 and 190:3f., 6ff.).

Line 40 of this text is most revealing in this regard. According to this line, the ritual will result in KI-*šú* GI.NA.MEŠ *i-tam-mu-ú*. Since this *Verheissung* predicts the results to be expected from a performance of the ritual, the meaning of this line must reflect the statement of purpose of the ritual found in 14ff., as well as the situation to be rectified by the ritual. Accordingly, this prediction should be taken to mean that those to whom the patient will address his requests will grant them, will turn them into "established facts" and will allow the patient to realize his needs or desires; and it should be translated approximately "They will say 'so be it' to him" (compare *annu kīnu* and Hebrew *kēn*). The prediction [... ŠÀ].SÈ.SÈ.KI([*ṣu*]*mmirāta*) KUR-*ad* KI-*šú* GI.NA.MEŠ *i-ta-mu-u* in l. 23 of the related text 4 *R* 55/2 clearly supports this interpretation, since *ittišu* GI.NA.MEŠ *itammû* is closely associated there with the statement "He will attain the desired ends." It must be emphasized that a translation "They will speak truthfully to him" for *ittišu* GI.NA.MEŠ *itammû* in either *STT* 256 or 4 *R* 55/2 would be meaningless.

[Note that when a suppliant prays for *kittu* to be placed in his mouth or for his utterances to be *kittu*, he is not asking the god for moral or ethical direction. Rather, he is expressing the wish that whatever he seeks will be realized; cf., e.g., *KAR* 92 rev. 31 // *LKA* 144 obv. 23 // Rm 247 rev. 11′: *mim-ma ma-la a-qab-bu-u kit-tú*(*LKA*: -*ti*) *lib-ši*, and see especially *AGH* 64:12f. and 106:13f.: *ema uṣammaru/akappudu lukšud šuškin kitti ina pîya* (*šubši amāt damiqti ina libbiya tīru u manzāzu liqbû damiqtī*). Note also the use of *kittu* in an address to Šamaš in his capacity of judge in an anti-witch incantation patterned on a court trial: *KAR* 80 obv. 24 // *RA* 26 40:13(B): *i-ziz-za-ma* [*ina*] *pi*(B: +-*i*-)-*ka li-za-kir kit-tu*(B: -*ti*). Here the petitioner is asking Šamaš to support his cause.]

The opposite of *ittišu* GI.NA.MEŠ *itammû* is *dābib ittišu kitta lā idabbub*. (Contra *AS* 16 290 n. 7, *da-bi-bi* in *da-bi-bi ittišu* ..., 4 *R* 55/2 obv. 3, should be interpreted as *dābib* and not as *da-bi-bu*. The final "*i*" vowel is due to the first "*i*" of *ittišu* [sandhi]. Cf., e.g. *STT* 247:9, K 2562 obv. 6 and the parallel texts Bu 91-5-9, 214:4′, *BAM* 316 II 6′ and *STT* 95 III 131.) The translation "if whoever speaks to him (is supposed to) speak nothing but untruths" (*AS* 16 290) is unacceptable, and this line should be translated: "the one who speaks to him does not say 'so be it' (i.e., does not agree to his requests)." Note especially the association of this statement with the statement that people are angry with the patient or hold him in contempt: cf., e.g., *STT* 247:9f. (*JNES* 26 190): *dābib ittišu kitta lā idabbub eli āmirišu mariṣ*, and *STT* 275 obv. I 6′f.: IGI.DU$_8$.A-*šú* [*n*]*é-kel-mu-šú u* KA.KA KI-*šú kit-tú la* KA.KA-*ub*.

In support of our interpretation of the type of dismissal referred to by *šuškunu*, we must emphasize that the setting of such passages as *AMT* 87/1 rev. 1ff., 4 *R* 55/2 obv. 1ff., *STT* 256:1ff. and (the original setting of) *KAR* 26:35ff. is that of goddess and have caused god, king, magnate and prince to turn away from me.

Lines 41-42, which immediately follow the lines just translated and which form the last two lines of the lament, contain a series of nouns referring to various evils. This series, which we previously encountered in the General Namburbis of the *JAOS* 59 13 group and in texts dependent upon them,[70] is itself followed by the relative pronoun *ša* governing a verb in the subjunctive. Lines 41-42, therefore, do not contain an independent finite verb. Since all the other entries in our lament, in contrast to the entries in the lists of evils in the aforementioned Namburbi group, form syntactically complete and independent sentences, lines 41-42 – if they are to conform to the pattern of the text, be integrated into its structure, and not stand, as it were, in limbo and be suspended in an incomplete state – must stand in relation to a finite verb and must be either the subject or object of that verb. Since these lines form the last entry in the lament, the only option open to us is that these lines are the object of a subject and verb found in the preceding line(s).

And, in fact, von Soden (*SAHG*, p. 309) took line 40 as containing that subject and verb and translated lines 40-42 as follows:

---

conflict with a *bēl lemutti/dabābi/amāti* who wishes to deprive his opponent of a sympathetic hearing and, thereby (at least originally), to win his suit. Compare especially *AfO* 18 298:15-17(= *ibid.*, pl. 15). (The following improvements may be suggested for these lines: read E[N!] INIM-*šú* in 15 instead of "(ras.) *pí-šú*" [cf. *STT* 89:91: ⌜DIŠ⌝ ⌜NA⌝ [*u*]*z-za*⌜*i*⌝*-šu* EN INIM-*šú i-ta-na*[*m-dar-šú*]]; and restore *lā* in 17 [in addition to *STT* 256:10 quoted above, cf. *BAM* 315 III 4 // 316 II 7′f.: *ina* É.GAL-⌜*šú*⌝ (*BAM* 316 omits -*šú*) GUB-*zu la mah-ra-šú* (cf. *BAM* 315 III 13 and 316 II 24′) and *STT* 95 III 133 // Bu 91-5-9, 214:6′: *ina* É.GAL-*šú la mah-ra-šú* (generally Bu 91-5-9, 214 agrees with *BAM* 315 III 1ff., while *BAM* 316 II 5′ff. agrees with *STT* 95 III 130ff.)].) *AfO* 18 298:15-17 read: [DIŠ NA] *id-da-na-bu-šú ina kiš-pi* E[N!] INIM-*šú* / [*it*]-⌜*ta*⌝*-na-ʾ-dar-šú ina* É.GAL GIN.GIN-*ku* / [*la ma*]*h-ra-šu* ....

(Our claim that *šuškunu* in *KAR* 26:38, *AMT* 87/1 rev. 4 and 4 *R* 55/2 obv. 5 does not refer to dismissal from service is, of course, not meant to deny that elsewhere the rejection by god and man may refer to loss of a position and to dismissal from service; see, for example, the consequences resulting from a communicable skin disease [cf. *JCS* 2 207 and *RA* 60 49 and see below Sec. C, 3.])

[70] See above note 3.

> Gott (und) König, Einflussreicher und Fürst liessen mich umgeben sein von bösen Kräften, bösen, gar nicht guten Vorzeichen, Eingeweidebefunden, die voller Fehler, erschreckend, schlimm (und) gar nicht gut waren, von ..., die Hindernisse vor mir auftürmte!

However, this translation, although commendable insofar as it represents an attempt at understanding the text, glosses over a number of difficulties. For not only is the causal relationship between "god, king, etc." and "evil signs, etc." posited by it unparalleled – to the best of our knowledge – elsewhere, but also – and even more important – "god, king, etc." cannot (have) be(en originally) the subjects of *ušashirūninni*, and the nouns in 41-42 cannot (have) be(en originally) the objects of that verb. For, as we have seen above, the subjects of this verb are (/were originally) "witchcraft, charms, spells, etc." found in 37, and "god, king, etc." are (/were originally) the objects of this verb.[71]

Therefore, lines 41-42 neither contain nor are themselves the subject or object of a finite verb. Since these lines are not integrated grammatically into the text (or, if they are integrated, it is a secondary and anomalous integration), they must be regarded as an intrusive addition to the text. Furthermore, since the entries in these lines recur without finite verbs as part of the Namburbi group mentioned earlier and since they reflect the interest in "signs" of these texts, these texts may be regarded as the source from which our lines were drawn.

So far we have seen that of lines 37-42, only 37-38a and 40 were original to the lament and that the lament, therefore, originally centered on witchcraft. Further support for this latter assertion is found elsewhere in the text. Before examining these supporting passages, we must first complete our survey of the lament and examine lines 35-36. These lines are introduced by an imperative and contain the request that the angry gods be reconciled with

[71] The insertions placed within parentheses are intended to cover the possibility that von Soden's translation is correct for the present redaction of the prayer. Let it be said, however, that we consider this possibility to be highly unlikely.

the petitioner.[72] While it is suggestive that the anger of the gods mentioned in these lines is due to events only described in later lines (38a and 40), this in itself is insufficient to impugn the originality of 35-36. However, considerations of literary form do suffice to establish their secondary nature; for, properly speaking, the kind of requests contained in 35-36 should be in the *Bitte* and not in the *Klage*. That this consideration constitutes legitimate evidence of the secondary nature of these lines is indicated by the absence of any other requests in 35-42. And it must be emphasized that our argument is in no way affected (perhaps, it is even supported) by the existence of requests in the preceding lines, 31-34. For, since the requests in 31-34 constitute an appeal to Marduk and Erua to be present[73] and to listen to the plaint, not only are the requests in 31-34, in contrast to those in 35-36, in their proper place, but also the two sets of requests are qualitatively different and those in 35-36 cannot be considered a continuation of those in 31-34.

Since 35-36 do not conform to the expected literary pattern and are the only lines in the lament to contain a request, they may justifiably be regarded as secondary. These lines are the expression of an attempt to make the anger of the god primarily responsible for the various evils encountered in the text – an attempt which is, in fact, contradicted by the original kernel of the lament (37-38a and 40) –, and it is for this reason that these lines were inserted at the beginning of the lament.[74]

---

[72] Assuming, of course, that the restoration ⌈*su*⌉-[*lim*] in 35 is correct; see above note 59.

[73] In 32 perhaps read [K]I-*ka al-si*!?(text: *ka*) (Ebeling, *ZDMG* 69 97, reads [*al*]-*ka al-ka*; von Soden, *SAHG*, p. 308, does not translate this part of the line), and compare 31b-32 (⌈*al*⌉-[*si*]-*ka bēlum ina qereb mušīti* [*it*]*tika alsi*! ᵈ*Eru'a hīrtu narāmtaka rabītu*) with, e.g., M I 1f.: *alsīkunūši ilī mušīti ittikunu alsi mušītu kallatu kuttumtu*.

[74] Possibly the use of imperatives and precatives in 31-34 supported the choice of this position.

2. Prayer and Scribal Framework

Our analysis thus far has revealed that the original lament centered on, and was concerned only with, witchcraft and its effects, but that it was reworked so as to include a number of other evils and to make the anger of the god the ultimate cause of all the difficulties. These conclusions, as well as the analysis upon which they are based, are supported, on the one hand, by the importance of witchcraft in the rest of the prayer and, on the other hand, by its virtual absence in the surrounding scribal framework, where, instead, the very evils which were inserted into the lament and the anger of the god which was made primarily responsible for them are of supreme importance. That is to say: whereas the basic prayer, though it has undergone significant revision, still reveals the intent of the original author, the surrounding scribal framework (in this case: the statement of purpose, the description of symptoms and circumstances and the accompanying amuletic prayer), which may, in principle, be treated as temporally posterior to the main prayer contained therein, expresses clearly the purpose for which the prayer has been revised and, therefore, the new purpose of the ritual.[75]

Prayer. Within the *Bitte* of the main prayer itself the importance of witchcraft is evident from the occurrence of a series of afflictions (HUL.GIG ZI.KU$_5$.RU.DA DI.BAL.A KA.DIB.BI.DA) almost exclusively associated with witchcraft (54a) and from the consistent occurrence and position of the witchcraft entries among the

---

[75] We take the following to be axiomatic:

(1) unless there is irrefutable evidence to the contrary, it must be presumed that if a prayer or incantation contains two (or more) major elements which can be shown to be redactionally distinct and if the scribal framework (ritual, statement of purpose, etc.) agrees with one of these, that one with which the scribal framework agrees is chronologically the later and expresses the purpose for which the prayer or incantation has been reworked;

(2) the scribal framework expresses accurately the purpose for which the prayer or incantation contained therein was recited at the time when that framework was written. If the connection between the prayer or incantation and scribal framework is not apparent or if the scribal framework seems to be partially or wholly contradicted by the prayer or incantation, it follows that either the prayer or scribal framework has been misunderstood by the modern interpreter or that the prayer has undergone revision and adaptation.

attributes describing the amuletic dog used in the ritual (48-50), the actions requested of it (53-54a) and the wishes found at the end of the prayer (rev. 1).

The attributes describing the dog are most instructive, for they point to its function and, therefore, to at least part of the function of the prayer. In *KAR* 26 obv. 48-50(A) // K 5937(B) we read:

48a [*ṭa*]-⌜*ri*⌝-*du lem-nu* GAL$_5$.LÁ[76] *u a*[77]-*a-ba*(B: -*bi*)
48b *na-si-hu kiš-pi* BÚR[78] *r*[*u*!-*he-e ru-se-e up-šá*]-*še-e*
HUL.MEŠ *šá a-me-*[*lu-ti*](B: LÚ-*ti*)
49 *mu-sal-lim* DINGIR *ze-ni-i* ^{d}XV! (restored from B)
ze-ni-⌜*tu*$_4$⌝ (B: -*ti*)
50 *ṣa-bit a-bu-ti a-na* ^{d}AMAR.UD *u* ^{d}A.EDIN
(B: [^{d}*ṣar-pa*]-*ni-tu*$_4$) *be-lí-šu*

The description of the dog in 48a-49 (the attribute in 50 is not germane to the question under study and need not be considered) clearly indicates that its function is to chase away the enemy, to uproot and release witchcraft and to reconcile the angry personal gods. This function must, of course, reflect the function of the prayer and the situation which has called forth the prayer. In fact, not only does the description set out the basic concern of the original prayer, but it does so in an order which reflects the chain of events which has brought the suppliant to his present state: the enemy (used) witchcraft (and thereby provoked) the personal god to be angry with his human ward.

The first two elements in this description of the dog, the enemy and witchcraft, recur in the same order and in the lead position among the actions requested of this same dog in obv. 53ff., and this recurrence confirms the impression gained from 48-50. In fact, the mention of the enemy in both these sequences and, especially, the initial position which he occupies in both support the propriety of our earlier analysis of obv. 37-40 on the basis of the comparison

[76] Contra *AHw* s.v., *gallû* in this line refers not to a demon but to a human enemy. Note that *gallû* is omitted in 53 (*lemna ajjāba kišpī* ...).

[77] So clearly B; in A we should probably read *u*! *a*!-*a-ba*.

[78] The break up of the stereotype *kišpī ruhê rusê* ... is strange. Could BÚR derive from an ancient misreading of the *ru-* of *ru-he-e*?

drawn between those lines and *AMT* 87/1 rev. 1ff. / 4 *R* 55/2 obv. 1ff.; for *AMT* 87/1 rev. 1ff. and 4 *R* 55/2 obv. 1ff. are concerned with acts, including witchcraft, initiated by an enemy.[79]

---

[79] Considering the occurrence of the enemy at the head of the sequence in both 48ff. and 53ff., we would not be at all surprised if the text originally had a line referring to the human enemy who practiced (or incited the practice of) witchcraft, in place of the present 35-36. Remnants of this line might be found in UŠ.MEŠ-*ni* at the end of 36. The occurrence of this word in its present context is somewhat surprising, for, while gods turn away in anger, we can recall no other instance within a prayer of the disenchanted personal god actively persecuting (*redû*, lit. pursues) his human ward in anger. (Moreover, it is possible that this line contains a further internal difficulty in that there seems to be a contradiction between the literal meaning of its first part and that of its verb: *ina su-*⌈*hu*⌉*-ur pa-ni* (*u ma-le-e lib-ba-te*) UŠ.MEŠ-*ni*, "they pursue me with 'turning away of the face' ...." While it is of course possible to eliminate this contradiction by translating the line idiomatically ["They pursue me in anger ..."], is it correct to do so?)

Apropos of an alleged persecution of a human ward by his personal god, a further passage requires some comment. Meier, *AfO* 14 143, followed by *CAD* E 394f. and I 95, translated *AfO* 14 142:38-39 (*ana upšāšê ša ili u il amēli ša ana šūtuqi ša annanna apil annanna qabû*) as "gegen die Machenschaften seitens eines Gottes und des Schutzgottes des Menschen, denen doch befohlen ist, (sie) an dem so und so, Sohne des so und so, vorbeigehen zu lassen, ...", and thus assumed that the personal god actively performed (or initiated the performance of) witchcraft against his ward. A number of objections must be raised against this translation: (1) As far as we know, there is no other instance of the explicit allegation that the personal god performed (or initiated the performance of) witchcraft against his ward. (2) The qualification that the gods are in fact acting in opposition to their own mandate ("denen doch befohlen ist,") is, to say the least, most unusual. (3) If these lines form the final entry in the list of evils which began in l. 34, *ana* should not occur at the beginning of 38, since *ana*, in the meaning "against (the evils)," occurs at the beginning of the list (34) and is nowhere else repeated. (4) The generic concluding entry *mimma i-ba-šu-ú* at the end of 37 argues against taking 38-39 as part of the list of evils.

The following alternative translation of these lines within the context of 34-40 may, therefore, be suggested: "Against (here follow various evils) ..., I have invoked you Lugalgirra by means of the magic of the god and of the personal god of the man, who have been commanded (or perhaps: who have commanded) to avert (the evils) from so and so, the son of so and so." Our translation assumes that *ana* is used in the meaning of *ina* and that *ana upšāšê ša ili u il amēli* is more or less equivalent to *ina upšāšê ša Asalluhi* (so restore *KAR* 355:2 [contra Mullo Weir, *LAP* s. *upšāšû*]: [*ina nar-bi*(*-e*) *šá* ᵈ*É*]*-a* (delete question mark in copy) *ina up-šá-še-e* ⌈*šá*⌉ [ᵈ*Asal-lu-hi*]).

It might be argued in support of Meier's translation that since 37 in his translation (36b-37: "jegliche 'Hand des Totengeistes', von seiten des väterlichen Schutz-

The occurrence and importance of witchcraft in the description of the dog and among the actions requested of it in the main prayer are the more striking and significant by contrast with the absence of any mention of witchcraft in the direct address to this same dog found outside the main prayer in rev. 28ff.

Scribal Framework. This striking contrast calls for an examination of the scribal framework of our prayer. We immediately notice that (with the exception of ŠU.NAM.LÚ.U_x.LU in the series of afflictions which was previously encountered as a secondary insertion in the prayer) witchcraft is mentioned neither in the description of circumstances and symptoms in obv. 1-10, in the address in rev. 28ff., nor in the rubric in rev. 7-8. In the light of this absence, it is significant that that series of afflictions which is restricted to inserted lines within the prayer (38b-39, 54b-55) occurs in the rubric, in the description of circumstances and symptoms (1-2) and in rev. 32 and that the generic HUL Á.MEŠ GISKIM.MEŠ, which headed the inserted Namburbi list (41) and is found nowhere else in the prayer, occurs also in the rubric. This rubric, Rm 2, 171 (+) Th. 1905-4-9, 117 + K 3268 + 8176 + 6033 rev. 6-8(A) // KAR 26 rev. 7-8(B), deserves closer attention:

INIM.INIM.MA *ki-mil-ti*[80] DINGIR(B adds: .MEŠ) DÙ.A.BI
BÚR-*ri* AN.TA.ŠUB.BA ᵈLUGAL.ÙR.RA ŠU.DINGIR.RA
ŠU.ᵈINNANA ŠU.GIDIM.MA
ŠU(B omits[81]).NAM.ERÍM.MA(B omits: .MA)
ŠU.NAM.LÚ.U_x.LU HUL Á.MEŠ GISKIM.MEŠ *a-na* NA NU
TE-*e*

---

gottes und der mütterlichen Schutzgöttin, alles was es gibt, ...") imputes unstated evil actions to the personal god of the father and mother, it is reasonable to expect 38-39 to develop this thought. However, 36b-37 should, perhaps, be translated differently: "every (?) (attack of) 'Hand of a Ghost' of the ghost of the father and the ghost of the mother (*il abi u ištar ummi*), every (evil) which exists, ..."

[80] INIM.INIM.MA *ki-mil-ti* is clear in A; B has *ana*? ⌜xx(x)⌝-*ti*. In view of the reading in A, it probably should be presumed that B also had *kimilti*, although it is presently unrecognizable in the traces in the copy. Note that Yalvaç, *AS* 16 331 n.5, restores here *ana*⌜*ṣi-ib-ta*⌝-*ti*. Unless his reading is based on a collation, it must be regarded as unlikely.

[81] B omits the ŠU in this ideogram also in obv. 55, but has it in obv. 2 and 39.

> The text to release the anger of all the gods so that AN.TA.ŠUB.BA ... not attack the man.

This rubric is especially revealing, for, in contrast to the prayer, it is explicit in making the anger of the god primarily responsible for the various evils.

3. Summary

To sum up: The main prayer to Marduk was originally concerned with attacks of witchcraft and the evil results thereof. This prayer has been reworked essentially by means of insertions. Through this reworking, the prayer has been "universalized" and adapted for use against a large number of unrelated evils, and the anger of the gods has been made primarily responsible for all the sufferings of the suppliant. The scribal framework expresses the new use to which the prayer has been put and evidences a clear verbal connection with those sections of the prayer which have been inserted, but very little connection with the original prayer.

C. BMS 12

1. Strategy

In examining *KAR* 26 we studied first the lament in the main prayer to Marduk and only afterwards the scribal framework. Since it is conceivable that this procedure colored our analysis and results, let us attempt an approximate reversal of that procedure in examining *BMS* 12[82] and study first the scribal framework and only then the lament in the main prayer to Marduk.

2. Scribal Framework and Prayer

Scribal Framework. The scribal framework in *BMS* 12 expresses in unambiguous terms the anti-witchcraft purpose of the text. This is evident from the following:

(1) According to the statement of purpose found in the first line of the text, the purpose of the ritual is: *ana* HUL.GIG DI.BAL.A ZI.KU$_5$.RU.DA KA.DIB.BI.DA KA.HI.KÚR.RA *ana* LÚ NU TE.[83]

[82] For editions of the whole or part of this text, see King, *BMS* 54ff., Hehn, *BA* 5/3 349ff., Ebeling, *AGH* 74ff. and von Soden, *Iraq* 31 82 and 84ff. See *SAHG*, pp. 302ff. (and 396) for a translation and Kunstmann, *LSS* nf 2 71. A further duplicate of *BMS* 12 (or part of a related text) may be the small fragment Sm 2149, which reads: 1′ [... Š]IM.LI / 2′ [...] *an-nu-ti* / 3′ [... AN].HÚL.MEŠ / 4′ [... GIŠ].MEŠ DÙ-*uš* / 5′ [...] ⌈a?⌉ GIŠ.ŠUR.MÌN HI.HI / 6′ [...] ⌈x⌉[(x)] ⌈x(x)⌉. The following correspondences between Sm 2149 (A) and *BMS* 12 (B) may be suggested: A 1′ // B 9; A 3′ // B 11; A 4′ // B 12; A 5′ // B 15. Note, however, that we have been unable to place A 2′, that, if the other correspondences are more or less as suggested, A 5′ should have corresponded to B 13 or to B 14 rather than to B 15, and, finally, that B 15 has *ina* Ì GIŠ.ŠUR.MÌN instead of ⌈a?⌉ GIŠ.ŠUR.MÌN found in A 5′ (we hesitate to read [...A.KA]L in A 5′ because a *hīl šurmēni* is unknown to us).

[83] HUL.GIG is to be read *zīru* or, possibly, *zērūtu* (see *CAD* Z 137) rather then *lumun murṣi* (*AGH* 74:1). Note that a variant writing for HUL.GIG is HUL.IG/K(.KI): thus *KAR* 35 obv.! 17! (= Ebeling's rev. 27) reads KI.ÁG.GÁ HUL.IG DI.BAL.A, for which the parallel text *KAR* 36:10f. + 261:1 has ⌈KI!⌉.[ÁG.GÁ HU]L!.GIG [DI].BAL.A. (Our reading of *KAR* 36 + assumes that Ebeling's line count in *KAR* 261 is incorrect and that there should be another line somewhere between his 2 and 5 which has left no traces in the copy. This assumption is based on the certain correspondence[s]: *KAR* 261:7 + 36:17: ^{d}DIŠ ^{d}UTU [...] [and 261:6 + 36:16, if the referent of the statement in *HKL* 97

This series of afflictions, as we already observed in regard to *KAR* 26:54a, is almost exclusively associated with witchcraft.

(2) The short independent incantation (105ff.) which was recited over an amulet after the recital of the main prayer is primarily concerned with witchcraft. Our understanding of this incantation is confirmed by the marked similarity between it and M VIII 90ff. (the last incantation in *Maqlû*) and *KMI* 76: K8505:17′ff.,[84] which were

---

s. 35 etc. ("n.36 16 entspricht n.261 6, lies *ṣal-lu*; Mitt. von vSoden") is the present 261:6 (whose sign *min* von Soden would then be reading as *ṣal*!) rather than 261:5(*ina*)] and the probable correspondence: *KAR* 36:10-11 + 261:1-2: ... ⌈KI!⌉.[ÁG.GÁ HU]L!.GIG [DI].BAL.A ZI.KURU$_5$.DA ⌈KA⌉.[DIB(.BI).DA ŠÚR.H]UN!.GÁ. Note that our interpretation of *KAR* 35 obv.! 17! is not affected if our reading of *KAR* 36 + is wrong.) This allows us to read *BAM* 214 III 11′ as ⌈HUL!⌉.IK.KI rather than as the more dissatisfying IG[I].NIGIN$_2$ *ik-ki*. We are uncertain of the phonetic implications, if any, of this ideogram. (We have assumed that it should not be emended to HUL.<G/KI>.IG/K(.KI).) Note also the Alalakh writing ú.hul.ki.ga.a cited *CAD* Z 137(now, *MSL* 10 112, note to l. 124). *KAR* 35 and *BAM* 214, a Middle Assyrian copy, have other deviant writings: in the former note KA.DIBI.DA (14) for normal KA.DIB.BI.DA and, in the latter note, e.g., NÍG.NAM for what must be NÍG.NA, and cf. also III 4′f. and 12′f., discussed below.

KA.HI(= DIM.MA).KÚR.RA is probably *šinīt ṭēmi*; cf. *Šurpu*, p. 58 and *AHw* 147b. It must be noted, however, that *BAM* 214 III 12′f. read: DÍM.MA.KÚR-*e u ši-ni-it ṭé-mi*. While we hesitate to posit an additional Akkadian value for KA.HI.KÚR.RA on the basis of *BAM* 214, because *u šinīt ṭēmi* there might conceivably be a misunderstood gloss (note II 7: *li-pi* Ì.UDU and the dittography of I 8f. in 11-13), still the phonetic complement in DÍM.MA.KÚR-*e* is unexpected if this ideogram represents *šinīt ṭēmi*, and this complement is, therefore, most suggestive.

[84]The incantation *KMI* 76: K8505:17′ff. is part of a witchcraft ritual which begins in 12′ and whose purpose is given in 15′. The text reads:

12′ DIŠ LÚ ME.DÍM.BI *it-*⌈*ta*⌉-[*na-aš-pa-ka*
13′ ŠÀ-*šú i'-ta-na-aš* ⌈*it*⌉-[*ta-na-ru*
14′ *a-si-id* ZAG-*šú* ⌈*ú*⌉-[*zaq-qat-su*
15′ *ana ip-ši* HUL.DIDLI *a-na* L[Ú NU TE
16′ *ana ṣíl-lí-šú*/ŠÚ *ša* ŠÀ *kal-li* [... (ÉN *attā ṣillī*)]
17′ *at-ta ba-aš-ti at-ti* ^{d}LA[MÁ
18′ *at-ta ṣíl-lí* GAL *at-ta* ^{d}A[LÁD
19′ *e tam-hur ša-ga-aš-tu*$_4$ *e tam-hur na-*[*kas napišti*
20′ *e tam-hur ú*!(text: *e*)-*pi-ši u rík-si lem-nu-ti* [
21′ [*mim*]-⌈*ma*⌉ HUL *a-a iṭ-hi-a-ka ina qí*!(text: *ku*)-*b*[*it*
22′ [GIM *an*]-⌈*ni*⌉-*a-am tàq-ta-bu-u a* [
23′ [xx] ⌈x⌉ ⌈*tú*⌉/⌈*na*⌉ *diš ma ra ki šu*? [
24′ [...] *ina* ⌈x⌉ [

unquestionably directed against witchcraft.

(3) The incantation *ez-ze-tú*, which in various forms is usually associated with witchcraft rituals,[85] is recited at the end of the ritual (117).

Prayer. Turning to the main prayer to Marduk in this text, we immediately notice that while witchcraft is, in fact, mentioned

---

Notes

12′-14′: A duplicate of 12′-14′ (which provides more restorations than those given in our transliteration) is to be found in *STT* 89, which is a collection of diagnoses. These diagnoses are, at least in part, extracted from texts which contain the full diagnosis and ritual. Thus, for example, compare *STT* 89:18-22 with *AMT* 90/1 rev. III 13ff. (Note further that *STT* 89:23-27 is a duplicate of *AMT* 90/1 rev. III 24ff.) The duplicate of our text is found in *STT* 89:38-42:

38 [DIŠ] ⸢NA⸣ ME.DÍM.BI ⸢it⸣-*ta-na-aš*-⸢*pa*⸣-[*ka* (x)] KÚ-*šu*
39 [x]-⸢*šú*⸣ U[ZU?] (or: bi [x]) ⸢*kul?*⸣⸢*šu*⸣/⸢*ku*⸣ DIB-*su* [ŠÀ]-[*šú*] ⸢*i'*⸣-*ta-na-aš*
40 ⸢*it!*⸣-*ta-na*-⸢*ru*⸣⸢x⸣(or: [x]⸢x⸣) 15-*šú* 150-<*šú*> *is*-⸢x x⸣-⸢*su*⸣
41 *a-si!*(text: na)-*id* 15-*šú* [*ú*]-⸢*zaq*⸣-*qat-su ana* ⸢NA⸣.B[I]
42 [*i*]*p-šú ep-šú*-[*šú*] *i-b*[*al*]-*luṭ*

12′: For the restoration: *it*-⸢*ta*⸣-[*na-aš-pa-ka*...](*KMI*)/*it-ta-na-aš*-⸢*pa*⸣-[*ka*](*STT*), cf. *BAM* 317 rev. 24: ME.⸢DÍM⸣.MEŠ-*šú* DUB.DUB-*ka* and *BAM* 231:2: *mi-na-tu-šu it-ta*-⸢*na*⸣-[*á*]*š-pa-ka* and disregard the restoration *it-t*[*a-na-at-ba-ka*] in *CAD* B 237b.

15′: For the restoration, see already *CAD* I 169.

16′, 18′: The reading *ṣíl-lí* was suggested by W. L. Moran.

16′: ŠÀ *kal-li*: since the preparations in this type of ritual usually involve a *burzigallu* (cf. *Maqlû* IX 188, the ritual for VII 90ff. [Tallqvist, *Maqlû*, II p. 93: K 7586: DUG.BUR.ZI.GAL.SAR; K 8879, Meier, *Maqlû*, p. 64 n. 2: [DUG].BUR.ZI.GAL], and *BMS* 12:14) and since *kallu* is equated with DUG.BUR.ZI.GAL in *MSL* 7 90:268, the signs šà kal li should probably be read *libbi kal-li* and translated "inside a k.-bowl."

17′: For the restoration, see already *CAD* B 143.

20′: The emendation is based on the frequent association of *upīšu* with *riksu*, which we will discuss elsewhere. For the time being, cf. *BMS* 12:109(= *Iraq* 31 89): *e* [*tam-hur*] (we delete von Soden's question marks) *ú-piš kiš-pi lem-nu!-ti!* (cf. *BMS* 12:62). It is possible that the emendation is unnecessary and that *epīšu* is a phonetic variant of *upīšu*; cf. the bilingual texts quoted in *CAD* E 191 s. *epēšu*, where we find níg.ag.a: *e-pi-šu* instead of normal níg.ag.a: *upīšu*.

21′-22′: For the emendation and restoration in *ina qi!-b*[*it* ... GIM *an*]-⸢*ni*⸣-*a-am*, cf. *BMS* 12:114f.

[85] For the use of this incantation in witchcraft rituals, see *AMT* 85/1 rev. VI (= obv. II!) 14, *AMT* 86/1 III 5ff., *Maqlû* V 139ff. (// *PBS* 1/1 13:48, *BBR* no. 26 V 75), *RA* 18 162:27 (?), *KAR* 298 rev. 42 // K 9873 rev. left col. 5′. For its use in different contexts, see *AMT* 95/2 II 16ff., *AMT* 97/1 8ff. and *BAM* 221 III 26ff.

a number of times (54-56, 62f., 81-83) it constitutes only one of the several concerns of the prayer (illness, witchcraft, sin, anger of god and man, evil omens). This is both surprising and perplexing in view of the clear and consistent anti-witchcraft character of the scribal framework, and this situation calls for a closer and more specific comparison between the scribal framework and the main prayer. This comparison reveals that:

(1) None of the witchcraft evils mentioned in either the statement of purpose (1) or in l. 108 of the independent address to the amulet occur in the main prayer itself.

(2) In the main prayer, the description of the results to be attained by means of the aforementioned amulet (67ff.)[86] does not include any mention of witchcraft. This absence contrasts sharply with the importance of witchcraft in the independent incantation (105ff.) which was addressed to that same amulet after the recital of the main prayer.

We notice immediately that the contrast in *BMS* 12 between the section dealing with the amulet in the main prayer and the independent incantation addressed to that same amulet found outside the main prayer is typologically comparable to the contrast in *KAR* 26 between the section dealing with the amuletic dog in the main prayer and the independent incantation addressed to that same amuletic dog found outside the main prayer (rev. 28ff.). In view of this parallel set of contrasts and of our experiences with *KAR* 26, the absence of agreement between the scribal framework and the main prayer to Marduk in *BMS* 12 strongly suggests that the prayer was originally not used (primarily) against witchcraft and that the scribal framework expresses not the original purpose of the prayer contained therein, but a new purpose to which this prayer has been applied.

3. Lament

The worth of this reconstruction is dependent simply upon how well it serves the purpose of explaining the aforementioned absence

[86]These results derive, in part, from the materials from which the amulet is constructed.

of agreement. Since this absence would be understandable if the present use of the prayer against witchcraft was secondary, the reconstruction fulfills its function more than adequately, and it therefore stands on its own merit. This is not, however, tantamount to final verification. Implicit in the reconstruction is the possibility that the prayer was reworked for that purpose which it now serves, i.e. combatting witchcraft. The reconstruction must depend, therefore, for its final verification upon the demonstration that if there is a significant mention of witchcraft in the main prayer, that mention is secondary and was not part of the original prayer. Since it can be demonstrated that the original lament (49-58) was not concerned with witchcraft and that the section dealing with witchcraft in the present text of the lament (54-55 +(?) 56b) was only secondarily inserted, this demonstration constitutes the aforementioned verification of the reconstruction and thereby of the explanation for the absence of agreement between the scribal framework and the main prayer.

We may best establish this point by closely examining lines 54-56 within their immediate context. Lines 49-57[87] read:[88]

49 *muruṣ marṣāku*[89]...
50 *sahpanni kīma šēti kutt[umanni kīma sa]pāri*
51 *alû dihu u tānihu la'bu ... [...] minātiya*
52 *murṣu lā ṭābu nīšu u māmīt ušah[m]û šīrēya*

[87]Cf. von Soden's edition of 49-55 in *Iraq* 31 87.

[88]For variants, see the editions.

[89]See *Iraq* 31 87. If von Soden's reading of B as [*mur-ṣ*]*u* and his deduction that NÍG.GIG in A should, therefore, be read *muruṣ* are correct–and on the face of it they seem reasonable–, we would suggest that NÍG.GIG, e.g., in *AGH* 16:19, 120:7, 108:8 and *TuL* 128:18, all of which attest the usage: *anāku* ... (*ša*/*šá*: *AGH* 16:19, 120:7) NÍG.GIG (...) *imhurannima* ..., also be read *murṣu*. In fact, if we require these lines to be syntactically identical, we could suggest that the two occurrences (*AGH* 108:8 and *TuL* 128:18) which apparently omitted the relative pronoun really read *šá* GIG. (If this is correct, it would confirm the reading of NÍG.GIG in these contexts as *murṣu*.) It has already been noted by von Soden, *Iraq* 31 88, that while *BMS* 12 has NÍG.GIG for *murṣu* in l. 49, it has GIG for it in l. 52. Similarly, *AGH* 16ff., for example, has NÍG.GIG in 16:19 but GIG in 16:20.24 and in 18:27.29. (While we prefer to regard this interchange as proof of von Soden's aforementioned deduction, the possibility must be admitted that it might call it into question.)

53 *šuklulti pagriya la'būma litbušāku kīma ṣu-bat*
54 *ilqû mê<ya?>*[90] *u ṣalmānū'a šunullū*
55 *eper šēpēya šabsū mindātiya leqâ*
56 *ba-aš-ti tab-la-tú ina ipšī lemnūti ša amēlūti lubbāku u lupputākuma*
57 *šibsāt ili u amēlūti bašâ eliya ...*

The acts of witchcraft described in 54-55 are directly (54a, 55a) or indirectly (54b, 55b) due to the actions of a subject who has practiced witchcraft. Furthermore, these acts presume a human, and not a non-corporeal, subject. The illnesses and demons listed in the previous lines can therefore not be that subject.[91] Since we have every right to expect the explicit mention at some point of the nominal or pronominal subject of these acts, its absence suggests that the lines within the lament dealing with witchcraft were secondarily inserted.[92] To determine whether this suggestion is, in fact,

[90]The two MSS which preserve line 54 disagree on its first half. They apparently read (cf. *Iraq* 31 87:54 and note to this line on p. 88):

A: *il*[*iš*]*-qu-u*
B: [x]*-qu-ú* A(*mê*) *ù* } NU.MEŠ-*ú-a šu-nu-ul-lu*

Von Soden, *ibid*, 88, notes: "A schreibt *iš* klein über *il*, in B ist das erste Zeichen abgebrochen. Zum Versrhythmus passt die Lesung *iš-qu-u mê* besser." Von Soden is certainly correct in assuming that the better reading would have included *mê*. It is clear from 55, each half line of which describes an independent act of witchcraft, that 54 should also be so divided and, therefore, that A must have omitted *mê*. However, the very parallelism of the two halves of 54, when viewed in the light of other texts, seems to indicate that the *Vorlage* would have had, not *išqû mê*, but *ilqû mê<ya?>*; cf., e.g., M IV 48ff., *AfO* 18 298:37b-38, *BAM* 231:15f., TCS II 69:12 // *BAM* 205:9'f., TCS II 66:12f., *TCS* II 66:25 // *LKA* 144 rev. 25. For the purposes of our discussion, however, it is immaterial whether the better reading is *ilqû* or *išqû*.

[91]Thus, one must disagree with Ebeling, *AGH* 79, who takes 54 as part of the previous section and punctuates the end of 53 with a comma, and must follow von Soden, *SAHG*, p. 304 and *Iraq* 31 88, who treats 54 as a new sentence.

[92]*A priori* one could assume that the previous lines, which center on illness, replaced a more original series containing a mention of the subject. Our analysis of the lament (see below) points to the connection of 53 and 56f. and, therefore, excludes this possibility. Furthermore, the use of the text in its final form primarily against witchcraft (see above) renders it highly improbable that the section dealing with illness is chronologically posterior to that dealing with witchcraft,

correct, we must examine the surrounding lines in order to determine the extent of the alleged insertion and to ascertain whether the lines surrounding the insertion take on a more unified and meaningful appearance when the lines dealing with witchcraft are treated as an insertion and are excluded.

The occurrence of *ina ipšī lemnūti ša amēlūti* in 56b would seem to indicate that the insertion extends through the end of 56. However it is difficult to simply treat 54-56 as a unit, because (a) 56 is considerably longer than either 54 or 55, and it neither parallels nor develops their poetic form;[93] and (b) more important, the enclitic *-ma* at the end of 56c places the last two verbs (*lubbāku u lupputākuma*) in 56 in a causal relationship, expressed accurately by "so dass" (*SAHG*, p. 304), with 57a, and there is no apparent reason to exclude 57a as secondary. This difficulty calls for a closer examination of 56 and especially of its last two verbs.

The first person stative form of the last two verbs in 56 and the fact that their referent is the pathological-physical state of the suppliant and not acts of witchcraft committed against him lead to the important observation that these verbs contrast sharply with those in 54-55, but are formally and semantically similar to those in 53 (... *la'būma litbušāku* ... *lubbāku u lupputākuma* ...).[94] Especially in view of the *-ma* connective linking 56c with 57, the formal and semantic connections between 53 and 56c and the contrast between these lines and 54-55 indicate that 56c is not part of the insertion, highlight the intrusive nature of the lines dealing with witchcraft and

---

for if that were the case, we would have every right to expect the statement of purpose (1) to be concerned with the illness mentioned in 49-53 and not with witchcraft. See above note 75.

[93]In 54-55 the verbs stand in a chiastic arrangement:

ilqû ... *šunullū*
X
... *šabsū* ... *leqâ*

i.e., 54 begins and 55 ends with a form of *leqû* and the two middle verbal forms begin with *š* and end with *ū*.

[94]Note the first person stative form in both lines; the use of *la'ābu* in the G theme in 53 and in the D in 56; the consistent occurrence of *l-b/p* verbs and the association here, as elsewhere, of *lapātu* with *la'ābu*/*lu''ubu* (for a complementary association, as here, cf. K 3394 [Gray, *SRT* VII] obv. 28′, quoted below in note 117; for *lapātu* as a replacement of *la'ābu*, cf. *JCS* 21 4:29, where one MS reads *ilputušu* instead of *il'ibušu* common to the other MSS).

thereby support the contention that 54-55 (and probably 56b: *ina ipšī ... amēlūti*) are an insertion.[95]

That these conclusions are correct can be finally and irrefutably demonstrated by the existence also of an inner connection between 53, 56a, 56c and 57a, of a direct development of a line of thought in these lines and of a unity of concern in these lines. This unity and the connection between these lines, as well as the very meaning and inner logic of the lament, follow from an understanding of the previously misunderstood nature of the suppliant's affliction described in lines 53 and 56c. The crucial word in these lines is *la'ābu*, which has traditionally been translated "to be/make feverish."[96] In line with this understanding of the word, l. 53, for example, has been translated: "meine Leibesgestalt ist (in) Fieber (versetzt), ...,"[97] or " ... halten meinen gut gewachsenen Leib in (schwerem) Fieber, ..."[98] That fever, however, is not the crucial concern here is apparent from the comparison drawn in this line between the effects of the disease upon the body (*šuklulti pagriya la'būma*) and covering the body with a garment (*litbušāku kīma ṣu-bat*). Especially since a similar simile is applied to the effects of leprosy (*saharšubbâ kīma ṣubāti pagaršu lilabbišma*[99]), the simile applied in 53 indicates that the line is describing the effects of a disease syndrome which severely disfigured the skin and that *la'ābu* is the disease action resulting in that effect.[100] This interpretation is supported by

[95]Further support for our argument that 54-55 are inserted may conceivably be found in the writing of the copula with *ù* in MS B of l. 54 (see *Iraq* 31 87:54). As far as we can ascertain from the published copies and the editions, the copula in all its other occurrences in this text is written with *u*. (Whether and to what extent orthographic features may be used as evidence in a "higher critical" study of SB prayers remains unclear to us and obviously requires a very detailed study.)

[96]Cf. Driver and Miles, *The Babylonian Laws*, II, pp. 227f. Also *la'bu-li'bu* have usually been translated as "fever" (see *ibid.*). More recently, however, it has been recognized that the referent of *li'bu* is "eine schwere Hautkrankheit" (*AHw* s.v.). For other and more recent translations of *la'ābu*, see below note 100.

[97]*AGH* 79.

[98]*Iraq* 31 88.

[99]For this and variant formulations, see JCS 2 205-207, *CAD* Ṣ 224 b2′ and *RA* 60 49.

[100](1) Our discussion of *la'ābu* and the conclusions reached therein are intended to necessarily deny neither the association of this illness with heat or with a burning sensation nor the possibility that fever may occur in crisis periods of

Šurpu VII 25f.,[101] *CT* 39 2:95[102] and paragraphs 148-149 of the *Code of Hammurabi*.[103] The skin effect of this disease probably involved both skin eruptions[104] and a pus-like secretion.[105]

As we mentioned above, the suppliant's physical condition as described in 53 is similar to the physical condition of the leper, and it is this similarity which ultimately leads to an understanding of the connection between 53/56c and 57a and allows us to define the exact force of the enclitic *-ma* which connects 56c and 57a. For the similarity between these diseases in terms of their physical effects suggests that we examine the social consequences or situations resulting from these effects.[106] In curses in which Sin is asked to bring about the affliction of leprosy, we find: "Que (Sin) leur fasse ainsi perdre leur

---

this illness (cf. *Or*NS 22 255f. and *CAD* and *AHw* s. *humṭu*; note that with *CAD* not only *la'bu*, but also *li'bu* is equated with *humṭu* [cf. *BAW* I 74 n. 23]). Nor are our remarks to be construed as a specific and proper diagnosis. (2) We regard also the translation "Strapazieren" (*AHw* s.v.) or "to tire out" (*ANET*[3] 598:66f.) for *la'ābu* as inadequate. (3) The general force of *la'ābu* has already been correctly expressed in Reiner's translation of *Šurpu* VII 25f. (see below note 105) and in the translation of 5 *R* 50 I 57f. (now *JCS* 21 4:29) (lú [d]DÌM.ME.KIL sa.ba.an.dih: *ša ahhāzu il'ibušu*) found in *CAD* A/1 185 ("whom the *a.*-demon has afflicted with a rash").

[101] See below note 105.

[102] See below.

[103] See below.

[104] That the effects of this disease included skin eruptions may be inferred from the fact that dih, which is translated by *la'bu*, *li'bu* and *la'ābu*, is also translated by *aṣû ša ziqti* (*CAD* s. *ziqtu*) and from the equation of *li'bu* with *zi*[*qtu*] (*AHw* s. *li'bu*).

[105] We base this guess on *Šurpu* VII 25f., which in Reiner's edition and translation read: [s]u.na im.mi.in.dih.eš zé.ta ba.an.sù.sù: [*zu*]*-mur-šú il-i-bu-ma mar-ta iz-za-ar-qu-šú*. "They ... covered his body with scab, sprinkled gall on him." Since in this passage "to sprinkle gall" on a person's body is best interpreted as a figurative way of saying that the body is covered with a yellow-green liquid substance, that is, with a pus-like secretion, it may be inferred from the association in this passage of *la'ābu* with "sprinkling gall" that the effects of the disease action to which *la'ābu* refers include a pus-like secretion. The possibility may also be noted that *la'bu*, when associated with the lungs, may refer to a phlegm-like excretion: *AMT* 55/2:4f.: [DIŠ NA HA]R.MEŠ-*šú* NE.MEŠ-*šú la-'-ba* SI.A *u* Ú[H *ina*(?) *pîšu*(?) ... NA.BI HA]R.MEŠ GIG UŠ$_{12}$ DIB-*uš*, "[If a man's lu]ngs are congested/inflamed and are full of phlegm(?), his spittle [... ; that man] is sick in the lungs, (because) witchcraft has seized him (i.e., he has eaten witchcraft)."

[106] For the social consequences of leprosy, see *JCS* 2 207f. and *RA* 60 49 and n. 4.

position au temple ou au palais,"[107] or "May Sin, the luminary of heaven and earth, clothe you in leprosy and (thus) not permit you to enter the presence of god and king; ..."[108] Thus leprosy results in the rejection of the leper by god and man, and for obvious reasons.

Turning to our own passage, we read: *šuklulti pagriya la'būma litbušāku kīma ṣubāt ... lubbāku u lupputākuma šibsāt ili u amēlūti bašâ eliya.* Here also we find the anger of god and man mentioned alongside the effects of a skin disease. In view of the *-ma* connective and on the analogy of leprosy, there can be no question that also here the two are intimately related, that the function of the *-ma* of *lupputākuma* is to express the existence of a causal relationship between them and that the physical effects of the skin disease action *la'ābu*, whose description begins in 53 and continues in 56c, led to the rejection of the sufferer by god and man ("... I have been afflicted and so the anger of god and man is incited against me"). These socio-religious results are probably due here, as with leprosy, not only to the effects of the disease upon the appearance, but also to its contagious nature; and Ungnad was therefore undoubtedly on the right track when he identified the disease from which the wife was suffering in the situation described in paragraphs 148-149 of the *Code of Hammurabi* as "Aussatz."[109]

Our examination of lines 53-57a has revealed that while 53 and 56c-57a logically and continuously develop the theme of the sufferings of a suppliant who was afflicted with a skin disease which severely marred his appearance, lines 54-55 and 56b, which center upon acts of witchcraft, develop an entirely different theme and therefore introduce a logically discordant element into an otherwise coherent narration. When we combine the discordant quality of the lines dealing with witchcraft with the formal and semantic contrasts

[107] This is Nougayrol's (*JCS* 2 207) translation of *BRM* 4 50:18, the first word of which he reads *ma!-za-sa-šu!-nu* (n. 15). *CAD* E 72, however, reads *zāirkunu ištu libbi* É.KUR É.GAL *luhalliq* [...], and translates "may your enemy (?) annihilate [you?] from temple and palace." What does *CAD* do with the *giš* sign before *za-*?

[108] *ANET*³ 538:419f.; we owe the reference to the original publication to *RA* 60 49 n. 4.

[109] We learned of Ungnad's identification from Driver and Miles, *op. cit.*, II, p. 227. However,we can obviously not agree with their judgment that "nor is it anything so specific as *Aussatz* (Ungnad), which has no philological support."

between these lines and those dealing with the skin disease, with the absence of the mention of an explicit subject for the acts of witchcraft and with the fact that the lines dealing with witchcraft are surrounded by lines dealing with a different and unified theme, it must be regarded as established that 54-55 (and probably 56b) are intrusive and were inserted secondarily into the text and that through this insertion the parts of an otherwise coherent and consecutive narration describing the various effects of a skin disease were separated from each other.

These conclusions find further internal support in the fact that they allow us to place 56a in proper perspective and thereby to explain one further anomaly in the text, viz. the unexpected construct form *ṣu-bat* at the end of 53. Since *baštī tablatu* (56a) occurs between the two explicit witchcraft entries, 54-55 and 56b, one might be inclined to construe it as part of the series found in 54-55.[110] However, this is immediately suspect because 56a differs in kind from the entries in 54-55: while the latter refer to mechanical techniques used by the witch,[111] *baštī tablatu* refers to a physical effect.[112] In fact, the loss of *baštu*, "a fine outer demeanor," is explicitly and understandably associated with *la'ābu*; thus, in *CT* 39 2:95 we read: *ina zumur bēlišu baštu innessīma* ᵈLAMA-*šú išannīma illa'ib*, "dignity will be removed from its (the dog's) master, and his looks will change and he will suffer from the *la'bu*-disease."[113] Accordingly, *baštī tablatu* is to be understood as a direct continuation of 53 and as the link between 53 and 56c.

Although we recognize that it is not completely unobjectionable, we would even go so far as to see the insertion of 54-55 as breaking a (secondary) construct. In view of our previous reasons for treating 54-55 as an insertion and 56a as a clear continuation of 53, the occurrence of the otherwise inexplicable construct form *ṣubāt* at the end of 53 and the existence of the substantive *ṣubāt bašti* are most suggestive and would seem to point to the possibility that *ṣubāt* in 53 and *baštī* in 56 formed at one time a construct *ṣubāt bašti*, which

[110] So, for example, *SAHG*, p. 304.

[111] Cf., e.g., *KAR* 80 obv. 30ff. and *passim* in the witchcraft corpus.

[112] This entry should not be confused with M VII 60 and 68.

[113] The text and translation of *CT* 39 2:95 are quoted from *CAD* B 142.

was broken by the insertion of 54-55. However, there are several objections against the assumption that the construct was original. The most formidable technical difficulty is the feminine form of the verb *tablatu*,[114] since it is not in concord with *ṣubāt*, a masculine noun. Since we are unprepared, under the circumstances, to treat *ṣubāt* <<...>> *baštī* as a pure result of chance, we must seek a solution to this problem. There are several conceivable solutions.[115] However, in view of the fact that a skin disease which covers the body is normally simply compared to *ṣubātu* and not to *ṣubāt bašti* and that the loss of *baštu* is associated with *la'ābu* in *CT* 39 2:95, quoted above, it seems preferable (albeit highly conjectural) to reconstruct the following three stages of development:

(1) ... *litbušāku kīma* TÚG(*ṣubāti*); *baštī tablat* ....

(2) A scribe seeing TÚG followed by *baštī* construed the two as forming the construct *ṣubāt bašti* and changed *tablat* to *tablatu* because of the *kīma*. The mutual association of these three words in this scribe's mind might have been reinforced by his knowledge of such a line as *ittabal ṣubāt balti ša zumriša*; *ammēni ... tatbal ṣubāt balti ša zumriya.*[116]

(3) Finally, the insertion of 54-55 broke the construct chain, but left vestiges of it in the construct form *ṣubāt* and in the -*u* of *tablatu.*

On the supposition that 66b, *ina ipšī lemnūti ša amēlūti*, is secondary,[117] the original form of the text may be tentatively reconstructed as:

---

[114]The subjunctive ending -*u* by itself would not constitute a formidable objection, for it might be due to the introductory *kīma.*

[115]E.g., *litbušāku kīma ṣubāt bašti* <*kīma baštu/ī*> *tablatu* (haplography); *murṣu lā ṭābu ... šuklulti pagriya la'būma litbušāku kīma ṣubāt bašti tablatu* (*sic*), "a sore illness, ... have covered my unblemished body with sores so that I am clothed (with them) as one is clothed whose good garment has been taken away (and who wears rags instead)," (the feminine form of *tablatu* would then be explained as an erroneous feminine due to concord with *bašti*, the second half of the construct); etc.

[116]*Descent of Ištar*: *CT* 15 46:60-61.

[117]Although this supposition remains perforce unproved because of M VI 116 and K 3394 (Gray, *SRT* VII) obv. 27′f., we still regard it as legitimate. In fact, we are prepared to venture the guess that the secondary association evident in our text between the skin disease action described by the verb *la'ābu* and witchcraft is ultimately responsible for the images in M VI 116 and K 3394 obv. 27′f. Note that K 3394 obv. 23′-29′ are now complete as a result of our having joined K 3394

šuklulti pagriya la'būma / litbušāku kīma ṣubāti! <*u*?>[118]
baštī tablat!
lubbāku u lupputākuma / šibsāt ili u amēlūti bašâ eliya

A sore illness ...
have covered my unblemished body with sores[119] so that I am covered with them as with a garment (and?) my good looks are taken away;
I am so covered with sores[119] and afflicted that the anger of god and man is incited against me.

---

to K 9866 (confirmed):
23′ *ar-ka-ti la par-*⌈*sa*⌉*-ku at-ma-a-*⌈*a*⌉ *la kul-la-ku*
24′ *dal-ha-ku dul-lu-ha-ku la-'-šá-ku par-da-ku ha-ma-ku da-ma-ku e-šá-ku*
25′ *mar-ṣa-ku ab-ka-ku na-da-ku na-as-*[*sa*]-⌈*ku*⌉ *u šu-ud-lu-pa-ku*
26′ *at-ta-na-'-ba-tú ù ú-zab-ba-lu e-*[*te-ni*]*r-ru-pu e-ti-né-eṭ-ṭú-u*
27′ *at-ta-nak-ta-mu ina* UŠ$_{12}$ UŠ$_{12}$ UŠ$_{12}$ *up-*[*šá-š*]*e-e* HUL.MEŠ NU DÙG.MEŠ
28′ *lu-'-ba-ku lu-up-pu-ta-ku* DINGIR-*ut-*⌈*ka*⌉ [GAL]-⌈*tum*⌉ ZU-*u* ^{d}UTU *at-ta-ma* ZU-*u*
29′ *ana-ku* NENNI ARAD-*ka ana pu-u*[*š-š*]*ur kiš-pi-ia*

(end of obv.; a full edition will appear elsewhere.) It may be of some significance for our study that the duplicate *LKA* 155 (which, we believe, joins 154; a further duplicate, which we have identified, is *LKA* 157) rev. 12-17 has a somewhat divergent text. On the assumption that the coordination of the fragments in the copy is correct, that text reads:
12 [E]GIR.MU *la pa*[*r-sa-ku atmā'a*] ⌈*la*⌉ *kul-la-*⌈*ku*⌉
13 [*e*]-⌈*šá*⌉-*ku* ⌈x⌉ [...] UŠ$_{12}$ UŠ$_{12}$ NENNI [...
14 [...] *šu lu* ⌈x⌉ [...] (perhaps: [... *lu-'-ba-k*]*u*! *lu-*⌈*up*!⌉-[*pu-ta-ku*)
15 [...] ⌈*ku*⌉/*šu* DINGIR *mám-ma* NU ZU-*u* [...
16 [... *at-ta*]*-ma ti-di* ^{d}UTU *ana-ku* ⌈x⌉(=? NENNI!) [...
17 [... *a*]*-na pu-uš-šur kiš-pi-ia* ⌈UŠ$_{12}$⌉ [...

Even if our supposition is disregarded and these passages are interpreted as supporting the primacy of *BMS* 12:56b, it must also be recognized that these passages support our argument that 54-55 are secondary, for they do not associate *la'ābu* with specific mechanics of witchcraft.

It seems to us that 56b, regardless of whether it is primary or secondary, was to be found in our text prior to the insertion of 54-55 and may, in fact, have attracted these lines. This chronology would explain, on the one hand, the separation of the lines dealing with witchcraft into two distinct sections (54-55; 56b) by *baštī tablatu* and, on the other hand, the choice of this awkward position for the insertion of 54-55.

[118] It may be preferable to place *baštī tablat*! at the beginning of the second line.

[119] "Sores" is used to convey the general force of the verb rather than its precise meaning (? sores, pimples, rash, etc.).

It would seem that the witchcraft entries were inserted into the lament in order to make witchcraft responsible for the illness and, therefore, indirectly responsible for rejection by god and man.

We neither need nor intend to extend our detailed analysis beyond these few lines of the lament, though eventually this should be done. Here we would only remark that the first part of the request (60ff.) would seem to support our analysis. The suppliant first asks Marduk to eliminate the illness and to reconcile god and man with him. Only after these two requests, which parallel the core of the lament which we have reconstructed, is witchcraft mentioned (62f.). Thus, witchcraft does not appear in the same relative position in the request as in the lament. Moreover, the witchcraft request is formulated in apotropaic form (*aj iṭhâ*). While this perspective agrees with that of the statement of purpose of the text (*BMS* 12:1) and of the prayer recited over the amulet (105ff.), it does not agree with the general import of the lament, for there the effects of witchcraft are viewed as already having been actualized. This discrepancy is due to the redactor's attempt to integrate witchcraft structurally and causally into the original lament, rather than to simply affix it as he did in the request, and therefore the context of the lament in which the witchcraft entry was to be embedded determined its form and meaning.

D. Conclusion

In examining *KAR* 26 and *BMS* 12 we discovered that the same type of relationship obtains in both these texts between the scribal framework and the main prayer to Marduk, that the scribal framework expresses not the original purpose of the prayer to Marduk contained therein, but rather the purpose for which that prayer has been reworked and that the framework agrees with the very lines which were secondarily inserted. Thus the scribal framework in *KAR* 26 expresses the "universal" purpose for which a prayer which originally centered on witchcraft and its effects was revised, and the scribal framework in *BMS* 12 expresses the anti-witchcraft purpose for which a prayer which orginally centered on a skin disease and its effects was revised. Although the development of the intention of these two texts is in opposite directions, the dynamics and formal expression of the development are essentially similar. The parallel configurations of the two texts confirm therefore the pattern and development we claim to have identified in each.

* * *

It is more than possible that a number of points made in our study of these Akkadian incantations and prayers will prove to be wrong. We hope, however, that our examination of these few texts will have provided some further, albeit limited, insight into the process of growth of Akkadian incantations and prayers and will have supported the claim that the understanding of these texts may often depend on an understanding of their literary history.

Excursus

We are presently unable to determine whether *KAR* 269 is a collection of incantations and rituals or a consecutive complex ritual, though we tend to think the latter more probable. In either case, it is closely related to *Maqlû*:

(1) Obv.(?) I 5′ (Ebeling's 4)-12′ is a parallel of M V 1-10. Note the absence of M V 4-5.[120]

(2) Obv.(?) II 1-3 = M VII 144-147.[121]

(3) Obv.(?) II 4-15 is related to the incantations in *Maqlû* which center on *kibrītu*. Cf. M VI 73-110 and compare especially obv. II 4 with M VI 78; obv. II 5 with M VI 73 (AN-*e* should probably be emended to DINGIR.MEŠ), 109 and Sm 352 rev. 16′; obv. II 6, 9 and 10 with M VI 105; obv. II 7 with M VI 80; obv. II 8 with M III 77, 88 and Tallqvist, *Maqlû*, II p. 96: K 8112 left col. 5: [*u anāku kīma* ᵈÍD *ina* KUR-*i*]*a lu el-le-ku.*

(4) Rev.(?) 1′-12′ is the parallel of M VII 119ff. discussed above.

One should study this Assur text in conjunction with *KAR* 226, part of which was edited above (Chapter 1). It is tempting to assume, though this remains completely uncertain, that these two texts form part of one sequence.[122]

We present below transliterations of these two tablets omitting those parts which have already been edited in the text of our study.

[120] Exegetical considerations seem to favor the originality of the absence.

[121] See above note 56 and below note 127.

[122] The frequent use of double dividing lines in *KAR* 269 seems to preclude the possibility that the two texts are from the same tablet.

KAR 226

Col. I (?)

1′]ka
2′] ⸢TU_6⸣.ÉN

3′]ZÌ.DA HUR.MEŠ ŠID-*nu*

4′ [...] *ki ka*-(?)*lu* UZU.MEŠ-*ia*
5′ [... -*i*]*a tu-ab-bi-ti bu-un-na-ni-ia*
6′ [...] *tu-kàs-si-in-ni tu-ṣab-bi-ti-in-ni*
7′ [x] ⸢x⸣-*ni man-ga ù lu-ʾ-ta tu-mal-li-in-ni*
8′ [x x] *ha-ah-ha ru-ʾ-ta ù su-a-la tu-šam-ri-ṣi-ni*
9′ [*nīš*] ŠÀ-*bi-ia te-ki-mi-ma* ŠÀ-*bi* KI-*ia tu-ze-en-ni-i*
10′ *e-mu-qi-ia tu-un-ni-ši a-hi-ia ta-áš-pu-ki bir-ki-ia*
11′ *tu-kàs-si-i ir-ta ù nag-la-ba tu-šam-ri-ṣi-ni*
12′ *mé-eš-re-te-ia ki-ma* ŠE+$MUNU_x$(= DIM_4)! *tah-šu-li*
13′ *mi-na-te-ia ki-ma i-ša-a-te tu-ha-am-mì-ṭí*
14′ *lip-šu-ru-ki* ^{d}*A-nu u An-tum* :(=GAM) *lip-šu-ru-ki* ^{d}BE *u* ^{d}*Nin-líl*
15′ *lip-šu-ru-ki* ^{d}*É-a u* ^{d}*Dam-ki-na* : *lip-šu-ru-ki* ^{d}IZI.GAR(=*Gira*?) *u* ^{d}ENŠADA
16′ *lip-šu-ru-ki* ^{d}SUMUKAN *u* ^{d}NIDABA : *lip-šu-ru-ki* ^{d}*A-nun-na-ku* DINGIR.MEŠ GAL.MEŠ
17′ A.MEŠ *ša naq-bi li-ni-ʾ-ú i-rat-ki*

Col. II (?)

1′ ⸢x⸣ [
2′ *mìm-ma š*[*a*?

3′ INIM.INIM.MA ⸢x⸣ [

4′[123] ÉN MÍ.UŠ$_{12}$ *ni*[*r-ta-ni-tu* ...]
5′ *a-šip-tu i*[*š-še-bu-tu* ...]
6′ *qa-diš-tu na-*[*di-tu* ...]
7′ *ṣa-a-a-di-tu ša* [...]
8′ *mu-la-ib-tu ša* A[N-*e* ...]
9′ *ka-si-i-tu ša pi-i* [...]
10′ *da-ik-tu ša* GURUŠ.M[EŠ ...]
11′ *ša-hi-ṭa-te e ša ṣab-*[*bu-ri-tu*
12′ *mu-ut-tal-lik-tu* [...]
13′ *ša a-na kiš-pi-ša ru-he-e-*[*ša*] [...]
14′ *e-nin-na a-na-ku a-ta-ma*[*r*?(*-ki*) ...]
15′ *uš-te-pi-lu-ki uš-ta-b*[*al*?*-kit*(*u*)(*-ki*) ...][123]

---

[123]For 4′-15′, cf. M III 31ff. (the two texts were already associated by Meier, *Maqlû*, p. 23, nn. 7-8 and *AfO* 21 74). Our restorations and textual notes are not intended to be exhaustive, and the reader is referred to M III 31ff.

Notes to *KAR* 226 II 4′ff.

7′: The *Maqlû* MS *STT* 82:46-47 has *ha-a-a-ṭi-tum*.

9′: This text probably agrees with the *Maqlû* MS *STT* 82:50-51 (*ka-si-tum šá* KA ^{d}*iš-tar*.MEŠ) against the other MSS.

11′: Compare M III 54. what is *e ša*?

12′: Absent in *Maqlû*.

13′: M III 55 has *ip-ši-šá* instead of *kiš-pi-šá*.

14′-15′: Compare M III 56-58, and note especially the variants provided by *STT* 82. M III 56-58 seems to have undergone corruption. We may note two possibilities of interpreting these lines. While it is more than possible that neither interpretation is correct, we are very attracted by the second.

(1) On the assumption that the verbs in M III 56-58 are first person verbs and on the analogy of 58, could the direct object of the verbs in 56f. originally have been terms for witchcraft? If so, read, e.g., *ki*(*špīki*) (abbreviation; cf., M IV 17ff., for which see *AfO* 21 76)/<*kišpī*>*ki* (haplography).

(2) Could the verbs in 56-58 originally have been third person verbs whose subject is witchcraft and whose object is the witch? This suggestion is supported by the *-u* suffix of the verbs and by the *i-* prefix documented for those in 56-57a (the other verbs have the ambiguous *u-* prefix): *i*-TAM-*ru-ki iṣ-ṣab-tu-ki i-te-ni-u-ki* (*STT* 82). If this suggestion is correct, we should read *i-tú-ru-ki* (*târu*), rather than *i-tam-ru-ki* (accordingly, *KAR* 226–if correctly restored–is a hypercorrection), and we should compare *i-tú-ru-ki iṣ-ṣab-tu-ki* (56) to, e.g., *li-tir-ru-ma li-iṣ-ba-tu-ki ka-a-ši* (M VII 160) and *ú-tar-ru kiš-pi-ki ru-hi-ki ú-ṣa-ab-ba-tu-ki ka-a-ši* (M VII 169).

Col. III (?)

1 *lu-ú ku-ri* ŠÀ-*ba-ša* ⸢x⸣ [...]
2 *lik-ru* ŠÀ-*ba-šá ka-bat-ta-*[*ša* ...]
3[124] *ki-ma kib-ru a-na k*[*ib*!?-*ri la iqerri/ubu* ...]
4 *ep-šu-ša up-ša-šu-*[*ša lemnūti* ... (*lā iṭehhûni*)]
5 *la-a i-qer-*[*ri/ru-bu-ni jâši* ...][124]
6 ⸢muš?⸣ ⸢x⸣ [
Break

Col. IV (?)

1 INIM.INIM.MA ⸢x⸣ [...] ⸢x⸣ *šul?*
2 ÉN 3-*šú* ŠID-*nu* [...]

For 3ff. see above Chapter 1 and note 2.

KAR 269

Obv.(?) Left Col.[125]

1′] ⸢x⸣
2′] ÍL-*ma*
3′] *ta-hap-pi*
4′] ⸢*ti*⸣/⸢*an*⸣

---

[124]This motif and related ones are also found elsewhere in the witchcraft corpus. They appear either in the form (as here): "just as X_1 cannot approach X_2, so too may witchcraft not approach me" (cf. M VI 64-68), or in the more common form "just as witchcraft cannot approach Y, so may it not approach me" (cf., e.g., M VII 54-57 and 182-185). A motif similar to that found in our text appears outside the witchcraft corpus, for example, in *JNES* 15 136:96f. (note that *i-ger-*[*r*]*u* there should almost certainly be emended to *i-qer-*[*r*]*u-*<*bu*>, since the simile as presently constituted is simply untrue and since *qerēbu* is frequently used elsewhere in similar contexts).

[125]Our line count in this column is one higher than that of the copy.

5'[126] [(...) *ēpišti u*] *mul-te-piš-ti*
6' [...] *ep-še-te-ia*
7' [*īpušā* (...) *bunnannīya*] *ú-maš-ši-lu*
8' [... *ṣalmīya i-ban*]-*na mi-na-*⌜*ti*!?⌝(text: ⌜ki?⌝)-⌜*ia*⌝
9' [*ubbirū* (...) *ipšī*/*epšēti tēpušā lū ša*] *at*!(text: it)-*tu-ki-na*
10' [... *mê tahbî lū*] ⌜*ša*⌝ *ra-ma-ni-ki-na*
11' [*šipatkina aj iqriba* INIM.MEŠ-*ki*]-*na*!?(text: ba?) *a-ia ik-šu-da-ni*
12' [...] *šú*? *ba la hi*[126]

13'] ⌜x⌝ *uš na* ⌜x⌝ *ka-a-ša*
14'] ⌜*su*?⌝ ⌜x x⌝ [x x *k*]*a*! *mi*
15'] *mi*
16'] *mi*
17'] ⌜*hu*⌝/⌜*ri*⌝
Break

Obv.(?) Right Col.

1 [^{d}AMAR.UD *ia-a-š*]*i ru-*[*ṣa-nim-ma lip-pa-áš-ru kiš-pu*]
2 [*ru-hu*]-*ú* ⌜*ru*⌝-*su-ú u*[*p-šá-šu-ú lemnūti ša amēlūti*]
3 [*ù*] *ma-mi-tu ša* SU-*ia* [...][127]

---

[126] Restorations are uncertain and are presented simply to indicate the similarities between this incantation and M V 1ff. For further possible restorations of several of the lines, see that text. It is possible that line 12' should be read: *a-a iq*]-⌜*ri*⌝-*ba* <*a-ia*> TE!-*hi*.

[127] The reading of this line is difficult, because *littaṣi* is consistently found between *māmīt* and *ša zumriya* in the other occurrences of this line (*Šurpu* V-VI 196; M VII 146). Since there seems to be space for approximately six to seven signs in the break at the end of *KAR* 269 obv. II 3, it is difficult to simply read: [*ù*] *ma-mi-tu ša* SU-*ia* [*lit-ta-ṣi*] or [*ù*] *ma-mi-tu* <*lit-ta-ṣi*> *ša* SU-*ia* [...]. Perhaps we should read: [*ù*] *ma-mi-tu* <<*ša* SU-*ia*>> [*lit-ta-ṣi ša* SU-*ia*].

4[128] [(ÉN) *kib-r*]*i-*^{d}ÍD *kib-ri-*^{d}ÍD *kib-ri-*[^{d}ÍD
5 *ma-*⸢*rat*!?⸣ *kib-ri*(-)⸢x⸣(= *it*?) *kal-la-at* DINGIR.[MEŠ GAL.MEŠ
6 ⸢x⸣⸢x⸣ *a-kul*!?(text: bat tap) *al*?(text: pa is)-*tu-ša ù si* ⸢x⸣ [
7 *i-*⸢xx⸣*-ma ul in-ni-pu-uš* ⸢x⸣ [
8 *ul* ⸢x x⸣ *ana-ku ki-ma* ^{d}ÍD *ina* KUR-*i*[*a lū ellēku*
9 ^{d}ÍD A *al-ti al*!?(text:⸢sar?⸣)-*la-biš* A ⸢*kib*⸣-[*ri*(-^{d}ÍD)
10 ^{d}ÍD A ⸢*al*?⸣-*tu-šú* A.MEŠ-*ia ṣu-ba*?-⸢*ti*!?⸣-[*ia*
11 *ù pár-sik-*⸢*ti*⸣*-ia* GIŠ.IG-*ti-ia* ⸢x⸣ [
12 *ina* GIŠ.IG KÁ-*ia* ⸢x x⸣ *e ia* [
13 ^{d}ÍD *ku-ul-*[*la*?*-at*?] [^{d}]ÍD *k*[*ul*?*-la-at*
14 *la-a-am kiš-pe-*⸢*e*!⸣ *ru-he-e* [
15 ⸢TU_6⸣ *ul ia-a*[*t-tu-u*]*n*! *ši-*⸢*pat*⸣ [^{d}*Ea* ...

---

16 [INIM].INIM.MA ⸢x⸣ [

---

17 [x] ⸢x⸣ [
Break

Rev.(?)

For 1′-13′ see above Chapter 2, Sec. B, 4.
14′] ⸢x⸣ [x] ⸢*ru*?⸣ *li i*[*a*/*ṣ*[*i*
15′] ⸢x⸣ [
16′ GI]G? ⸢x⸣ [
Break

[128] Emendations and restorations are tentative.

PART TWO

Maqlû I 1-36: An Interpretation

Chapter One

Introduction

A. Background

In a paper delivered before the American Oriental Society in 1971, we indicated that the original nucleus of *Maqlû* was a short incantation sequence and that I 73-143 represented the opening and V 156-184 the closing sections of that sequence. The gradual growth of the series from an original nucleus of ten incantations into the present sequence of almost one hundred incantations was paralleled by the emergence of a new pattern. Two separate changes in the time of performance of the ceremony were decisive–and in good part responsible–for the growth of the series and for the emergence of this pattern: (1) the change of the time of performance of the original nucleus of I-V (or an already extended form thereof) from the morning to the evening; and (2) the subsequent extension of the time of performance to include the whole night and the following morning. The latter change is reflected in the addition of tablets VI-VIII to the series, and we will examine these tablets elsewhere. In this part we shall concern ourselves with one of the developments in the text of the series resulting from the change of the time of performance of I-V from the morning to the evening.

This change led to the replacement of Šamaš by Nusku in the opening incantation (I 73-121) of the original sequence and to the addition of a number of incantations addressed to the fire god. However, the most meaningful and significant innovation during the development of the text of the first five tablets into their final form was the composition of a new introduction, I 1-72. This introduction begins with an address to the gods of the night sky and expresses thereby the new setting in time of the ritual. An internal analysis of this new introduction, which is composed of five incantations, shows it to be divided into three sections: 1-36, 37-60 and 61-72, each of which develops a specific theme. In fact, this division is formally articulated in the text itself by the presence of the *ina qibīt* formula at the end of each of these three sections.[1] The most significant act in I-V and, for that matter, in the whole of *Maqlû* is the trial of the witch in I 73ff. The introduction to *Maqlû*, I 1-72, concerns itself with the activities leading up to this trial. It begins with the initial accusation and indictment of the witch and ends with a summons to witnesses to be present at the trial in support of the plaintiff.

This part is devoted to an examination of I 1-36, the opening incantation of *Maqlû*. Within the context of this examination, we shall also treat I 73-121.

B. First Reading

I 1-36 is an oft read, quoted and translated incantation. The importance of this address to the gods of the night sky lies in its not insignificant literary qualities, as well as in the fact that as the first incantation in *Maqlû* it sets the tone for the work. Because of its importance, we propose to essay a detailed exegesis and literary analysis of this apparently simple incantation.

A reading of Meier's edition and translation of the incantation[2] would probably lead the casual reader to the following understanding:

1) The plaintiff calls on the gods of the night because a witch has injured him (1-12).

2) He asks these gods to judge his case (13-14).

---

[1] While the occurrence of this formula at the end of the first incantation might, by itself, prove nothing, its presence in 72 is suggestive because that line is shown to be a major dividing point by the fact that the original version of *Maqlû* started in 73. When it is noticed that this formula occurs at the end of the first (36) and fifth (72) incantations and also at the end of the fourth (60), but that it is absent at the end of the second and third incantations (37-49), in other words, that its distribution agrees with the division of these incantations into sense units, our interpretation of the distribution of this formula becomes virtually certain.

[2] Meier, *Maqlû*, pp. 7f. and 66; *AfO* 21 70f. For other translations, see, for example, Tallqvist, *Maqlû*, I (this translation has not been accessible to us during the writing of this part); Thompson, *Semitic Magic*, p. XXVII (ll. 27-36); Landsberger in Lehmann-Haas, *Textbuch zur Religionsgeschichte*, 1st ed., pp. 124f., 2nd ed., pp. 321f. (henceforth: Landsberger, *Textbuch*); Mendelsohn, *Religions of the Ancient Near East*, pp. 215f.; etc.

3) He brings the witch to court (in effigy), presents his case (15-18) and asks that the witch die but he live (19), that the witchcraft be released (20) and that several plants render him clean, pure and free (from witchcraft) (21-24).

4) He then asserts that he has become pure and clean before the gods of the night (i.e., that the wish articulated in 21-24 has been realized).

5) Having succeeded in changing his own status, he concentrates next on the witchcraft and the witch (27-35): he asserts that previously uttered imprecations are evil and have come to nought (27-28); he asks the gods to strike the witch on account of her witchcraft and to release the witchcraft (29-30); he articulates the wish that the witch who has performed the evil deeds melt like wax and dissolve like salt (31-33); he asserts that the witch's machinations and imprecations have come to nought and are ineffective (34-35); and he pronounces the *ina qibīt* formula (36).

C. Questions

If we now re-read the incantation, we notice that this understanding leaves a number of questions unanswered. A few examples should suffice to illustrate this point.

1) How are we to explain the temporal-aspectual sequence in 19-35? More specifically, why does the speaker shift from precative verbal forms (19-24) to perfects (25-26) and statives (28), back to precatives (29-33) and again to statives (34-35)? In view of the fact that 25-26, 28 and 34-35 express not the circumstances which have caused the petitioner to address the gods, but some of the major objects to be achieved through the address, the use of perfects and statives in these lines is most disturbing. For here, in contrast to most addresses to the gods, the objects whose achievement is the *raison d'être* of the address are treated as having already been achieved; and this difficulty is only compounded by the fact that 29-33, which also express objects to be achieved through the address, contain precative verbal forms and thus agree with the aforementioned addresses in seeing these objects as not yet having been achieved and in refer-

ring their achievement to the future. Certainly, we cannot follow the lead of an earlier student of this text who interpreted the statives in 28 and 34-35 on the analogy of the Hebrew prophetic perfect and referred them to future time.[3]

2) Furthermore, how are we to explain the fact that the plant-purification motif (21-24), which in other texts is limited to expressions of hope (precative), culminates in our text in the speaker's assertion (25-26) that he has become (G perfect) pure?

3) Moreover, how are we to explain the fact that the motifs contained in 28ff., which appear together elsewhere as members of a common sequence and there occur in a set order and in a uniform "tense," are placed in our text in an order which deviates from the one normally found and are formulated in both stative and precative forms?

4) Is there a logical connection between 21-26 and 27ff., and, if so, what is it?

5) Why is the speaker concerned alternately with witchcraft and *amātu*, and why does he accord equal weight to both? What, in fact, does *amātu* in 28, 32 and 35 mean?

6) Why does the speaker repeat essentially the same idea in 20 and 30 (cf. 34) and in 28 and 35, when, on the surface at least, the repetition appears to be meaningless and to destroy any semblance of logical continuity?

These and other questions not only establish the need for a closer examination of the incantation and define a few of the tasks of that examination, but also point the way to further possibilities of interpretation and to a fuller understanding of the situation described in and underlying the incantation.

---

[3]Tallqvist, *op.cit.*, p. 119; cf. Thompson, *op.cit.*, who translates 28 (... *turrat* ... *kaṣrat*) as "Her word shall turn back to her mouth, her tongue shall be cut off."

Chapter Two

Declaration of Innocence and Repudiation of Witch's Accusation

A. Lines 27-30: Exegetical Inferences and Suggestions

Let us begin with 27-30. The text reads:

27 *tûša ša kaššapti lemutte*
28 *turrat amāssa ana pîša lišānša kaṣrat*
29 *ina muhhi kišpīša limhaṣūši ilī mušīti*
30 3 *maṣṣārāti*[4] *ša mūši lipšurā*(!)[4] *ruhîša lemnūti*

In this passage 28 is treated as temporally prior to 29f.; or, to put it differently, the effects described in 28 do not depend on the actions requested in 29f. of the gods and watches of the night. In fact, one might infer from this incantation that 28 and 29f. are not closely bound together, since 28 contains a description of an achieved state and 29f. describes actions whose fulfillment still lies in the future. However, other passages in which these motifs occur teach us not only that the actions described in 28 and 29f. are closely bound together, but also that the sequence is normally reversed with the

[4]This line (Tallqvist, *Maqlû*, II, p. 4:30) reads: 3 EN.NUN.MEŠ *šá mu-ši lip-šu-ru ru-hi-šá lem-nu-ti*. In spite of the masculine form of the verb, the feminine noun *maṣṣārāti*, the traditional reading of EN.NUN.MEŠ in this line, should be retained (and should not be replaced by the masculine *maṣṣārū*) because of the obvious similarities between M I 3 + 30 and *AGH* 40:12-16, on the one hand, and the occurrence of unambiguous feminine forms in the latter passage, on the other hand. *lip-šu-ru*, therefore, must be an error for *lipšurā*. This error was, perhaps, made under the influence of the following word (*ruhîša*), whose first syllable and sign is *ru*. A contributing influence may have been the use of a masculine form in 29. That the form *lipšurū* is the result of error and that the following word is the probable source of the error seem to find support in the equally incorrect variant reading *lipšur* found in a Sultantepe MS (*STT* 78: [...] ⌈*mu*⌉-*ši lip-šur ru-hi-šá* HUL.MEŠ). Note that the incorrect replacement of a feminine verb form by a masculine one is attested also for line 34 of our incantation, the correct reading of which is found in the aforementioned Sultantepe MS; see below note 104.

"turning back of the witch's *amātu* into her mouth" (28)[5] temporally posterior to, and, probably, effectually dependent upon, the striking (29) and the releasing (30).

Compare the following occurrences, which, with one exception (*KAR* 71), are all found in witchcraft incantations.[6]

M VI 62:
[*mahṣā*] *lēssa tirrā amāssa ana pî*[*ša*]

M VI 17f.:
li-[*im-ha-ṣu*[7]] *kaššāpī/a u kaššaptī/a* [*litirrū amāssa*] *ana pîša*

Sm 352 rev. 10′:
i-mah-ha-ṣu TE-⌈*ki*⌉ [*ú-tar-ru*] INIM-*ki ana* KA-*k*[*i*]

Tallqvist, *Maqlû*, II p. 96: K 8162:10f.:
an-na-ši-mi kaš-ša-ap-tum ša ú-da-ab-ba-bu eṭ-lam
ú-lab-ba-an-ni ina HUL!(text: ši + ib)-*te mah-ṣa le-es-sà*
us-ha li-šá-an-[*šá*]
(12: traces)[8]

M V 27f.:
dajjānša[9] *kīma nēši lissâ eliša*
limhaṣ lēssa litīr amāssa ana pîša

---

[5]Idiomatically, *amāssu ana pîšu turru* is best translated "to force one to swallow his 'words'." Cf. *JCS* 15 10, where several examples of *awāta turru* in the meaning "to reply" are given (cf. also *JCS* 16 38).

[6]The passages to be quoted indicate clearly that *limhaṣūši* is identical with *limhaṣū lēssa.*

[7]The other passages quoted justify our restoration of *li*-[*im-ha-ṣu*] in 17, rather than Meier's *li*-[*du-ku*(?)]. 18 was already restored by Meier.

[8]While we are unable to restore meaningfully the traces in 12, the last line before the break, it may be presumed that *tirrā amāssa ana pîša* is found there.

[9]Text: DI.KUD-*šá*; following *GAG* § 33h, we see no reason to accept Meier's *daiânu-šá.*

Sm 756 obv. 14′ff.(A) // *RA* 22 155 rev. 10ff.(B) // *KAR* 81:13′f.(C):[10]

Ú.IGI.LIM *lim-ha-aṣ* (B: *li-im-ha-ṣa*) *le-es-sa* (so B;
  A: ⸢TE?⸣-[*sa*)
GIŠ.KAN.U$_5$ *li-pa-áš*(B: omits)-*ši-ra kiš-pi-šá*
GIŠ.UGU-*kul-la li-tir*(B: +-*ra*) INIM-*sa ana*
  pi (so B, = (?)*pi*/KA)-*šá*
ù gam-lum li-paṭ-ṭi-ra ki-ṣir qí-bi-it ŠÀ(-*bi*(?))-[*šá*]

Finally, *KAR* 71 rev. 1ff., an Egalturra incantation previously edited in *MAOG* 5/3 32 reads:[11]

[*šá*] AN-*e qu-u-*[*la*]
šá qaq-qa-ri ši-ma-a pi-ia
a-di ana-ku šá EN KA.KA-*ia*

---

[10]These three texts are part of the genetically related incantation group *RA* 22 155 rev. 1ff.; Sm 756 obv. // *KAR* 81 // Rm 252 r. col.; *AMT* 32/1:13ff., identified by Meier, *Maqlû*, p.6, n.31 and Reiner, *Šurpu*, p.59. The corresponding part of Rm 252 r. col. and of *AMT* 32/1 are destroyed and fragmentary respectively (it is even uncertain whether *AMT* 32/1 had a similar section). A further text which might be compared is *RIAA* 312 rev.(!) 7′-10′. However, this text is so badly copied that we hesitate to use it. *RA* 22 155 rev. 1ff., published by Scheil, was given only in transliteration. Sm 756 suggests a number of changes that must be introduced into Scheil's transliterations. Restricting ourselves to the lines quoted, we note the following: 11: for Scheil's GAN-MAZ(?) read: [GIŠ].KAN.U$_5$; 12: for S.'s [(*šam*)IN]-NU-U[Š] read: [Ú.UGU]-*kul-*[*la*] (S. read *kul* as NU-U[Š]); 14: for S.'s [*urra*] *u muša* read: *ga*]*m-lum* (S. read *ga*]*m* as *u* and *lum* as MI); for S.'s *li-im ṭi-ra* read: *li-paṭ-ṭi-ra* (and delete this occurrence from *AHw* s. *madāru*); for S.'s *ku-uṣ* read: *ki-ṣir*. S. gives the following signs as "*ki*(?) *pi-it*(?) *libbi* ...." While these words are preserved in none of the other texts (with the exception of *k*[*i* in Sm 756 obv. 17′), we have, perhaps wrongly, read *qí-bi-it*, and not *ki-pi-id*, because all examples of *kipdu* cited in *AHw* s.v. are plural and our form is singular construct. Cf. M III 89f.: *ša iq*<*b*>*û amāt lemuttiya ina libbiša*. For *lipaṭṭira kiṣir qibīt libbi*[*ša*] of Sm 756 and duplicates, cf. *KAR* 80 rev. 35 // *RA* 26 41:13(B).: *ú-paṭ-ṭar* ⸢*ki-ṣir*⸣(B: omits) *qí-bit* ŠÀ(B: +-*bi*)-*šú-nu*. Note also that S.'s transliteration: "*libbi* ..." does not allow us to determine whether there are traces or how the word is written. Sm 756 also indicates that *KAR* 81:14′, the last preserved line in this text, must be read and emended: [GIŠ.KAN].⸢U$_5$⸣ *li*!(text: *lu*)-*pa-áš-ši-ra*!(text: *ma ra*[*t*) [.

[11]We believe that obv. 26-28 are the opening lines of this incantation. However, we are unable to restore them sufficiently, and we therefore omit them.

NENNI A NENNI *a-ṭè-ru-u* TE-*su*
a-né-et-ti-pu EME-*šu*
ú-tar-ra INIM-*su ana* KA-*šu*
pi-i-šú a-na da-ba-bi su-uh-ha-šu
a-na ṣa!(text: *a*)[12]-*ra-a-ti ul a-nam-din*

[IN]IM. INIM.MA É.GAL.TUR.RA

[DÙ].DÙ.BI *ana* UGU ŠU.GUR URUDU ÉN 3-*šú* ŠID-*nu-ma*
[*ana*] ŠU.SI-*ka* GAR-*an ana* IGI NUN TU-*ub-ma* NUN *ha-di-ka*

A comparison of our *Maqlû* passage with these others results in certain observations and exegetical presumptions and permits us to advance several suggestions.

1) Normally, the motif contained in M I 28a is found together with those contained in 29f. This implies that these lines must be part of a related chain of events (we return to this below) and that the general setting of both 28 and 29f. should be identical. The context of our incantation (cf. 13-17) and a passage like M V 27f. clearly indicate that the gods and watches are addressed in I 29f. in their capacity of judges and that the action requested in 29 is of legal import. Since the motif contained in 28 is normally found with that of 29, the courtroom setting of the latter should also apply to the former. Obviously, then, a juridical frame of reference should be determinative in deciding the meaning of these two lines. Hence, whereas, by itself, 28 might mean that the witch's imprecations have come to nought and that she is no longer capable of uttering them and whereas, by itself, the striking (of the cheek) in 29 might be just a "symbol of humiliation,"[13] a more specific meaning in line with the courtroom setting is required here for both lines.

Let us leave 29f. for later and concentrate on 28. The Egalturra incantation *KAR* 71 rev. 1ff. is most helpful in allowing us to understand this line. This incantation reflects a very specific situation apparent both in the content of the utterance and in the ritual in-

---

[12]For this emendation, see *CAD* A/2 305.
[13]Cf. *JAOS* 79 169 n. 10.

structions and *Verheissung*. It is especially relevant, as we shall see elsewhere, that this incantation and M I 61-72 are essentially comparable and that *amātu* has virtually the same meaning in I 28, 35, 68, 70f. and *KAR* 71 rev. 6. This Egalturra incantation is recited prior to an audience or, better, confrontation at court (11) and is directed against an adversary who has levelled accusations against the speaker, or is presently doing so (3ff.). In this incantation the speaker asserts that he will not permit his opponent to utter a sound (7f.) and that he will repudiate the accusations (4ff.) by means of testimony backed up by witnesses (1f.).[14] This situation is, of course, reminiscent of K 8162 quoted earlier. In K 8162 our sequence is preceded by the statement: *annašimi kaššaptum ša udabbabu eṭlam ulabbanni ina lemutte*, which may be translated tentatively as "this is the witch who accuses the young man; she is unjustly besmirching me (?)."[15]

The juridical frame of reference of M I 1-36, generally, of 28-30, specifically, and of the passages just discussed suggests that a meaning "accusation" may reasonably be proposed for *amātu* in 28 and that the line may be rendered: her accusation has been (effectively) disproved[16] and she is now unable to reaffirm it.[17]

2) A comparison of M I 28-30 with all the other passages shows that our passage has reversed the normal sequence[18] and that our passage, which has statives in 28 and precatives in 29-30, is the only one in which all members of the sequence are not in the same "tense."[19] These deviations from the norm may represent an inno-

[14] This incantation will be translated and more fully discussed in our treatment of M I 61-72.

[15] *CAD* D 12 translates: "This is she, the witch, that pesters the young man." We derive *ú-lab-ba-an-ni*, perhaps wrongly, from *la'ābu* (i.e., *ulabbanni*). It is possible that it should be derived from *lawû* or from *lu"u* (i.e., *ulabbânni*) or that it should be read *ú-rib-ba-an-ni* and derived from *râbu*.

[16] Cf. *CCT* 3 36a:11f. as quoted and translated in *JCS* 15 10: *kīma niāti awatam ta'er*, "Reply for us to the (false) accusations."

[17] Lit.: "Her word has been turned back into her mouth and her tongue has become constricted." See below Chapter 3, Sec. A, 3, and note 62.

[18] Referring to the four elements 28a, 28b, 29 and 30 as *a*, *b*, *c* and *d* respectively, we note that the order of corresponding entries in these other passages is: *c*, *a* (M VI 62, VI 17f., Sm 352, M V 27f.); *c*, *b*, *a* (K 8162 [*a* restored] *KAR* 71); *c*, *d*, *a* (Sm 756 and duplicates).

[19] The other sequences are in either the imperative (M VI 62, K 8162), the

vation. In any case, they must be regarded as purposeful, as exegetically significant and as implying a meaningful divergence from a normal pattern of events. The exegetical presumptions which may be inferred are as follows:

a) Since 28 does not stand in its normal position within the sequence, but at the head, since it does not refer to future time as 29f., but to an achieved state and since the shift to this temporal and aspectual perspective already began in 25-26 (G perfect; contrast the precatives in 21-24), a clear relationship between 25-26 and 27-28 must exist and this relationship should provide a clue for the understanding of the function of 25-26 within the sequence 21-26.

b) Since an intimate relation, be it circumstantial or causal, obtains between 27 and 28,[20] 27 should serve as the bridge between 25-26 and 28.

c) Since 28 is part of the sequence 28-30 and since the existence of a relationship between these lines has already been established, the relationship between 25-26 and 27-28 should provide the reasons for the reversal of the sequence in 28ff. and should enable us to define the relationship between 28 and 29f.

B. Lines 21-26: Exegetical Inferences and Suggestions

Bearing these observations and presumptions in mind, let us examine 21-26. The text reads:

21 *bīnu lillilanni ...*
22 *gišimmaru lipšuranni ...*
23 *maštakal libbibanni ...*
24 *terīnatu lipšuranni ...*
25 *ina mahrikunu ētelil kīma sassati*
26 *ētebib azzaku kīma lardi*

---

precative (M VI 17f., V 27f., Sm 756 and duplicates) or the present-future (Sm 352, *KAR* 71).

[20]This relation is made explicit, for example, by Meissner's translation (*Babylonien und Assyrien*, II, p. 227) of 27f.: "Die Beschwörung der Hexe ist böse; darum kehrt ihr Wort in ihren Mund zurück ...."

In lines 21-24 the speaker requests that a number of plants "purify," "cleanse" and "release" him. These lines represent a stock motif frequently encountered in Akkadian magical literature.[21] Since 25-26 share with 21-24 the two verbs of purification and cleansing (*elēlu*: 25, 21, *ebēbu*: 26,23) and since in 25-26, as in the earlier lines, this cleansing is related to the properties of plants, there can be no doubt that 21-24 and 25-26 share a common setting and that 25-26 develop a line of thought already begun in 21-24. However, the usual "magical" meaning of the motif, viz. "may plants purify and cleanse me of certain evil forces," does not do justice to our lines. The formulation of this motif is normally restricted to the expression of hope that plants will purify the speaker.[22] While our passage also contains that formulation in 21-24, it contrasts with the other occurrences of the motif in continuing with the further statement that the wished for result has been attained in the presence of the addressee; viz., "I have now become pure, clean ... in your presence." That the composer of our text has transformed a stock motif (21-24) by adding lines 25-26 is evident not only in the expanded time range and in

[21] For the plant-purification motif found in I 21-24, cf., e.g., *BMS* 12:84, *TCS* II 28:5-7, *OECT* 6 24: K 2999:10, Laessøe, *Bît rimki*, p.58:90f., *JCS* 21 10:6+a-9+a, *TuL* 142:23 (as emended in *ZA* 43 269), *ZA* 51 174:18, *JAOS* 59 14:24ff., *Or*NS 34 116:10, *Or*NS 36 273:10, *STT* 251 (// *STT* 72):36. A further example is found at the end of a Marduk prayer and ritual which we have reconstructed on the basis of *AMT* 21/2 + K 3648 + Sm 1280 // K 1853 + 6262 + 6789 + 13358 + 13813 (+) 7201 + 10819 (+) 3000 (+) 9216 (+) 431 + 11260 (+) 6996 // *BAM* 232 // K 8965 // 5088 // *RT* 24 104 // *STT* 129 // 130 // 135 // 262 // 328. (All Kuyunjik joins have been confirmed; several of the Sultantepe fragments probably join each other, but these joins have not yet been confirmed.) (For a form of the motif different from those cited above, see *BAM* 244 rev. 58ff.)

On a ritual level, the cleansing and purification are achieved through contact with the plants. Compare *bīnu lillilanni* ... (M I 21) with *marṣu bīna ikabbas*(!) (*STT* 83:11′ [the reasons for this emendation and reading are given in our "Textual notes to the ritual tablet of *Maqlû*"]), the ritual prescription for M I 1-36. Even without the specific evidence of *STT* 83, we would still reject the opinion (Levey, *Chemistry and Chemical Technology in Ancient Mesopotamia*, p. 123) that the plants in our incantation are used as a detergent as being far too simplistic. Whatever the functional origin of the cleansing properties ascribed to plants, purification may be attained by simple contact with (touching, holding, standing on) these plants and their extracts. In fact, simply looking at plants (cf., e.g., *JCS* 21 10:7+a-8+a) may be sufficient for this purpose.

[22] See the passages cited above note 21.

the resultant contrast mentioned above, but also in the absence of *zakû* in 21-24, but its presence in 26, and in the lack of identity between the plants mentioned in 25-26 and those mentioned in 21-24. More important than the simple expansion of the motif is the fact that the innovation represents a reinterpretation of the motif and its transference to a new setting.

To understand the meaning of 21-26 we must look to those lines whose very occurrence represents the innovation, i.e., 25-26. Previously we noticed that the shift to a perfective perspective in 25-26 and its continuation in 27-28, in which lines this perspective also represented an innovation, establish a connection between 25-26 and 27-28. This suggests that 25-26 express the conditions necessary for 27-28. Since we have supposed a juridical setting for 27-28, the connection supports the impression that a purely "magical" frame of reference is insufficient for an understanding of 25-26 and, therefore, also of 21-24 and suggests that the meaning of these lines is to be sought within a very specific juridical setting. If, then, we examine 25-26 closely, we find a number of usages reminiscent of usages known from legal contexts.

1) Compare *ina mahrikunu ētelil* ... *ētebib* ... with *ina mahar* DN *ubbubu*, "to clear oneself by an oath sworn before the gods."[23] It goes without saying that the second person plural pronominal suffix in *mahrikunu* refers to the gods and watches of the night who constitute the court.[24]

2) We noticed above that *zakû* is absent in 21-24 but present in 25-26 and that this discrepancy is due to the transformation of the stock motif represented by 21-24 by the addition of 25-26. Accordingly, the presence of *zakû* in 26 constitutes a significant feature of the new setting in which the meaning of our lines is to be sought. Compare, then, the use of *zakû* in the sense "to be cleared by an ordeal."[25] Most suggestive is the relation between *zakû* and an oath found especially in *KAR* 134 rev. 3f., which should be translated: "They draw water, drink, swear (*itammû*) and are cleared (*izakkû*) ...

[23]For this meaning of *ina mahar* DN *ubbubu*, cf. *CAD* E 7.

[24]Cf. Landsberger, *Textbuch*[1], p. 125, n. 1 on "Vor euch" (*mahrikunu*): "Den angerufenen Göttern."

[25]For this meaning of *zakû*, cf. *CAD* Z 26b.

I drew water, drank, swore (*attame*) and was cleared (*azzuku*: G perfect as in M I 26)."[26]

3) Our discussion thus far has clearly implied that the cleansing achieved through the use of plants in 21-26 is an element in that juridical process in which our incantation is set. It is, therefore, significant that the ritual cleansing undergone prior to an oath described in *MSL* I 77:39-44 (see especially 41-44) includes the use of a plant substance as part of the cleansing.[27] It is especially noteworthy, and probably significant, that the plant substance *lardu* used there (*MSL* I 77:42) is identical with one of the two plants which are mentioned in 25-26 and which are absent in 21-24.

We have seen that:

(1) the contrast between 21-26 and the other occurrences of the motif establishes a sound exegetical presumption that the motif has a special meaning in 21-26;

(2) the general context of the incantation indicates that this meaning is to be sought in the juridical realm;

(3) the temporal-aspectual connection of 25-26 and 27-28 indicates that 25-26 should establish the conditions which render the statements in 27-28 ("(because) her *tû* is that of an evil witch,[28] her accusation has been (effectively) disproved and she is unable to reaffirm it") feasible; and

(4) several usages in 25-26 are similar to usages which are found in legal contexts and which relate to the establishing of innocence by means of an oath and an ordeal.

---

[26] Contra *CAD* Z 26a: "They ... speak the incantation (and) become pure ... I spoke the incantation (and) became pure." With this passage compare Numbers ch. 5 and note especially the occurrence of *hšby'* (19, 21), *hšqh* / *yšqh* (24, 26f.) and *wṭhrh hw' wnqth* (28). Both *KAR* 134 and M I 25-26 use *zakû* within a legal context specifically relating to an oath (see below). This is, of course, not to deny that *zakû* may simply be used in prayers and incantations in the meaning "to be cleansed"; cf. especially *Šurpu* VIII 83.

[27] For the meaning of these lines, see Landsberger's discussion, *MSL* I 223ff.

[28] For this translation of *kaššapti lemutte* (27), see already Landsberger, *Textbuch*[1], p. 125: "Die Zauberformel der bösen Hexe, ..." In contrast to his earlier translation ("Die Beschwörung der Zauberin (ist) böse: ..." [*Maqlû*, p. 8]), Meier, *AfO* 21 71, now also translates: "Ihre Beschwörung (ist) die einer bösen Zauberin." We discuss the implications of *kaššapti lemutte* below Chapter 4, Sec. A.

Accordingly, it may be suggested that:

(1) the speaker in 25-26 asserts that he has cleared himself, in the presence of the gods and watches of the night who constitute the court, of an accusation brought against him;

(2) the cleansing by means of plants constitutes here a functional equivalent of the oath or ordeal (or perhaps symbolizes simply the quality of innocence to be attained through an oath or ordeal);

(3) the speaker in 21-24 expresses the hope that the plants (as the oath or ordeal) will vindicate and clear him;

(4) this use of the plant-purification motif in 21-24 exemplifies a legal reinterpretation of a common magical motif, a reinterpretation rooted in an established juridical institution wherein cleansing and establishing of innocence were associated.

Chapter Three

Behavior of Witch: Verbal Adversaries and Witchcraft

A. Verbal Adversaries: Lines 4-12 and their Implications

1. Introduction

Although our examination thus far has not resulted in absolutely definitive conclusions, it has suggested the following interpretation of 21-28: the speaker takes an oath and establishes thereby his innocence of an accusation; this proof of his own innocence allows him to declare that the accusation made against him by the witch is false and is, therefore, disproved. In order to test this interpretation we should examine the initial description of the witch's actions in lines 4-12 to see whether the nature of the harm inflicted on the speaker, as described in these lines, agrees with the interpretation suggested for his address to the judges in 21ff. Lines 4-12 read:

4 Because (*aššu*) *kaššaptu ukaššipanni*
5 *elēnītu ubbiranni*;
6 she has (thereby) caused my god and goddess to be estranged from me (and)
7 I have become sickening in the sight of those who behold me;
8 I am therefore unable to rest day or night;
9 *qû imtanallû pīya*
10 *upunti pîya iprusu*
11 *mê maštītiya umaṭṭû*;
12 my song of joy has become wailing and my rejoicing mourning, ...[29]

[29] For our understanding of 4, see below Sec. A, 3; for 5 see immediately below; for 9-11, see below Sec. A, 3. We take all verbs in 4-12 to be singular subjunctives dependent upon *aššu* in 4 (see below Sec. A, 3, and notes 76-77).

2. Denunciation of Victim (Mouth and Words): Line 5 and Parallel Lines

Meaning of Line 5. Lines 4-12 constitute a distinct unit which forms a *Kausalsatz* introducing 13-14, the request to the gods to take up the case. Lines 4-5, the opening section of the unit,[30] contain a statement of the actions which have been performed against the speaker and which have led to the situation described in 6ff.[31] Previous students of the text have translated 5 essentially in one of two ways:

(a) 4 weil die Zauberin mich bezaubert hat,
5 der Alp mich gebunden hat;[32]

(b) 4 because a witch has bewitched me,
5 a deceitful woman has denounced me.[33]

---

[30] Contra Meier, *Maqlû*, p. 7, lines 4-5 should not be connected syntactically with 1-3. Lines 4-12 form a long *Kausalsatz* introduced by *aššu* in 4. See below Sec. A, 3, and note 77.

[31] For this understanding of 6-7, see immediately below; for 9-11, see below Sec. A, 3.

[32] So Meier, *Maqlû*, p. 7. Von Soden (who listed our line in *AHw* s. *abāru* III d 1 "umspannen") and Mendelsohn (who translated *ubbiranni* in our line as "... has paralyzed me" [*op. cit.*, p. 215]) agree with this translation.

[33] So *CAD* E s. *elēnītu* A. Compare Landsberger, *Textbuch*[1], p. 125: "... mich ... gebannt hat." Landsberger's translation should be interpreted in the light of his later comments. In his discussion of the relation of *nugguru* and *ubburu* (to denounce, accuse), Landsberger, *JCS* 9 124, pointed out that "the Sumerian correspondence of *ubburum* is ... lá, basically 'to tie,' that is, 'to inflict a ban on a person'." It may be presumed that he uses both Germ. "bannen" and Engl. "to inflict a ban" in the sense of placing under a liability or restriction. The use of lá (cf. *ibid.* n. 19 on Lipit Ištar parag. 17): *ubburu* in the meaning "to accuse by words" does not derive from the act itself, but from the resultant state of the accused (in contrast to Engl. "to ban," which derives its legal force from the act of proclaiming or summoning [according to *The Oxford Universal Dictionary*[3], s. Ban, v., Germanic *Bannan is formed from the root ba-, cognate with Greek $\phi\alpha$-, Latin fa-, "to speak"]). This usage may perhaps be compared with Engl. "to bind" in the meaning "to constrain with legal authority," "to subject to a specific legal obligation" and it must certainly be compared with the idiom "to bind over for trial."

To decide which of these translations of line 5 is to be preferred, we may examine some of the effects of the actions described in 4-5. The following lines, 6-7, inform us of the first and main consequence of these actions: the alienation of the victim's personal gods and his loss of social stature. In texts concerned with witchcraft we often encounter a similar reaction on the part of a victim's superiors and/or equals.[34] For the purposes of our present discussion, it is of the utmost importance and significance (1) that a number of these and related texts center on the activities of a *bēl lemutti/dabābi/amāti* and frequently, implicitly or explicitly, construe the aforementioned consequences as resulting from a combination of witchcraft activity and verbal denunciations; and (2) that several of these texts contain ritual and incantation parallels to the first section of *Maqlû*.[35]

---

[34] See our analysis of *KAR* 26 in Part One, Chapter 3, and note the passages quoted there in the text and in notes 64-65 (*KAR* 26 obv. 37ff., *AMT* 87/1 rev. 1ff. // *BAM* 315 II 42ff., 4 *R* 55/2 obv. 1ff., M IV 64, *AfO* 18 293:66ff., M I 109, II 86ff., *KAR* 80 rev. 6); among many additional examples, see the texts cited below in note 35, as well as M III 114f., IV64ff., V 73, *STT* 89:76-79, 87-90, 91-95 and *STT* 275 I 6′ff. (note that the units which follow this entry in *STT* 275 [I 16′f., 20′] deal with *kišpū*, *māmītu*, *zikurrudû* and *dibalû*).

[35] An examination of the text type which has been called "Beschwörungen gegen den Feind" by Ebeling, *ArOr* 17/1 172ff., will suffice to demonstrate and document these statements. Examples of this type are 4 *R* 55/2 (*ArOr* 17/1 186ff.), Assur photo 4129 and VAT 13909 (*ArOr* 17/1 190ff.), *STT* 256 (already compared to the above texts by Gurney, *STT* II p. 12, no. 256) and probably VAT 13740:7ff. (*ArOr* 17/1 202f.), which is probably duplicated by K 2562:1ff. These texts normally describe the patient's misfortunes in an opening statement introduced by *šumma* and usually repeat them in an elaborate statement of purpose, which contains a description of the situation to be rectified and the positive goals to be attained. In trying to determine the real cause of the patient's plight, the interpreter is hindered by the frequent absence of a distinct formal articulation of the aetiological diagnosis (e.g., NA.BI ...) and by the lack of syntactic coordination between the individual elements in the description of the misfortunes.

I. Let us ignore, for the moment, the rare diagnosis and the accompanying rituals and only examine the remaining sections of these texts. This examination leads to the following observations (*STT* 256 and *ArOr* 17/1 190ff. are examined separately below in Section II, and the material in these texts is not frequently used in this section).

1) The description of the patient's plight centers on the social difficulties encountered by the patient and on his rejection by divine and human authorities (insofar as the patient's own behavior is described, it can best be understood as a

reaction to what must have appeared to him to be an unjustified and calamitous situation), and the statement of purpose and prognosis essentially describe the social and religious rehabilitation of the patient.

2) The opening section of these texts (i.e., the description of the patient's plight or, when this is missing, the statement of the purpose of the ritual) frequently begins with the mention of a *bēl lemutti.* In the course of the description of misfortunes and of the statement of purpose this *bēl lemutti* generally turns out to be a *bēl dabābi*: see, e.g., *STT* 256 discussed below.

3) Standard witchcraft terms occur. An examination of these occurrences reveals the following:

a) Witchcraft may be the cause of rejection by authority: see, e.g., 4 *R* 55/2:3-5 discussed below and cf. the texts listed above in note 34.

b) The use of witchcraft is explicitly imputed to the *bēl dabābi*: see VAT 13740 (*ArOr* 17/1 203):10 // K 2562 obv. 3: *upšāšê bēl dabābišu* and cf., e.g., *AMT* 89/1 II (= rev. V!) 16 // K 249 + V! (*KMI* 51f.) 14: DIŠ NA EN KA-*šu* (K 249 +: -*šú*) *kiš-pi* NIGIN-*šu*; *AMT* 89/1 II 19 // K 249 + V! 17: DIŠ NA EN KA-*šu* (K 249 +: -*šú*) *kiš-pi* NIGIN-*šu* (K 249 +: -*šú*); *KAR* 80 obv. 6ff.(A) // K 1853 + I 2'ff.(B): LÚ.BI EN [K]A.KA-*šú* (B: E]N KA-*šu* ⌜x(x)-*šú*⌝ (= (?) ⌜EGIR-*šú*⌝)) *kiš-pi* NIGIN-*šu* (-*šu* is from B) *kip-di lem*[*nūti ik-p*]*u-du-šú ana kiš-pi šú*(B: *šu*)-*nu-ti* BÚR-*ri ana* IGI ^{d}UTU NÍG.NA ŠIM.LI GAR-*an mi-ih-ha* BAL-*qí* NU UŠ$_{12}$.ZU *u* (A: UŠ$_{12}$.ZU! *u*!) MÍ.UŠ$_{12}$.ZU ... DÙ-*uš* (B: +-*ma*) (see below note 37). Note that the use of witchcraft by the EN KA is consistently expressed through the verb NIGIN in the texts just quoted, as well as, e.g., in *AMT* 87/1 rev. 1ff. // *BAM* 315 II 42ff. This should suffice to prove that the *bēl lemutti* = *bēl dabābi* in 4 *R* 55/2 1-5 (DIŠ NA EN HUL-*tim* TUK-*ši* ... UŠ$_{12}$ UŠ$_{12}$ UŠ$_{12}$ NÍG.AG.A.MEŠ HUL.MEŠ *ina* NU ZU NIGIN-*šú* DINGIR LUGAL ... KI-*šú ú-šá-áš-ki-nu-ma* ...) is responsible for the use of witchcraft and is the understood subject of NIGIN-*šú* (and that *kišpī*, etc., is in the oblique case [contra *ArOr* 17/1 188, *CAD* I 29 and *AS* 16 290]).

c) Furthermore, there is explicit evidence that the *bēl dabābi* will use witchcraft in order to bring about the aforementioned rejection: see especially 4 *R* 55/2 quoted above and cf., e.g., *AMT* 87/1 rev. 1ff. // *BAM* 315 II 42ff. (It is within this context that we should interpret a text like *STT* 271 I 7f.: DINGIR-*šú* KI-*sú* SILIM-*im* NA.BI UGU EN KA G[U]B-⌜*az*⌝.)

4) The victim is harmed not only by magical acts, but also by being maligned, accused and denounced. In 4 *R* 55/2 obv. 1-2 we read:

1 DIŠ NA EN HUL-*tim* TUK-*ši* EME *sah-*[...]-*tu* UŠ.UŠ-*šú*

2 *dib-bi-šú i-dab-bu-bu* INIM.MEŠ-*šú uš-tan-nu-ú* EME.SIG.MEŠ-*šú* KÚ.MEŠ.
That the *bēl dabābi* is responsible for this is clear from a comparison of line 2 with the speech addressed to a *bēl dabābi* by his victim, as he renders the *bēl dabābi* harmless by depriving him of his powers of speech, in the following texts: VAT 35:1-5 (see below note 59): [*a*]*ṣbat pâki* ... *attasah lišān p*[*îki*] *ana lā dabābi ša dibbiya ana lā šunnê ša amātiya*; *ArOr* 17/1 191:4-6: *aṣbat pâka ana lā qabê* <(?) *ša amāt* > *lemuttiya* (for our emendation, see below note 52) ... *aktanak šaptēka* [*ana l*]*ā šūlê ša šumiya.*

The final words of this last text recur in a similar context in *AfO* 11 pl. V (A) and its duplicate *LKU* 27 rev. (B) which we have identified. (This text is an incantation addressed to a witch; A was previously edited in *AfO* 11 367f.)

A 10 presently reads: [xxx] *šu-ṣi-i šá šu-mi-ia*

B 7′ presently reads:]*ud la is li i šá ba me* ⌜*ia*⌝ [

A comparison of these lines with each other and with *ArOr* 17/1 191:6 and a reconsideration of the context result in the reading (contra the edition of A): [*a-n*]*a la šu-li-i šá šu-mi* (B: *me*)-*ia*. (Notes: A: The previous edition reads: [*a-na*] *šu-ṣi-i*: The spacing of A and the *la* of B require that A be restored: [*a-na la*]; for *ṣi* read *li*! B: for *ud* read *n*]*a*; for *is* read *šu*!; for *ba* read *šu*! [note that the same sign form recurs in B 8′: *ha-šu*!-*ut-tú* (cf. A:11-12); we have assumed that the form is a slight error only because of the more standard form of *šu* in *LKU* 27 obv. 9; it can just as well be taken as a legitimate paleographic variant]. Note also that B 6′ reads: *a-na ub-bu-*[*ri*]-[*ki* and thus indicates that the beginning of A 9 must be restored: [*a-na u*]*b-bu-ri-ki*. Accordingly, disregard [*a-na du-u*]*b-bu-ri-ki* in the edition in *AfO* 11, as well as [*ana dup*]*puriki* in *CAD* Ṣ 9.)

The context of *AfO* 11 pl. V 10 // *LKU* 27 rev. 7′ and of *ArOr* 17/1 191:6 indicates that the act referred to as *šuma šūlû* is injurious to the *bēl dabābi*'s victim and that the *bēl dabābi*'s mouth is instrumental in its performance and suggests that *šuma šūlû* here is to be translated: "to summon to court." (Cf. PN *šūlû*, "to summon as a witness" [*CAD* E 127b] and PN *elû*, "to go to court" [E 119b] and "to start a lawsuit" [E 123b]. We know of no other example of this usage. Should *šum* DN/LUGAL *šūlû*, "to take an oath by DN/king" [E 135] be compared? [Obviously one must not compare *šuma ullû*, "to extol" (E 126b).])

We may conclude this part of our examination of this text type by quoting *AfO* 18 298:15-17 (for which we are able to suggest two important improvements: the reading E[N!] KA-*šú* in 15 instead of the edition's "(ras) *pî-šú*" and the restoration *la* in 17; see Part One, note 69). This text sums up a few of the features which we have previously recognized: 15 [DIŠ NA] *id-da-na-bu-bu-šú ina kiš-pi* E[N!] KA-*šú* / 16 [*it*]-⌜*ta*⌝-*na-*'-*dar-šú ina* É.GAL GIN.GIN-*ku* / 17 [*la ma*]*h-ra-šu* ....

II. An examination of 1) *STT* 256 and 2) *ArOr* 17/1 190ff. confirms the observations made in Section I and leads to a somewhat sharper delineation of the situation described in our text type.

1) a) Gurney, *STT* II, p. 12, no. 256, has characterized *STT* 256 as a "ritual with incantation against 'hand of man' (*qāt amēlūti*, 11) i.e., calumny and hostility on the part of neighbours and the authorities." Most of the misfortunes enumerated in 1ff. describe social difficulties encountered by the patient. Those others which center on the patient's own behavior are best understood as reactions to persecution and rejection: 1f.: ⌜DIŠ NA⌝ EN HUL-*ti* ⌈TUKU⌉ ŠÀ-*ba-šú šu-*'-*du-ur* K[I ...] INIM.MEŠ-*šú im-ta-na-áš-ši* ..., "If a man has an enemy and, therefore, is afraid, [...] *stutters* (lit.: he continually forgets his words), ..." (Cf., e.g., *STT* 247 [edited *JNES* 26 190] where the statement that the patient *ta-di-ra-ti ul-ta*-DAR (4) follows a description of his rejection and of the spreading of rumors about him (1-3).)

b) Almost all of the entries in 14ff., the statement of the purpose of the ritual, center on regaining the esteem and favor of the gods and of superiors. The *Verheissung* found in line 40 sums up the earlier statement of purpose (14-19) with the prediction: KI-*šú* GI.NA.MEŠ *i-tam-mu-ú*. As we have shown elsewhere (Part One, note 69), this means that the patient will find favor and that all of his requests will be granted and become "established facts" (cf. 4 *R* 55/2:23 [*ArOr* 17/1 187]).

c) The enumeration of misfortunes is introduced by the statement ⸢*šumma amēlu*⸣ *bēl lemutti* ⸢*iraššî*⸣ (1), which would seem to imply that the *bēl lemutti* is ultimately responsible for the various misfortunes. This is confirmed by the formal diagnosis which follows the enumeration of the misfortunes: NA.BI ŠU.NAM.LÚ.U$_x$.LU ⸢UGU⸣-[*šú* GÁL-*ši*] (11); for this diagnosis states explicitly that the various misfortunes are due to machinations and activities performed by another human being. (Note that this is the only example of a formally articulated diagnosis found in the texts listed at the beginning of this note.) Within the lengthy statement of purpose of the ritual we find the entry: UGU EN KA-*šú* <*ana*> GUB-*zi* (17). This entry is the only one in the whole statement of purpose which relates, not to the regaining of things lost, but to victory over an opponent. It may, therefore, be presumed that this *bēl dabābi* is responsible for the various misfortunes, that the *bēl lemutti* of line 1 is to be understood as *bēl dabābi* and that this adversary's actions are termed *qāt amēlūti* in the diagnosis. Turning to the ritual, we find that the objects of the destructive part of the ritual are none other than the warlock and the witch: 2 NU.MEŠ LÚ.UŠ$_{12}$.ZU *u* MÍ.UŠ$_{12}$.ZU *šá* IM DÙ-[*uš* (34). Since the warlock and the witch are referred to as kúr.kúr: *nakara* in the accompanying incantation addressed to the fire god (41ff. [cf. *ArOr* 17/1 191:25ff. and K 8107:1′ff.]), it is more than likely that the *bēl dabābi* (= *bēl lemutti*) and the warlock are identified with each other in this text. This situation is paralleled exactly by *KAR* 80 obv. 6ff. // K 1853 + I 2′ff., quoted above.

d) The situation, then, in *STT* 256 is that of a man who is rejected by his superiors, who suffers losses, etc., because of the actions of an enemy (*bēl lemutti*/*qāt amēlūti*/*bēl dabābi*/*kaššāpu*/*nakru*) who uses witchcraft against him.

e) Finally, it must be noted that the ritual in *STT* 256 is a miniature version of several crucial acts in tablet I of *Maqlû*. Thus, after various preparatory rites (20-28), the priest prepares statues of a warlock and witch (34), places an offering before the gods of the night (*ilī muštti*, 35), destroys the statues (36; cf. M IX 85, the text of which we have established in our "Textual notes to the ritual tablet of *Maqlû*") and recites an incantation to the gods of the night (37 = 29ff.; cf. M I 1-36) and another to the fire god (37 = 41ff.; cf., e.g., M I 135ff.). (See below Chapter 4, Sec. C, and note 115.)

2) We may now turn to *ArOr* 17/1 190ff. (The main text edited there is Assur Photo 4129. Ebeling listed VAT 13909 as a duplicate, and cited variants from it on p. 192:a-e [cf. also p. 195]. Note, however, that the two tablets have different layouts. An examination of a rough mixed transliteration and handcopy of the obverse of VAT 13909 [Geers] indicates the following correspondences: VAT 13909:1′-6′ = *ArOr* 17/1 191:34-38; VAT 13909:7′ cites the incantation *ArOr*

In view of these other texts, the emphasis in our incantation on the adversary's "mouth" (28, 31, 32 [see below]) and "word" (28 [cf. *tû*, 27], 32, 35), the close association in our text of the "word" and witchcraft (e.g., 31-35 [see below]) and the fact that the activities in 4-5 lead to the alienation of the victim's personal gods and to his loss of social stature strongly suggest that we should translate:

17/1 191 rev. 2-8 by incipit only; VAT 13909:8′ (NU.BI ⌈ÍL!⌉-*ma*! *ana*! d!UTU! ⌈x⌉[])-10′ = *ArOr* 17/1 191 rev. 9 - 192 rev. 11. Here, after a dividing line, VAT 13909:11′-15′, which Ebeling edited on p. 192 as a-e, follow. While these five lines [preparation and burning of statues and recital of an incantation to the fire god] are functionally equivalent to *ArOr* 17/1 191:15b-32, it is unclear whether they are part of the same ritual as the preceding lines on the tablet or whether they constitute the beginning of a new ritual. [The absence in these lines of any mention of such preliminaries as the setting up of the apparatus would seem to favor the former alternative.] In any case, it may be presumed that the concern with a *bēl dabābi* in VAT 13909:1′-10′ extends to 11′-15′.)

If the edition is correct, the text of Assur Photo 4129 begins with the statement of purpose of the ritual and does not contain a description of the situation. Central to this statement is the desire to achieve victory over an opponent and to regain the favor of the authorities. According to the *Verheissung*, the performance of the ritual results in victory over a *bēl dabābi* (192:12, 22-23; cf. 191:35 and rev. 2). That the *bēl dabābi* maligned the patient is clear from the ritual (191:35ff.), which prescribes that the mouth of a statue of the *bēl dabābi* be sealed, and from the accompanying incantation (191 rev. 2ff. [see above I 4)]), which states that the reason for sealing the *bēl dabābi*'s mouth is to stop him from maligning the patient. That the *bēl dabābi* also performed (or initiated the performance of) witchcraft against the patient is rendered probable by the fact that the ritual in *ArOr* 17/1 190ff. evidences a number of similarities to and connections with those in the witchcraft corpus, generally, and in *Maqlû*, specifically. Thus: the preparation and burning of statues in 191:14ff. and in 192:a-d (= VAT 13909:11′-14′) are in a form standard for the witchcraft corpus (cf., e.g., *AfO* 18 296:1ff. and *KAR* 80 [and duplicates] obv. 8ff. and rev. 15ff.); the incantation in 191:25ff. (// *STT* 256:41ff. // K 8107:1′ff.) is directed against a witch (who is, thereby, identified with a kúr.kúr: *nakara*) in *STT* 256 (see above II 1)) and mentions *zikurrudû*, a form of witchcraft; the function and formulation of the dousing of the fire in 191:33-35 (emend *it-tu* in 34 to *it-tu-*<*hu*>) are comparable with *AfO* 18 297:10 and M IX 86ff.; the incantation cited by incipit in 192:e (= VAT 13909:15′) is identical with M II 19ff. = IX 29 (see already *ArOr* 17/1 195); the incantation addressed to the *bēl dabābi* in 191 rev. 2ff. and the corresponding ritual in 191:37 may be compared, for example, with M III 89ff. (for the reading of 89, cf. *AfO* 21 80 on IX 47) and IX 47f. (the ritual for III 89ff. [for 48, see *CAD* B 102 and A/2 301]) respectively. (In contrast to *Maqlû* and to *STT* 256, *ArOr* 17/1 190ff. did not contain an address to the gods of the night, because it was performed in the daytime [cf. 191:38].)

4 Because a witch has bewitched me,[36]
5 a deceitful woman has accused me (or: a denouncer has denounced me), ...[37]

It must be emphasized that this translation of line 5 is based on established meanings of *elēnītu*, *elītu* and *ubburu.*[38]

This understanding of line 5 is rendered certain by more explicit usages in other incantations and by the evidence of later sections of our own incantation.

Evidence of Other Incantations. Elsewhere in the witchcraft corpus we find the explicit association of ***elēnītu*/*ubburu*** with "words" (*amātu*/*qibītu*) and the concomitant occurrence in parallelism of *elēnītu*, *ubburu* and *amātu*/*qibītu* with ***kaššaptu***,***epēšu*** and ***kišpū*/*riksu***, respectively. Note especially the legal setting of *LKA* 154 rev. 8′-9′ quoted below.

4 *R* 59/1 rev. 11-13:[39]
ša MÍ.UŠ$_{12}$.ZU.MU GAZ KEŠDA-*sa*
ša e-le-ni-ti-ia$_5$ *su-pi-hi* INIM.MEŠ-*šá*
tir-ra kiš-pi-šá a-na me-he-e INIM.MEŠ-*šá ana* IM
(compare M I 34-35: *kiṣrūša puṭṭurū ipšētūša hulluqā*[40]
kal amātūša malâ ṣēra.)

---

[36]For the meaning of *ukaššipanni* in this line, see below Sec. A, 3.

[37]In view of the documented association of witchcraft, a legal adversary and *kipdū*/*kapādu* (see below and cf., e.g., *AMT* 89/1 II [= V!] 11-22 // K 249 + V! [*KMI* 51f.] 8-20; K 249 + V! 21-24), we consider such statements as *ša kiš-pi i-pu-šu-ni ik-pu-du-ni nu-ul-la-a-*[*ti*] (4 *R* 17 rev. 20) or EN [K]A.KA-*šú kiš-pi* NIGIN-*šu kip-di lem*[*nūti ik-p*]*u-du-šú* (*KAR* 80 obv. 6f. and duplicate; for a fuller quote and for variants see above note 35) to be parallel formulations of M I 4-5 and of *LKA* 154 rev. 8′-9′ discussed below. We would translate 4 *R* 17 rev. 20, for example, as "who has performed witchcraft against me and has conjured up baseless (charges) against me." (Note further the final word in each of the lines 27-29 of this text: ... *kip-di-*[*šú-nu*] ... *kiš-pe-e* ... *ʾ-il-ti.*)

[38]Cf. *CAD* E s. *elēnēti*, *elēnītu* A, *elītu* mng. 9 (for *elītu*, see also *Nabnītu* L:265 cited *CAD* A/2 29b), *JCS* 9 124 (*ubburu*, *ākil karṣi*) and *AHw* s. *abāru* III D 2 (for the lexical equation lá, lá.lá = *ubburu ša amāti* cited there, see the translation of *Nabnītu* M:175f. in *CAD* A/2 29b and *ŠL* 481.2).

[39]See below Chapter 4, Sec. C.

[40]See below note 104.

M VI 44-48:
e kaššaptiya elēnītiya

....

....

....

[*u*]*sappah kišpīki u*[*târ amātīki ana pîki*][41]

Sm 352 obv. 17′:
[*ša kaššapti hipi*] ⌜*ri*⌝-*kis-sa šá eli-ni*!(text: *sa*)-*ti te-er* INIM-*sa* ⌜*ana*⌝ [*pîša*]

LKA 154 rev. 8′-9′:
...UŠ$_{12}$! DÙ-*šú-ni ina qí*-⌜*biti*⌝
[*u-tab/ub*]-*bi-ru-in-ni* ^{d}UTU *ina di-ni-ka* GAL-*e di-na-ni-ma* UGU-*šú-nu lu-ziz.*

(Note the courtroom setting, and for UGU-*šú-nu lu-ziz*, see, e.g., *STT* 271 I 8: NA.BI UGU EN KA G[U]B-⌜*az*⌝ ; and compare *LKA* 154 rev. 8′-9′ with *BWL* 200:16-17: *eninna ina qibīti ubburat napištī* / ^{d}*Šamaš ina dīnika murtudû aj ūṣi* [also compare *LKA* 154 rev. 10′ff. with *BWL* 200:18].)

Other Lines in this Incantation: Lines 31-33, 34-35, 28. Our understanding of M I 5 as referring to the oral delivery of accusations or denunciations against the speaker is confirmed by lines 31-33, 34-35 and 28. Although the nature of the argument in each case is essentially identical, the reader will perhaps forgive us if we present each argument separately and in detail.

---

[41]The correctness of Meier's restoration of M VI 48 is apparent from a comparison with M V 4f. It is possible that V 53 should serve as the basis for the restoration of VI 47; if so, read: [*hašû ti'ut ma-a*]-*ti*. In VI 45 Meier read: ".. *a*(?)-*bu la taš-ku-ni tu-qu-un-tu*." If Meier's reading ".. *a-bu*" is correct, then the mention of *tuquntu* and the association of these types of texts with those relating to an adversary suggest the possibility that *ayyābu* or, more probably, a derivative should be restored.

a) Lines 31-33 read:

pûša lū lipû lišānša lū ṭābtu
ša iqbû amāt lemuttiya kīma lipî littatuk
ša īpušu kišpī kīma ṭābti lihharmiṭ(!)[42]

Before we can make use of these lines, we must correct the previous translations of 32-33. Recent students of these lines have assumed that the witch is the subject of 32-33.[43] For example, Meier, *Maqlû*, p. 8, translates:

Ihr Mund sei Talg, ihre Zunge sei Salz:
Die die böse Zauberformel gegen mich gesprochen, wie Talg zergehe sie!
Die Zauberei gemacht hat, wie Salz löse sie sich auf![44]

However, this understanding is incorrect; for the subject of 32, represented by *ša*, is *pû*, "mouth," mentioned in 31a, and the subject of 33, also represented by a *ša*, is *lišānu*, "tongue," mentioned in 31b.[45] Since the mouth is identified with fat in 31a and the tongue with salt in 31b and since the subjects of 32 and 33 are then compared to fat and salt respectively, it is, to say the least, rather unlikely that the subjects of 32 and 33 respectively could be anything but the mouth and the tongue. Furthermore, the actions ascribed to the subjects of 32 (*ša iqbû amāt lemuttiya*)[46] and 33 (*ša īpušu kišpī*)

---

[42]For this emendation, see *AS* 13 61f.

[43]E.g., Meier, *Maqlû*, p. 8, Mendelsohn, *op. cit.*, p. 212, von Soden *apud* Meier, *AfO* 21 71. Some translations (cf. Thompson, *op. cit.*, p. XXVII, Landsberger, *Textbuch*[1], p. 125 and Heidel, *AS* 13 61f.) take the "word" and "magic" as the respective subjects of 32 and 33.

[44]Below we indicate that the subjects of 32 and 33 are the mouth and tongue respectively. That Meier did not take these as the subjects (and, therefore, that he construed the witch as the subject) is evident from the feminine relative pronoun "die" and the feminine third person pronoun "sie" used in his translation of 32, since "Mund," the correct subject of 32, is a masculine noun.

[45]Our translation of these lines was communicated in February, 1969 to Prof. A.L. Oppenheim and was introduced into a draft of the dictionary article on *kišpū*. [See now *CAD* K 455 a).]

[46]Cf., e.g., *ArOr* 17/1 191:4: *aṣbat pâka ana lā qabê* <(?) *ša amāt*> *lemuttiya.*

express functions of these two organs rather well. Finally, the preserved part of the ritual for this section, *STT* 83:12′-14′, prescribes the recitation of lines 32-33, the placing of salt in the mouth of the statue and the application of a torch to it.[47] The ritual thus assumes that these lines express the wish that the mouth and tongue of the witch, and not the witch herself, be destroyed and, therefore, that the subjects of 32-33 are these organs.

The speaker in lines 31-33 expresses the wish that the witch's mouth and tongue be destroyed. They are to be destroyed because these are the very organs which she used to harm him (*ša iqbû amāt lemuttiya ... ša īpušu kišpī*) and which she may be expected to use again for the same purpose. Through this destruction the plaintiff is avenged for past harm and protected against future harm, since the witch is now rendered powerless and unable to initiate harmful actions. This should be compared not only with such passages as *ArOr* 17/1 191:4-6 and VAT 35:1-5, where the victim renders his *bēl dabābi* harmless and unable to malign him by depriving him of his powers of speech,[48] or with such others as M VII 109f. // 116f., but also with those laws which stipulate that an organ responsible for a damage is to be destroyed; it has already been said of paragraph 218

The reasons for our emendation are given below note 52.

[47]The ritual, *STT* 83:12′-14′, reads:

12′ ÉN *al-si-ku-n*[*u-š*]*i* 3-*šú* ŠID-*nu* M[UN

13′ *šá iq-bu-u a-mat* HUL-*ti-ia i-*<*qab*>*-bi šá* [*īpušu kišpī*

14′ ⌈x⌉ [x x] ⌈x⌉ MUN *ina* KA-*šú* GAR-*nu*/NU *ina ap-pi* GI.IZI.LA[L

The reasons for our reading of 13′ will be found in our "Textual notes to the ritual tablet of *Maqlû*." Moreover, it is noted there that the ritual tablet has split our incantation into two parts and has prescribed a different set of ritual actions for each of these parts. The treatment of our incantation in the ritual tablet points up an important principle which should be kept in mind when reading incantations: An incantation describing progressive ritual actions may in fact have been accompanied by the performance of these very actions. An incantation of this type need not be static, and the action may progress step by step and achieve its intended result within the incantation itself. Accordingly, a later part of the incantation may express, assume or derive from the fulfillment of an earlier part. This dynamic is especially evident in our incantation. The reader will remember, for example, that the speaker in 21-24 requests that various plants cleanse and free him. In 25-26 he states that he has been cleansed. 25-26 assert that the earlier actions have been performed and that the hoped-for result is now an established fact. The later parts of the text then start from that result.

[48]See above notes 35 and 46 and below Sec. A, 3.

of the Code of Hammurabi that:

> If, however, either of the first two operations is unsuccessful and the patient dies or loses his eye, the doctor, if the patient is a free man, loses his hand and therewith his ability to remain in practice; he is punished in the offending organ for the satisfaction of the patient, and the general public is at the same time protected against future risk at his hands.[49]

We have seen that the tongue and mouth of the speaker's adversary are to be destroyed because they are the organs with which that adversary has harmed him. More specifically, the tongue has *īpušu kišpī* (33) and the mouth has *iqbû amāt lemuttiya* (32). We are now ready to return to lines 4-5. Since 4-5 describe the actions by which the speaker's adversary originally harmed him, it may be supposed that 4-5 and 32-33 parallel each other and refer to the same actions (but see below Sec. B). Given this supposition, the sufficiently apparent parallelism between *lišānša ... sa īpušu kišpī* (31b.33) and *kaššaptu ukaššipanni* (4) and the association, established above, of *elēnītu* and *ubburu* with *amātu/qibītu* permit us to conclude that *pûša ... ša iqbû amāt lemuttiya* of 31a.32 parallels *elēnītu ubbiranni* of 5 and that both refer to the same action. Accordingly, 5 must refer to an action involving the spoken word, and *ubburu* here must be translated "to accuse/denounce."

b) Lines 34-35 read:

kiṣrūša puṭṭurū ipšētūša hulluqā
kal amātūša malâ ṣēra.

Since 4-5 describe the actions which the speaker's adversary has performed against him and since 34-35 contain the court's declaration that (the results of) these actions are nullified, it may be supposed that 4-5 and 34-35 parallel each other and refer to the same actions. Given this supposition, the sufficiently apparent parallelism between *kiṣrūša puṭṭurū ipšētūša hulluqā* (34) and *kaššaptu ukaššipanni* (4) (see below Sec. A, 3.) and the association of *elēnītu* and *ubburu*

[49] Driver and Miles, *The Babylonian Laws*, I, pp. 417f.

with *amātu/qibītu* permit us to conclude that *kal amātūša malâ ṣēra* of 35 parallels *elēnitu ubbiranni* of 5 and that both refer to the same action. Accordingly, 5 must refer to an action involving the spoken word, and *ubburu* here must be translated "to accuse/denounce."

c) Line 28 reads:

turrat amāssa ana pîša lišānša kaṣrat.

28 parallels 31-33 in that 28a and 31a.32 are directed against the witch's mouth and word and 28b and 31b.33 are directed against the witch's tongue. 28 also parallels 34-35 in that 34 nullifies an effect of an action performed by the witch and 28b causes that same effect to take hold of the witch (see below Sec. A, 3) and both 28a and 35 declare that a "word" spoken by the witch has been rendered ineffective. Accordingly, 28 also reflects the original actions of the witch. Since 4-5 describe the witch's original actions (and since 4-5, 31-33 and 34-35 are parallel), it may be supposed that 4-5 and 28 parallel each other and refer to the same actions or types of actions. Given this supposition, the parallelism between 28b, 31b.33 and 34 and between 31b.33, 34 and 4 indicates that 28b parallels 4 (see below Sec. A, 3). The parallelism between 28b and 4 and the association of *elēnītu* and *ubburu* with *amātu/qibītu* permit us to conclude that *turrat amāssa ana pîša* of 28a parallels *elēnītu ubbiranni* of 5 and that both refer to the same action. Accordingly, 5 must refer to an action involving the spoken word, and *ubburu* here must be translated "to accuse/denounce."

Summary: Line 5 and Lines 21-28. It may be considered as established that *ubburu* in 5 means "to accuse/denounce," that in this line the speaker states that orally delivered accusations or denunciations have been directed against him, and that these accusations are responsible for his having been rejected by god and man. This understanding of 5 confirms both our interpretation of *amātu* in 28 (as well as in 32 and 35) as referring to an accusation which had been brought against the speaker and our interpretation of 21-26 as representing the speaker's attempt to clear himself of an accusation by means of (a functional equivalent of) an ordeal or oath. Given this confirmation and the exegetical presumptions concerning the relation of 21-26 to 27-28 and of 27 to 28 established earlier (see above Chapter 2), we may summarize our understanding of the inner logic of this part of the plaintiff's address to the court as follows: The speaker-plaintiff has had an accusation brought against him by the witch (5: *elēnītu ubbiranni*). By clearing himself by means of an "oath" of the accusation (21-24: *bīnu lillilanni* ...), the speaker has demonstrated his innocence to the court (25-26: *ina mahrikunu ētelil* ... *ētebib azzaku* ...). If he is innocent, the accusation must be false and must have been motivated by evil intent. This being the case (27: *tûša ša kaššapti lemutte*), the accusation is disproved or rebutted (28a: *turrat amāssa ana pîša*), and the accuser is silenced and unable to press the charge (28b: *lišānša kaṣrat*).

For a convincing parallel to this situation, we need only remember that in the Code of Hammurabi the act referred to by the verb *ubburu* normally causes the accused to undergo some kind of ordeal in order to establish his innocence.[50]

3. Silencing of Victim (Tongue): Lines 4, 9-11 and Parallel Lines

Silencing. In our text the speaker and the witch are to be viewed as legal adversaries (*bēl dabābi*) who harm each other by means of accusations and counter-accusations. In addition to accusations, there is a further component in a controversy of the type found in our text, and we must now turn to this component. In this type of confrontation the adversaries are understandably concerned with their opponent's ability to speak, because it is this ability which allows one party to make the initial charge and the other to disprove it. For this reason, the parties not only accuse each other, but also attempt to silence each other. One may silence an opponent by presenting the evidence in a manner that will confound him and will thereby

[50]In connection with the occurrence in paragraphs 1-2 of the Code of Hammurabi of forms derived from *ubburu*, Driver and Miles, *The Babylonian Laws*, I, p. 59, ask: "Does this mean that the man who brings the charge prosecutes the other man in a court of law or merely that he is publishing a defamatory statement about him?" They answer the question as follows:

force him to remain silent and/or by magically impairing his speech organs. (We should not see these as totally separate means, since the use of magic to silence an opponent is often no more than a concretization of the hope that the evidence will be so overpowering as to force him to keep silent.)

This silencing, however achieved, finds literary expression in statements involving the tongue and mouth of an adversary. In texts dealing with this type of conflict we have already encountered such statements as *anettepu lišānšu* (*utarra amāssu ana pîšu*) (*KAR* 71 rev. 5f.) and *ushā lišān*[*ša*] [(K 8162:11),[51] and we may also quote

> The other passage where it is found is §131, which says that a woman's husband 'has charged her' (Bab. *ûbbirši*) with infidelity; and it seems that this charge must be brought in a court of law as the woman is required to purge herself by the ordeal by oath, which is a mode of proof frequently ordered by a court where there is no direct evidence. In §132, again, where the wife is accused by common report, she is required to undergo the ordeal; here, too, there must be a trial before some court which sends her to the ordeal. In §126, too, the proof before a god that nothing has been lost seems to require the order of a court, and in §127, which is in content not unlike §§1-2, the proceedings take place before the judges. It appears, then, that this verb in §1 implies an accusation before a court of law, and that in §2 the 'man' (Bab. *awīlum*) who brings the charge of witchcraft is also a prosecutor as he is called in l. 44 the 'accuser' (Bab. *mûbbirum*). (*ibid.*)

Without necessarily rejecting this conclusion, we must take exception to the argument on which it is based. The argument boils down to this: since the act of *ubburu* leads to an ordeal or to some other court-instituted procedure, *ubburu* must refer to the bringing of a formal accusation before a court of law. However, the authors themselves compare paragraphs 131 with 132 and note that 132 also requires an ordeal. But, since the functional equivalent of *ubburu* in 131 is accusation "by common report" in 132, the comparison would seem to vitiate the argument because it indicates that a formal determination of innocence or guilt need not result only from a formal accusation brought before a court of law. Note, for example, that in the Middle Assyrian Laws, Tablet A, paragraph 17, Numbers ch. 5 and Deuteronomy 22:13ff. an initial non-formal suspicion and accusation led to an ordeal (the first two) or to a court investigation and decision (the last). It may be that in those communities in which these laws developed the distinction between a formal and informal accusation, which gave rise to the authors' original question, was not significant and that both types of accusations would have had the same effect upon the accused's standing in the community.

[51] See above Chapter, 2, Sec. A.

from a patient's address to his *bēl dabābi* (*ArOr* 17/1 191 rev. 2ff.) which he delivers as he magically impairs the speech organs of his *bēl dabābi* (cf. *ibid.* 35ff.):

ṣalam bēl dabābiya attāma ...
aṣbat pâka ana lā qabê <(?) *ša amāt*> *lemuttiya ...*
aktanak šaptēka ana lā šūlê ša šumiya.[52]

In our incantation we find the same idea expressed: after the plaintiff has proved his innocence and has established the presumption that the accusation brought against him is false, he states:

(*turrat amāssa ana pîša*) *lišānša kaṣrat* (28).

As we have seen, the plaintiff declares in this statement (a) that the witch's accusation has been disproved (*turrat amāssa ana pîša*) and (b) that her speech organ has thereby been disabled (*lišānša kaṣrat*).

Meaning of Line 4. Since we may assume that the plaintiff's (= the speaker) actions essentially parallel those of his detractor (= the witch) and reverse their effects, since one of the two components present in this type of conflict can be documented for both the detractor and the plaintiff, viz. the bringing of an accusation by the witch (*elēnītu ubbiranni*, 5) and its refutation by the speaker (*turrat amāssa ana pîša*, 28a), and since the other component can be documented for the plaintiff, viz. the silencing of the witch by the speaker (*lišānša kaṣrat*, 28b [cf. also 31a.32]), it is reasonable to surmise that also the detractor originally attempted to silence the plaintiff, that *kaššaptu ukaššipanni* (4) refers to this attempt and is parallel to *lišānša kaṣrat*, and, therefore, that the witch's initial action against the speaker would have involved not only the bringing

[52] Our emendation of *aṣbat pâka ana lā qabê lemuttiya* to ... *ana lā qabê* <*ša amāt*> *lemuttiya* is based on: the parallelism between this line and *aktanak šaptēka ana lā šūlê ša šumiya*; the structure (*ana lā* + verb + *ša* + term for utterance (+ ...)) of the latter line and of such similar lines as VAT 35:4-5 quoted below; and the similarity in function as well as in linguistic content of the emended line to M I 32: *ša iqbû amāt lemuttiya* (cf. M III 89f., for which see *AfO* 21 80 on M IX 47).

of an accusation, but also an attempt to impair his speech organs and to render him speechless.

To determine whether this is correct we must turn again to the description of the witch's actions. Several considerations indicate that 4 is in fact to be interpreted in the light of 28b and that it refers to the disabling of the speaker's speech organs by the witch for the purpose of ensuring the success of the accusation. We may refer in the first instance to the formal configuration of elements in our text. It may be taken as established that 28a (*turrat amāssa ana pîša*) parallels 35 (*kal amātūša malâ ṣēra*), that both parallel (i.e., refer to the situation created in) 5 (*elēnītu ubbiranni*) and that 34 (*kiṣrūša puṭṭurū ipšētūša hulluqā*) parallels (i.e., refers to the situation created in) 4 (*kaššaptu ukaššipanni*). From these equations and from the occurrence of forms of *kaṣāru* in 28b (*lišānša kaṣrat*) and in 34 (*kiṣrūša puṭṭurū*), it may be inferred that 28b and 34 are parallel (i.e., 34 nullifies an effect of the witch's action, 28b causes that same effect to be imposed on her) and that, since 4 and 34 are parallel, 4 and 28b must also be parallel. It follows from these inferences, especially since the witch's *kiṣrū* in 34 must be due to that action of the witch referred to as *ukaššipanni* in 4, that 4 refers to the same type of action as 28b, that an action which creates a state described by forms of *kaṣāru* must be understood as being subsumed under the statement *kaššaptu ukaššipanni* and that this action had as its purpose the disabling of the speaker's speech organs so as to ensure the success of the accusation which was subsequently brought against him in 5.[53]

Lines 9-11. This interpretation of 4 is rendered certain by the continuation of the description of the plaintiff's state. In 9-11 we read:

9 *qû*[54] *imtanallû pīya*
10 *upunti pîya iprusu*[55]
11 *mê maštītiya umaṭṭû*

[53] See below Sec. B for the place of 31-33 in this configuration of elements.

[54] *qu-ú* is to be preferred to *qu-lu* found in one MS. See below note 78. For the meaning of *qû*, see below.

[55] The omission of a macron over the final *u* in *iprusu* is not inadvertent. See below.

These lines were translated by Meier, *Maqlû*, p. 7, as:

> Mit Zauberknoten haben sie meinen Mund gefüllt,
> mit Mehl mir den Mund verschlossen,[56]
> mein Trinkwasser verringert.

Let us leave 10-11 for later and concentrate on 9. According to von Soden,[57] "Die Übersetzung von Meier setzt anscheinend voraus, dass *im-ta-na-al-lu-ú* ein Hörfehler für *um-ta-na-al-lu-ú* 'sie füllen immer wieder' ist. Im I, 1 und I, 3-Stamm ist *malû* neutrisch (s. zu Z. 23). Der Text muss hier verderbt sein."[58] Underlying this translation and emendation of 9 are the incorrect assumptions that the *qû* had not been placed in the speaker's mouth prior to its mention in 9, that the function of 9 is to describe that placing, that the main purpose of placing it in his mouth was to prevent him from eating and drinking and that *imtanallû* is a plural verb whose grammatical subject is the witches.

In VAT 35,[59] a text which had as its purpose the victory over a legal adversary (see 18, the statement of purpose of the ritual: *ina muh-hi* EN INIM-*šú* GUB-*zu*; cf. 7: NU EN *da-ba-ba* ... DÙ-⌜*uš*⌝), we find the speaker addressing a statue of his *bēl dabābi* as follows:

1 [*a*]*ṣ-bat* KA-*ki ú-tab-bil* EME-*k*[*i*]
2 *aṣ-bat* ŠU^{II}-*ki ad-di qa-a a-na* KA-[*ki*]
3 *ap-te-te* KA-*ki at-ta-sah* EME K[A-*ki*]
4 *a-na la da-ba-ba šá dib-bi-ja a-na* [*la*]
5 *šu-un-ni-e šá a-ma-ti-já*

---

[56] Von Soden *apud* Meier, *AfO* 21 71 now translates: "Das Mehl für meinen Mund hielten sie fern."

[57] *Apud* Meier, *AfO* 21 71.

[58] Cf. *AHw* s. *malû* IV Gtn 2: "*qû im-ta-na-al-lu-ú pî-ja Maqlû* I 9 (Fehler?)."

[59] We learned of this text from quotations in *CAD* D 3f. A transliteration of the full text prepared by Prof. F. Köcher is in the possession of the Oriental Institute, and we quote from that transliteration. Most of the lines quoted below have already appeared in *CAD* (18: D 4; 7: D 3; 1: A/1 31, Ṣ 21; 4-5: A/2 31).

Lines 1-3 may be translated as follows:

> Having seized your mouth (and) dried out your tongue,[60]
> (and) having (then) seized your hands (and) placed a *qû*
> (see below) into your mouth,
> I have now held your mouth open (and) torn out your tongue
> (i.e., having held your mouth open [by means of the *qû*],
> I have now been able to tear out your tongue), ...

The text explicitly informs us that these operations on the *bēl dabābi*'s speech organs were carried out in order to silence him and thereby to prevent him from maligning and accusing the speaker. These operations include the insertion of a *qû* into the *bēl dabābi*'s mouth in order to force him to keep his mouth open, in order to prevent him from moving his tongue and in order to force his tongue into a position in which it may easily be grabbed and torn out.[61]

However, if one inserts a *qû* into an adversary's mouth, it is not really necessary to also tear out his tongue, because the *qû* by itself would achieve the desired result of silencing him. The insertion of a *qû* into an adversary's mouth causes his tongue to be *kaṣrat*, "constricted,"[62] and this physical condition makes it somewhat difficult to speak (cf. TDP 62:19: *šumma lišānšu ikkaṣir dabāba l[ā*

[60] For this translation of 1b, see *CAD* A/1 31 and *AHw* s. *abālu* I D 3.

[61] For addresses to a *bēl dabābi* similar to the one in VAT 35, see above note 35 I 4). The sequence of actions in lines 1-3 can be best understood in the following way (we refer to the speaker as A and the *bēl dabābi* as B): A causes B's tongue to be parched in order to force B to open his mouth. (It may also be that a parched tongue is more easily torn out than a moist one.) When B opens his mouth, A grabs B's hands in order to prevent him from offering any resistance and inserts the *qû* into B's mouth. (Consider that it would require both of A's hands to grab B's hands and to place the *qû* in his mouth. This left A with no hands free to hold B's mouth open. Since the *qû* could only be inserted if B's mouth was open, A had to resort to a means which would force B to keep his own mouth open, and so he first dried out B's tongue.) The *qû* forces both B's mouth to remain open and his tongue to be in an accessible position. A, then, tears out B's tongue. See below note 63.

[62] See already Kraus, *AfO* 11 226:66, who translates *kaṣrat* when said of the tongue as "zusammengezogen." Cf. *AHw* s. *kaṣāru* G 6b and N 3 for further examples; *kaṣāru* in this usage is translated there as "verhärten" (G 6) or "gebunden, verkrampft werden" (N 3).

ilê and *ZA* 45 26:8: [*l*]*išānšu ikṣurma atmâ ul utarra*). As the Mesopotamians were no less economical in their actions than we are, more often than not they would have placed a *qû*, or a similar device, into an adversary's mouth and have left it at that. This is clear, for example, from the address to a witch in M VII 109f. // 116f.: *pîki lemnu epera limli* (var.: *limla*) *lišānki ša lemutti ina qê likkaṣir*[63] or from the rubric *STT* 72:40 // 251:6′: INIM.INIM.MA *ki-ṣir qa* EN(*bēl*) DI(*dīni*) DU$_8$-*ri*(*puṭṭuri*), "to relax the constriction (of a tongue caused by) a *qû* (placed into the mouth by) a legal adversary."[64] Contrary to accepted opinion,[65] *qû* in these passages does not simply refer to a string with which the tongue was tied. Rather, it refers to some kind of gag or bridle, the mouthpiece of which was probably placed under the tongue and pushed as far back in the mouth as possible. *qû* should be compared, for example, with *napsamu*. Compare specifically *addi qâ ana pî*[*ki*] (VAT 35:2) with *ina pî ... iddi napsama* (*BWL* 56:q) and *lišānki ... ina qê likkaṣir* (M VII 110 // 117) with *napsamu: makṣaru ša pī sīsî* (the commentary to *BWL* 56:q).

Returning to our *Maqlû* incantation, we note immediately that *kiṣrūša puṭṭurū* (M I 34) is exactly parallel to *kiṣir qâ bēl dīni puṭṭuri* (*STT* 72:40 // 251:6′) and that *lišānša kaṣrat* (M I 28b) is exactly parallel to *lišānki ša lemutti ina qê likkaṣir* (M VII 110 // 117).

In view of the function of the *qû* just documented and of the association of *qû*, *kaṣāru*[66] and *lišānu* in magical texts having a background similar to that of our incantation, the occurrence in our in-

[63]VAT 35 (see above note 61) points to the possibility that dirt/dust (*epru*) was placed in the witch's mouth in order to dry out her tongue and, thereby, to facilitate the insertion of the *qû*.

[64]In *STT* 72 DI is immediately followed by DU$_8$-. In *STT* 251 there are traces between these signs, and we are uncertain whether these traces represent a damaged sign (in which case perhaps read DI.⌈KUD⌉ or *di*-⌈*ni*!?⌉ in this MS) or an erasure. While we have disagreed with Reiner, *JNES* 26 191, who transliterated and partially translated the rubric as INIM.INIM.MA *ki-ṣir qa* EN DI *paṭāri*, "incantation to undo a knot of ...." in taking DU$_8$-*ri* as *puṭṭuri*, we have done so only because of *kiṣrūša puṭṭurū* of M I 34, and it is still possible that *paṭāri* is correct.

[65]E.g., Meier, *Maqlû*, pp. 7:9, 50:110, 51:117; *AHw* s. *kaṣāru* N 3.

[66]The underlying association of *qû* and *kaṣāru* is also evident in the phrase *mušalliṭu qê lumni* (cf. 4 *R* 17 rev. 17, *RA* 48 8:16, *Iraq* 18 62:18), since *qê lumni* is obviously comparable to *kiṣir lumni* (e.g., 4 *R* 55/2:6).

cantation of *lišānša kaṣrat* (28b) and *kiṣrūša puṭṭurū* on the one hand and of *qû imtanallû pīya* on the other clearly indicates that the *qû* in our incantation was placed in the speaker's mouth in order to silence him and to deprive him thereby of his ability to defend himself against accusations. And we must compare this situation with the one described, for example, in lines 68-75 of the first tablet of *Ludlul bēl nēmeqi*:

Their hearts rage against me, and they are ablaze like fire.
They combine against me in slander and lies.
They have sought to muzzle my respectful mouth,
So that I, whose lips used to prate, have become like a mute.
My sonorous shout is [reduced] to silence,[67]
My lofty head is bowed down to the ground,
Dread has enfeebled my robust heart.
A novice has turned back my broad chest.[68]

The G (neutral) tn (iterative) form of *malû* (in contrast to a factitive non-iterative form of the verb) in the statement *qû imtanallû pīya* in 9 excludes the possibility that this line describes the insertion of the *qû* into the speaker's mouth, indicates that the verb is a singular whose subject is *qû*[69] and requires that this line describe a continuous situation ("a *qû* continually fills my mouth") which resulted from the aforementioned action. Therefore, the speaker in 9 must take this action for granted; the action must have taken place at a point prior to 9; and the description of the action must be implicit in one of the earlier lines in the text. Since there is no reason to assume that it is implicit in 1-3 or in 5-8,[70] since we previously

[67] Cf. M I 12.

[68] Lines 68-69 and 71-75 are quoted from *BWL* 35, and line 70 is quoted from *ANET*[3] 596.

[69] See below where we show that the *-u* ending is a subjunctive morpheme.

[70] That a description of this action is not implicit in 1-3 and 6-8 is too obvious to require comment. Moreover, we reject categorically the possibility that it is either explicit or implicit in 5 (*elēnītu ubbiranni*). While we believe that our previous arguments relating to 4 and 5 are sufficient to establish this, the reader might be inclined to raise an objection from the rubric *AfO* 18 296:26-28, and, therefore, we must examine this rubric. The present edition and translation of this rubric read:

established the presumption from the parallelism between 4, 28b and 34 and between 5, 28a and 35 that the act of silencing was implicit in *kaššaptu ukaššipanni* of 4 and that this act created a state described by forms of *kaṣāru* (*kiṣru*, *kaṣrat*) and since we have also established that the main purpose of inserting the *qû* into the speaker's mouth in our text was to silence him and that the state created by this use of a *qû* is also described by forms of *kaṣāru* (*kiṣru*, *nakṣuru*), we are completely justified, and probably even required, to conclude that the act of inserting the *qû* into the speaker's mouth in order

---

26 INIM.INIM.MA *kaššāpti*(MÍ.UŠ$_{12}$.ZU) *šá kiš-pi ma-'-du-tú i-pu-*[*šu*]
27 *sahārim*(NIGIN)-*ma ṣa-ba-ti šá kaššāpti*(MÍ.UŠ$_{12}$.ZU) *šá ru-he-e i-pu-šu-šu pi-i-*[*š*]*a*
28 *ár-hiš ub-bu-ri*

Incantation for finding and seizing a sorceress who has performed much sorcery, for speedily binding the mouth of the sorceress who has performed charms against him.

We consider the text of this rubric to be corrupt. The present edition and translation of the duplicate, *ibid.* 8-9, read:

8 INIM.INIM.MA [..] *kaš-šap-tu ša kiš-pi ma-'-*[*du-ti īpuša*(DÙ-*šá*)]
9 *sahārim*(NIGIN)-*ma ṣabāti*(DI[B) [*šá ru-*]*he-e šá ru-se-e īpuša*(DÙ-*šá*) *ú-še-pi-š*[*á* ..]

Incantation [..] for finding and seizing a sorceress who [has performed mu]ch sorcery, [who] has performed and has had performed [.. cha]rms and spells.

1) Since the duplicate reads *īpuša*(DÙ-*šá*) *ú-še-pi-š*[*á*] (9) instead of *i-pu-šu-šu pi-i-*[*š*]*a* (27) and since lines 26-28 contain the only occurrence of *pâ ubburu* known to us, it is probable that the original text did not have *pīša* and that 27 should be emended to *i-pu-šu* ⸢*ú*!⸣-<*še*>-*pi*-<<*i*>>-[*š*]*a*.

2) Line 8 of the duplicate indicates that something has been omitted in 26 between INIM.INIM.MA and MÍ.UŠ$_{12}$.ZU. A glance at *LKA* 154 (+) 155 (not yet confirmed) // *LKA* 157 // K 3394 (Gray,*SRT* 7)+ K 9866 (confirmed) is most instructive in this regard:

LKA 157 I 21 // *LKA* 154 obv. 9(B):
[*kiš-pi e*]*p-šú-šú sa-ha-rim-ma ana* DÙ-*šú-nu ṣa-*⸢*ba*⸣(B: (?)+-⸢*a*⸣)-*ti*(B: *te*);
K 3394 rev. 15 // *LKA* 155 rev. 27:
INIM.INIM.MA *kiš-pi sa-ha-rim-*[*ma ana* DÙ-*šú*]-*nu ṣa-ba-ta*.

These two passages, and especially the second, indicate that *kišpī* should be restored in 8 and inserted in 26. 26-27a should be translated "to cause <witchcraft> to turn and seize the witch (*kaššapta*) who has performed much witchcraft." (For the *sahāru*/ *târu*-*ṣabātu* motif in this meaning in witchcraft texts, cf., also, M VII 159f., 169, *AMT* 85/1 II 13f. // *BAM* 208 II 8f., K 2395:2.)

(3) We leave open the question whether the first *ša* in 27 should be attached to *ṣabāti* or whether it was inserted after *ušēpiša* had been corrupted to *piša* and should, therefore, be eliminated.)

to silence him and to prevent him from rebutting the accusation is implicit in *kaššaptu ukaššipanni* in 4.

Our interpretation of 9 as describing a situation which resulted from an action of the witch, rather than the action itself, not only explains the Gtn form *imtanallû* and thereby eliminates the need of an emendation, but also allows us to remove a disturbing anomaly from lines 6-12. According to the previous translations of 9-11,[71] these lines describe actions of the witch. However, since 4-5 describe actions of the witch and since 6-8 and 12 describe the effects of these actions on the victim, 9-11, as understood by these translations, do not fit into the sequence and create a structural and logical disturbance. By showing that 9 describes a situation which resulted from an earlier action, we have eliminated that part of the problem created by 9. But we are then left with the following interrelated questions about 9-11:

1) If the witches are not the subject of *imtanallû*, what is the function of the -*u* ending in this verb?

2) Since 9 describes a situation which resulted from an action whose purpose was to silence the speaker and since no mention is made of any speech impairment in this and the following lines, why does the speaker in 9 even bother to describe this situation?

3) If 9 describes an effect of an action performed in an earlier part of the text, should not 10-11 also describe such effects?

The reader will recognize that if we can answer these questions satisfactorily, our interpretation of 4 and 9 will be further confirmed.

To answer these questions, we need only realize that the same *qû* which was placed in the speaker's mouth in order to silence him would not have allowed him to close his mouth or to use his tongue and, therefore, would also have had the added effect of not allowing him to eat or to drink. The purpose of 9-11 is to describe this added effect. In presenting this description, the speaker first explains why it is that he is unable to eat or to drink, viz. *qû imtanallû pīya*, and, thereby, also ascribes ultimate responsibility for this inability to the witch who had placed the *qû* in his mouth (4). However, it is not

---

[71] Cf., e.g., Meier, *Maqlû*, p. 7, quoted above; von Soden *apud* Meier, *AfO* 21 71, quoted above and in note 56; Landsberger, *Textbuch*², p. 322 ("Mit Kleister (?) haben sie meinen Mund vollgestopft, ...").

the witch, but rather the *qû* (9) that is immediately responsible for the speaker's inability to eat and to drink (10-11). This immediate responsibility is implicit in the proximity of 9 to 10-11 and in the situation underlying our text. And we may again refer to a description of a comparable situation in *Ludlul bēl nēmeqi*, though this time found in tablet II (*BWL* 42-45:84-87):

> A snare is laid on my mouth,[72]
> And a bolt bars my lips,
> My 'gate' is barred, my 'drinking place'[73] blocked,
> My hunger is prolonged, my throat stopped up.

Moreover, the speaker in our incantation expressly describes the situation exactly as we have construed it. For, by using the preterite-specific form of the verb in 10-11 and by contrast the present-iterative form in 9, a usage which indicates that the events described in 10-11 are attendant upon the circumstance described in 9, the speaker also explicitly ascribes the immediate responsibility for his inability to eat and to drink (10-11) to the *qû* (9).

The verbs in 9-11 (*imtanallû, iprusu, umaṭṭû*) have been interpreted by the previous translators of 9-11[74] as plural verbs whose subjects are the witches. The considerations presented thus far in our treatment reveal, however, that this interpretation is incorrect and that not the witches, but the *qû* is the subject of all three verbs in these lines. Moreover, the aforementioned considerations do not exhaust our reasons for contending that "the witches" cannot be the subject of these verbs. We may also introduce the -*u* ending in these verbs as further evidence in support of this contention; for if "the witches" (*kaššaptu* + *elēnītu*), a feminine plural referent, were the subject, the pronominal affix expressing the subject of these verbs should then have been -*ā* (**imtanallâ*, **iprusā*, **umaṭṭâ*) and not -*u*. This -*u* ending is a subjunctive morpheme, and the subjunctive form of these verbs is due to *aššu* in 4, which word governs 4-12. This is

[72] *ina pîya nahbal nadīma*. In the context of our discussion, note, for whatever it is worth, that *nahbalu* is translated *qû nahbalim* in *MSL* VI 76:98 and 79:43 (cited *AHw* s. *nahbalu*).

[73] See below note 79.

[74] See above note 71.

proved by the variant *am-ru-ṣu* in 7,[75] since *amruṣu* obviously cannot be a plural verb and the *-u* must be the subjunctive morpheme. All the verbs in 4-12 are in the (singular) subjunctive form,[76] and these lines form a *Kausalsatz* introducing 13-14.[77]

The verbs in 9-11 are singular subjunctives whose subject is the *qû* mentioned in 9,[78] and these lines are to be translated:

> A gag(?) continually filling my mouth
> has kept food distant from my mouth (and)
> has diminished the (amount of) water (which passes through) my drinking (organ).[79]

[75] Meier, *Maqlû*, p. 7, n. 7.

[76] Thus, "the witch" and not the witches is the subject of *ušessû* (6). From the speaker's point of view, the *kaššaptu* and *elēnītu* of 4 and 5 are simply designations of a single opponent.

[77] This, of course, proves that 4-5 are not a syntactically independent unit or syntactically connected to 1-3.

[78] According to Meier, *Maqlû*, p.66, an Assur MS has *qu-lu* instead of *qu-ú* in this line. Even if *qu-lu* were to be shown to be the better reading, our interpretation of 4 would not be essentially affected, since 9 would then be quite explicit in describing the speaker as being silent and would, therefore, still take a prior action of silencing for granted. (Also our interpretation of the verbs in 9-11 as singulars would remain unaffected, though the subject of 10-11 would then probably have to be the witch.) However, we consider *qu-ú* to be the better reading for a number of reasons. These reasons are all implicit in our discussion of 9-11 and their relation to other parts of the incantation, and here we need only summarize several of these reasons.

1) Texts like *BWL* 34f.:68-75, quoted above, establish the association of maligning with silencing the accused by means of a mouthpiece.

2) In view of the association of *kaṣāru, lišānu* and *qû* in, e.g., M VII 110 // 117, the clear occurrence in our incantation of the first two (28b, 34) argues in favor of seeing the third in 9.

3) Since 9-11 deal with the mouth, it is a legitimate presumption that there is a close relationship between 9 and 10-11. *qû* fulfills the terms of this requirement and establishes a relationship between 9 and 10-11 identical with the one between *BWL* 42f.:84 and 42-45:85-87. *qūlu*, on the other hand, does not fulfill the terms of this requirement.

[79] Since *upunti pîya* (10) and *mê maštītiya* (11) are parallel, *maštītiya* is best taken here as a term for the whole or part of the mouth. Compare the use of *mašqû'a* in *BWL* 42:86 (*ba-bi e-di-il pi-hi maš-qu-u-a*), quoted above.

4. Lines 4-5: Summary and Further Illustration.

We have tried to show that lines 4-5 (*aššu kaššaptu ukaššipanni elēnītu ubbiranni*) are to be understood in the following way: In order to effectively denounce the speaker, the witch inserted a *qû* in his mouth and thereby constricted his tongue (*kaṣrat*; cf. 28b and 34) and silenced him. She then denounced him. We may conclude this part of our analysis by citing a bilingual incantation, edited without translation in *ZA* 45 25f.[80] Not only does this incantation provide a parallel to the treatment suffered by the victim in M I 1-36 at the hand of his witch, but it also shares with it a number of linguistic usages. It will be sufficient for our purpose to quote and translate the Akkadian version of the first eight lines, and we may safely leave it to the reader to notice the similarities and to draw the necessary conclusions.

2 [*kaš*]*šaptum ana tappê ubburi ṣalam ibni*
4 [*l*]*išānšu mušāṭu ukarrik mešrētūšu uktessi*
6 *pīšu iṣbatma pīšu ul ipetti*
8 [*l*]*išānšu ikṣurma atmâ ul utarra*

2 In order to denounce a comrade,[81] a witch made a statue (of him).

[80]A further duplicate of this incantation is Rm 491 obv. 1′-11′. These lines correspond to obv. 5 - rev. 7 of the edition. Note that the incantation in this MS seems to be unilingual. This MS provides several variants. (In listing these variants, we utilize Falkenstein's alphabetic notations of variants whenever possible and repeat the information given there.)

obv. 12 ù-me-ni-sì: Rm 491: u- for ù-.
obv. 15 ba-ni-íb-gi$_4$-gi$_4$: Rm 491: mu-un-ab-gi$_4$-[.
rev. 1 note d: "Rm II 314 mu-na- für ba-."; Rm 491: mu-un-na- for ba-.
rev. 3 kuš-ni-ta: Rm 491: šu- for kuš-.
rev. 3 note f: "Rm II 314 hat zi-zi für ba-an-zi."; Rm 491: zi [for ba-an-zi.
rev. 6 sig$_5$-ga: Rm 491: sig$_6$- for sig$_5$-.

[81]For intra-*tappû* denunciations, cf. *BWL* 34:86 and *JCS* 9 123. For a different translation of *ubburi* in this line, see *AHw* s. *abāru* III D 1 ("umspannen").

4 She gagged his tongue with wool combing[82] (and) bound his members.
6 She seized his mouth so that he would be unable to open his mouth.
8 She constricted his tongue so that he would be unable to refute (her) accusation.[83]

B. Two Images of Witchcraft

1. Tongue-Mouth/Words

For reasons which will become evident, we have refrained thus far from introducing lines 31-33 into our discussion of line 4. We previously showed that the speaker in 31-33 expresses the desire that the mouth (31a.32: *pûša lū lipû ... ša iqbû amāt lemuttiya kīma lipî littatuk*) and tongue(31b.33: *lišānša lū ṭābtu ... ša īpušu kišpī kīma ṭābti lihharmiṭ*(!)) of his opponent be destroyed. We need only compare these lines with 28: *turrat amāssa ana pîša lišānša kaṣrat* to notice that both 31-33 and 28 are concerned with the mouth and tongue of the adversary, that 28a (... *amāssa* ... *pîša*) parallels 31a.32 (*pûša* ... *amāt* ...), that 28b (*lišānša* ...) parallels 31b.33 (*lišānša* ...) and that both 28b and 31b.33 have as their purpose the disabling of the witch's tongue. Given the parallelism between 28 and 31-33 and between 28, 34-35 and 4-5, it may be supposed that 31-33 parallels 4-5. In view of the parallelism between 5 and 31a.32 (see above Sec. A, 2), it may be concluded that 4 and 31b.33 are also parallel. The mention of the witch's tongue in 31b supports, therefore, our interpretation of 4 as involving an action which disabled the speaker's tongue.

In terms of this interest in the tongue and mouth, the unit 31-33 fits with the other units in our text, and together they form the pat-

[82] For this translation, see *CAD* K 199 (correct "he" there to "she"; see below note 83).

[83] Contrary to a previous translation of lines 7-8 (*JCS* 15 10: "He (the demon) has bound his (the patient's) tongue so that he is unable to reply."), the subject of these lines is a witch and not a demon.

tern: 4-5 // 28 // 31-33 // 34-35. Each of these four units is made up of two components, one of which always centers on the tongue and the other of which always centers on the mouth and/or words (i.e. accusations):

A. the tongue
- 4: the tongue of the speaker is harmed,
- 28b: the tongue of the witch is harmed,
- 31b.33: the tongue of the witch is harmed,
- 34: the tongue of the speaker is healed.

B. the mouth and/or words
- 5: the witch harms the speaker by uttering words (with her mouth),
- 28a: the witch's words are "turned back into her mouth,"
- 31a.32: the witch's mouth, which uttered the words, is harmed,
- 35: the witch's words are scattered to the wind.

In both A and B, the recipient of the action in the first and last units is the speaker (with the first describing the harm done to him and the last declaring that it has been undone), while the recipient in the middle two units is the witch. It is interesting that while the two units which center on the harm done to the speaker have the order A(4; 34) – B(5; 35), the two which center on the witch reverse this order and have B(28a; 31a.32) – A(28b; 31b.33). Both of these orders probably reflect, and are therefore probably due to, a speaker-oriented chronological perspective:

A-B: the actions performed against the speaker are described and their effects are eliminated in the order of their performance.

B-A: Those performed against the witch are given in an order which is determined by (1) the closeness to the speaker of the effect emanating from the organ to be harmed – for this reason, the witch's tongue is harmed only after the "word" which "touches" the speaker is returned to the witch's mouth or only after the mouth which utters this "word" is destroyed – and (2) the actual order of events – only by disproving the accusation is the speaker able to silence the witch.

2. Lines 31-33: Another Conception of Witchcraft

The tongue-mouth/word pattern constitutes the dominant theme in our incantation. However, while lines 31-33 fit into this pattern, the fit remains imperfect because of 31b.33: "may her tongue be salt, ..., may that (= the tongue) which performed 'witchcraft' (*ša īpušu kišpī*) dissolve like salt." Since the act described in 4 resulted in the constriction of the speaker's tongue, the destruction of the witch's tongue in 31b.33 can be understood as an "eye for an eye" type of revenge. But, whereas *kaššaptu ukaššipanni* (4) assumes that the witch manually manipulated the speaker's (statue's) mouth in order to disable his tongue (just as 31-33 assume that the speaker manually manipulated the witch's (statue's) mouth and tongue in order to disable them[84]), lines 31b.33 assume that the witch's tongue is to be destroyed because it has *īpušu kišpī*, and, therefore, these lines also assume that the witch performed *kispī* with her tongue and not with her hands.

This contradiction is symptomatic of the fact that our incantation contains an uneven mixture of two sets of images of the witch and witchcraft and that these images reflect two distinct situations: (a) the conflict with a witch and (b) the conflict with a legal adversary.

In much of the SB Akkadian and late Sumerian prayer and incantation tradition, experiences originally unrelated to law or the law court are perceived through, molded by and integrated into a view of reality generalized from the legal sphere of life and are expressed in images drawn from that sphere. Thus, for example, evil demons who "are forms given to the numinous power experienced in sudden illness and pain, or other situations of uniformly terrifying nature"[85] are perceived as criminals, and the experience of being in conflict with a demon takes on the character of a conflict whose resolution lies not only in the realm of "sympathetic magic," but also in the law court.[86] Where the gods were asked originally only for magical

[84] The ritual tablet (*STT* 83:12′-14′; see above note 47 and reference there) confirms this interpretation of 31-33, since it expressly prescribes such manipulations.

[85] Jacobsen, "Formative Tendencies in Sumerian Religion," *The Bible and the Ancient Near East*, ed. G. Ernest Wright (1961), p. 271.

[86] Cf. Frankfort *et al.*, *Before Philosophy*, pp. 221f. and Laessøe, *Bît rimki*, pp. 87f.

assistance, the entreaty now becomes a lawsuit and the gods become judges. It is well known that the theme of turning to the god as judge and seeking a decision from him dominates many Akkadian prayers and incantations.

Central to the original perception of witchcraft was the witch's spittle, and it is possible that this perception derives from the image of the witch as a (disturbed) woman who, among other things, slavered at the mouth. It is well known that the sign $UŠ_{12}$ is composed of the elements KAxÚŠ and represents not only the standard words for witchcraft, but also such others as *imtu*. A most revealing passage is *BAM* 318 II 38f.: DIŠ NA *kiš-pi u ru-mi-ka-ti ik-bu-us a-na kiš-pi u ru-mi-ka-ti* BÚR, "If a man steps in *kišpī* or (lit.: and) in (discarded) washwater; in order to release the (effects) of (stepping in) *kišpī* or (lit.: and) (discarded) washwater." In view of *rumīkātu*, it is not unlikely that also *kišpī* in this passage refers to a liquid substance[87] and that this substance is spittle. It is possibly with this meaning of *kišpū* in mind that the witch is said to give her victim bewitched food to eat and bewitched liquid to drink (i.e., food and drink mixed with spittle).[88,89]

---

[87]It is possible, though in our opinion doubtful, that this inference is disqualified by *JNES* 15 142:43′-47′.

[88]Cf., e.g., Laessøe, *op. cit.*, p. 38:11ff. and n. 86, M I 103f., 4 *R* 59/1 obv. 15f. // K 9285 + 13861:2′f. (Note that Laessøe's statement, *op. cit.*, p. 15, n. 19, that *ramāku* in 4 *R* 59/1 obv. 16 refers to washing with beer is wrong, since it simply ignores the break in the middle of the line. This line must read: *ina* KAŠ *lu*! [*iš-qu-šú ina* A.MEŠ] *lu ú-ra-me-ku-šú*. The duplicate, K 9285 + 13861, has: [... *ina* KAŠ *lu* NAG-*šú*] *ina* A.MEŠ *lu* TU_5-*šú*.)

[89]Note that the medical texts frequently associate symptom syndromes centering on the stomach, lungs and mouth with witchcraft diagnoses. Since some of these texts expressly state that the patient has eaten and drunk *kišpū* (e.g., *BAM* 190:22f. and the texts cited in *BAM* II p. XXI for these lines; *AMT* 87/1 obv. 8ff.; 48/4 rev. 8f.; *STT* 102:1ff.), this is probably also to be assumed for those others which simply say that *kišpū* has seized the patient or that the patient is *kašip* (e.g., *BAM* 193 I 8′ff., 90:12′f., *AMT* 50/3 obv. 11, 55/2:4f., 31/4:14ff., *AfO* 1 23:1ff.). Note *BAM* 90:5′ (cf. *AMT* 48/2:13f.): NA.BI *lu-a-te* KI NINDA KÚ *u* KAŠ [NAG.

3. Integration

While this perception of witchcraft and the witch remains alive throughout the life of the tradition, in many texts it has been placed into a legal setting, redefined in terms of this new setting and overlayed by, mixed with, and even submerged by images drawn from this new setting and sphere. This legal setting can be described as the conflict at law with an adversary.[90] We need only examine the many anti-witch Šamaš incantations to see and appreciate the transformation. In these incantations the speaker addresses Šamaš, or one of his replacements, as a judge, refers to the witch by such terms as *bēl ikkiya*, *bēl ṣirriya*, *bēl dīniya*, *bēl amātiya*, *bēl dabābiya*, *bēl lemuttiya*, etc., denounces the actions of the witch, claims that, while he has not harmed her, she has harmed him unjustly and asks the god to give a judgment in his favor.[91]

In this new setting the witch and victim become legal adversaries and the conflict becomes a legal conflict. For our purposes it is necessary to emphasize that also the means normally used by legal adversaries are attributed to both the victim (i.e., the plaintiff) and the witch (i.e., the defendant). This development in the image of the witch is especially apt, because in both the older and younger conceptions one of the witch's main instruments of harm is her mouth. For this reason, the development did not require that the older terminology used to describe the witch's actions be eliminated or even that it undergo radical transformation. Often the addition of new terms and the subtle shift in meaning of older ones sufficed to create a literary idiom for the new conception. And perhaps it is not to be attributed to textual error that in the witchcraft incantation *PBS* 1/2 120(A) // Sm 275 + Rm 329 (confirmed)(B), *ina pîša našât*

[90] The fact that a witch might be called upon to assist a party to a "real" conflict may have contributed to this. Cf. *JCS* 23 29:20-26, where both the plaintiff and the defendant accuse each other of having been assisted by witches (see *ibid.*, p. 28). (Note that the last paragraph on p. 27 is to be disregarded, because "le texte cité comme l'unique exemple de magie noire par Ebeling, *Orientalia*, NS, 20, 167 ss., n'est en vérité qu'un serment niant une dette ou l'accusation d'un détournement de fonds." [Reiner in *Le Monde du Sorcier*, Source Orientales 7, p. 97, n. 10.])

[91] Cf. e.g., M I 73ff., *KAR* 80, *AfO* 18 289ff. (A full list of the representatives of this incantation type will be presented elsewhere.) See below Chapter 4, Sec. D.

amāt maru[*š*]*ti* (A obv. 4 // B 9′) of the description of the witch's actions is paralleled by *uskī imat* HUL-*ti ša pîki* (A obv. 15 // B 16′) of the speech to the witch.[92]

This new conception of the witch pervades our incantation, and the conflict between her and her victim has taken on the guise of the type of legal conflict described earlier, to the extent that not only the victim but also the witch has recourse to the standard techniques, both magical and non-magical, used in this type of conflict. But even here, the older conception has not been completely eliminated and it finds particular expression in lines 31-33, and we should probably translate 31b.33 as: "her tongue ... which has made spittle ...."[93]

[92]We identified Sm 275 as a duplicate of *PBS* 1/2 120 on the basis of Geers' copy, and guessed that Rm 329 both duplicated *PBS* 1/2 120 and joined Sm 275 on the basis of Bezold, *Cat.*, p. 1604 s. Rm 329, where we came across the entry "One section begins: ÉN *an-nu-ú šu-ú an-ni-tu ši-i i-la-as-su-ma* [ ]." We communicated our surmise to Mr. C.B.F. Walker of the British Museum, who checked and confirmed the suggested join. Because a copy of Rm 329 was not available to us, Mr. Walker most graciously prepared a preliminary transliteration, and we wish to express here our deep-felt gratitude to him not only for this but for all his assistance. An edition of this text will be presented elsewhere.

[93]Compare 31-33 with M III 89-92 (for the correct reading of 89, cf. *AfO* 21 80 on IX 47).

Chapter Four

Meaning of I 1-36 and Observations on *Maqlû* I 73-121

A. Legal Construction: Force and Function of Lines 4-12 and their Implications for the Incantation

Lines 4-12. In view of our lengthy discussion of lines 4-12 and of our understanding of the incantation as representing a legal conflict between two adversaries, it is necessary to determine the legal force and function of 4-12. It is obvious that these lines form a *Kausalsatz* which serves to introduce 13-14 (*aššu ... izizzānimma ilī rabûti šimâ dababī dīnī dīnā alaktī limdā* [94]) and that they explain and justify the plaintiff's request to the court that it convene, hear the case and examine the evidence. Our question, then, is whether the plaintiff's description of the actions performed against him by the witch and of the injuries which he suffered as a result of these actions constitutes, as such, evidence of the witch's guilt or whether it has no legal force beyond that of setting out the grounds for the above-mentioned request.

The description in 4-12 simply presents the facts of the case as they appear at the beginning of the trial. These facts constitute neither proof of the witch's guilt nor an accusation against her. In fact, the witch would not deny these facts. She and the speaker would differ solely on their interpretation, and she would claim that

[94] For the technical meaning of *uzuzzu*, cf. *JNES* 2 163f. and especially 164 n. 24. We shall discuss the meaning of *alaktu* and *alakta lamādu/tamû* elsewhere. For the time being, note the following: (1) the usual translations of *alaktī limdā* in our line (cf., e.g., Meier, *Maqlû*, p. 7, Landsberger, *Textbuch*[1], p. 125, Mendelsohn, *op. cit.*, p. 216, *CAD* A/1 297) are probably wrong. Note that *alaktu* is a synonym of *šīmtu*, *ṭēmu* and *urtu* and that *alakta lamādu* is a synonym of *purussâ parāsu* and *dīna dânu*. The approximate meaning of *alakta lamādu* is "to infer a ruling about (the nature of) one's destiny." (2) Saul Lieberman, *Hellenism in Jewish Palestine*[2], p. 83, n. 3, discussed the origin of the term *Halakha* (*hlkh*) and suggested the possibility that it had its origin in the name of the fixed land tax *hlk/hlk'*, which in turn derived from Akk. *ilku*. In our opinion, it is more likely that *alaktu* and *alakta lamādu* in the sense used in our incantation were the points of origin of *hlkh/hlkt'* and *lmd hlkh* respectively.

her actions were legally justified. Moreover, the witch is initially not required to defend her construction of the facts, and the burden of disproving her construction is imposed on the plaintiff (= speaker) who convenes the court in order to demonstrate that, far from being justified, these actions are criminal and actionable.

That the actions ascribed to the witch in the plaintiff's statement of the facts need not be criminal and that their criminality depends on evidence above and beyond a simple description of the actions are apparent in the first instance from the following considerations:

1) It is obvious from the Code of Hammurabi that *ubburu*, "to denounce/accuse," is not, as such, an illegal action;

2) The use of magic to influence other people was permitted in Mesopotamia;[95]

3) The witch's actions do not differ in kind from those of a normal litigant or from those of the speaker; and

4) In any case, the witch qua *bēl dabābi* is not presumed to be a criminal any more than is a normal litigant.

***Lemēnu* : Significance of Absence and Presence.** This understanding of 4-12 is confirmed by the conspicuous absence of any form of *lemēnu* in 4-12 in contrast to its marked presence in later parts of the incantation (18, 27, 32). Having convened the court, the speaker in 18 states: *aššu īpuša lemnētiište'a lā banâti* (*šī limūtma* ...). Here the speaker states for the first time his construction of the facts presented in 4-12 and his own accusation against the witch. We cannot help but observe the structural similarity between 4 and 18 and, therefore, the significance of the replacement of *aššu* ... *ukaššipanni* ... *ubbiranni* by *aššu īpuša lemnēti iste'a lā banâti.*

[95]Several texts which center on relations between the sexes may be cited as examples. They are *ZA* 32 164ff. (to build up a prostitute's clientele), *TCS* II 70ff. (to attract a woman) and *STT* 257 rev. 2ff. In this last text, which we have identified as a duplicate of *RA* 18 21 face (*STT* 257 rev. 11-16 // *RA* 18 21 face I 1-10; *STT* 257 rev. 17ff. // *RA* 18 21 face I 11ff.), a woman attempts to win back her estranged husband, who is angry with her because she is not pregnant (see *RA* 18 22 obv. II 9 and 14). (Note that *STT* 257 rev. 2ff. and obv. 1′ - rev. 1 are not part of the same ritual. Their inclusion in the same tablet is to be explained by their mutual concern with problems which cause a husband to be angry with his wife. It is to be presumed that in obv. 1′ - rev. 1 a rival—called *ēpi*[*šti*] in rev. 1 and *muppišti* in obv. 18′ and 22′ and charged with the practice of witchcraft in obv. 1′-4′—has come between a husband and wife.)

Moreover, it is only after the plaintiff establishes his own innocence of any accusation made against him by the witch (21-26) that he states: *tûša ša kaššapti lemutte*, "ihre Beschwörung (ist) die einer bösen Zauberin."[96] Only clear evidence of his own innocence can constitute proof of the evil intent of the witch who has accused him (*elēnītu ubbiranni*, 5) and of the falsity of her accusation; and it is only this proof that can then allow him to state that her accusation has been refuted (28) and to request the court to take action against her (29f.). We cannot help but observe that as a consequence of his having cleared himself of the witch's accusation and of his having proved its falsity, the *kašsaptu* of 4 becomes the *kaššapti lemutte* of 27.

Accordingly, the speaker in 4-5 simply states that a *kaššaptu* has performed magical acts against him and that an *elēnītu* has accused him. The actions mentioned in these two lines, which are the cause of the injuries described in 6-12, are inherently neither legitimate nor illegitimate. Their legitimacy depends solely on their having been used for legitimate ends. Having seen that the legal status of the act described in 5 (an *elēnītu*[97] has accused me) depends on the truth or falsity of the witch's accusation of the speaker, we should now define that upon which the determination of the legal status of the act described in 4 depends.

The contrast between *aššu ... ukaššipanni* (4) and *aššu īpuša lemnēti ...* (18) and between *kaššaptu* (4) and *kaššapti lemutte* (27) and the consequences derived therefrom indicate that the author of our incantation used *kaššaptu* and *kuššupu* as legally and morally (though probably not emotionally) neutral terms and that at least here the person designated *kaššaptu* is not by definition an evil-doer or criminal and the action designated *kuššupu* is not by definition evil or illegal and actionable. The neutral use of these terms is probably to be explained not only by the fact that the image of a *bēl dabābi* is superimposed on, or replaces, that of a witch, but also by the fact that sometimes the services of at least some segments or members of the *kaššāpu-kaššaptu* group were employed for legitimate causes

[96] *AfO* 21 71; see already Landsberger, *Textbuch*[1] p. 125: "die Zauberformel der bösen Hexe, ..."

[97] Did *elēnītu* originally designate a type of informer?

and that, therefore, they and their actions were sometimes deemed unobjectionable from a legal and moral standpoint.[98]

***Kišpū* and lines 21-35.** However, while *kaššaptu* and *kuššupu* are legally neutral terms in our incantation, *kišpū* is not. For that magic designated by the term *kišpū* is by definition evil and a crime.[99] The issues to be decided in this hearing are not only whether the accusation brought by the witch against the speaker-plaintiff is false, but also whether the magical acts performed by the witch are evil and constitute legitimate grounds for indicting the witch on a count of practicing that type of illicit magic designated as *kišpū*. Just as the witch would not deny that she had accused the speaker, but would deny that this accusation was false, so too she would not deny that she had performed magical acts against the speaker, but would deny that these magical acts were *kišpū*.

We previously saw that the speaker in 21-28 established his innocence of the witch's accusation (21-26) and used this innocence as proof of the falsity of that accusation. To fully understand lines 21-30 and to explain the deviant order of elements and mixture of "tenses" in 28ff.,[100] we must realize that – and this is the key to the problem – the determination of whether or not the witch's magical

[98]See above note 90. See especially M VII 84-105 (= IX 155-159). Our analysis (for the present see our "Ritual and Incantation: A Consideration of *Maqlû* VII 58ff. and IX 152ff.," which was delivered before the American Oriental Society in 1969) has shown that in that incantation a *kaššāpu* and *kaššaptu* (VII 94f., IX 158), working together with other "magical" personnel (VII 92-100), side with a bewitched man against another *kaššaptu* (VII 85-100, IX 156f.). We hope to present additional evidence and to discuss the sociological implications elsewhere.

[99]While we do not wish to claim universal applicability for this distinction between *kaššaptu*/*kuššupu* and *kišpū*, it would explain, and be supported by, usages found elsewhere. We may restrict ourselves to one example. Both the Code of Hammurabi, parag. 2 and the Middle Assyrian Laws, Tablet A, parag. 47 (*KAV* 1 VII 1ff.) take for granted that "witchcraft" is a crime, that its performance is illegal and that the performer is guilty of a crime. The issue at stake in both laws is whether the accused did in fact perform that crime. In the light of our discussion, it is therefore noteworthy that: (1) that act which is taken for granted to be a crime is termed *kišpū*; (2) the performers who by definition are culpable are called *muppišāna ša kišpē* (*KAV* 1 VII 6) and not *kaššāpu* (contrast Exodus 22:17: *mkšph l' tḥyh* and Deuteronomy 18:10: *l' ymṣ' bk ... wmkšp*); and (3) the performance of this crime is described as *kišpē uppišūma* (*KAV* 1 VII 2)/*kišpē epāša* (7) and not as (*kišpē*) *kašāpu*/*kuššupu*.

[100]See above Chapters 1-2.

acts were evil and were, therefore, *kišpū* is wholly dependent upon the determination of whether or not the accusation in whose service these acts were performed was true or false.

We can see this most clearly from a consecutive reading of lines 21-30:

21 *bīnu lillilanni ...*
22 *gišimmaru lipšuranni ...*
23 *maštakal libbibanni ...*
24 *terīnatu lipšuranni ...*
25 *ina mahrikunu ētelil kīma sassati*
26 *ētebib azzaku kīma lardi*
27 *tûša ša kaššapti lemutte*
28 *turrat amāssa ana pîša lišānša kaṣrat*
29 *ina muhhi kišpīša limhaṣūši ilī mušīti*
30 3 *maṣṣārāti ša mūši lipšurā*(!)[101] *ruhîša lemnūti*

In order to prove that the witch's magical acts were *kišpū* and that they, therefore, constitute a criminal offense, the speaker must clear himself by means of an oath of the witch's accusation (21-26) and establish thereby the evil intent of his adversary and the falsity of her accusation (27-28). Only when he has discredited the accusation and established thereby a sound evidential basis upon which to base the claim that the witch's magical acts were *kišpū*, is he able to – and only then does he – ask the court to charge the witch on a count of *kišpū* (29). That the designation of the magical acts as *kišpū* depends upon the evil intent and falsity of the accusation and that this notion determines the sequence of elements in 21-30 would seem also to be supported by the order in lines 31-33:

31 *pûša ... lišānša ...*
32 *ša iqbû amāt lemuttiya ...*
33 *ša īpušu kišpī ...*

Because his refutation of the witch's accusation is a prerequisite for his request that the court charge the witch with the crime of *kišpū*

[101] See above note 4.

and release the witchcraft, the "returning of the word to the mouth" motif (28) must precede the "striking" (29) and "releasing" (30) motifs. Furthermore, whereas the motifs in 28 can be formulated in stative form because the refutation follows from the speaker's own innocence, the motifs in 29 and 30 must be formulated in precative form because the power to charge the witch and nullify the magic resides solely in the court.[102,103]

This analysis of 21-30 also allows us to explain the apparent repetition of 28.30 in 34-35. It is evident from 36, which cites the source and authority of the statement contained in the preceding two lines, that 34-35 contain the announcement of the court's decision:

34 *kiṣrūša puṭṭurū ipšētūša hulluqā*[104]
35 *kal amātūša malâ*[105] *ṣēra*
36 *ina qibīt iqbû ilī mušīti* TU$_6$.ÉN.[106]

[102]This explanation of the deviant order of elements and mixture of "tenses" in 28ff. is related to the further observation that 28ff. differs in one other regard from all the examples quoted above for the joint occurrence of these motifs. It is the only one in which there is an active interplay between two parties (the plaintiff and the judges) and in which all the actions described by these motifs are not assigned to only one party. Contrast this, for example, with the performance of all the actions by the judge in M V 27f., by the plants in Sm 756 and duplicates, by the litigant in *KAR* 71 and by the gods in M VI 17f.

[103]The meaning "to charge, to indict" for *mahāṣu* in 29 is inferred from (and required by[?]) the context and the relationship of our incantation to M I 73ff. (see below Sec. C). It is possible that this inference finds external support in the occurrence of *māhiṣ qaqqadišunu* in the meaning "leur accusateur" in Dossin, "Un cas d'ordalie par le dieu Fleuve," *Symbolae Koschaker* (Studia et Documenta 2), pp. 114f.:15, 22f., 27 (cf. p. 118). (We owe our knowledge of this text to Yochanan Muffs.)

[104]Following *STT* 78: *[hu]l-lu-qa,* rather than *hulluqū* preserved in the main text used in the edition.

[105]*STT* 78 has *lim-la-a*. Because l. 34 has statives and because the Sultantepe MS also has a stative in that line, we retain *malâ* as the better reading for the final version of the incantation. For the possibility that Sultantepe's *limlâ* is a vestige and represents the reading of an earlier and shorter version of the incantation, see below note 113.

[106]We remain unconvinced by Landsberger's explanation, *ZDMG* 74 441, of TU$_6$.ÉN; for we are unable to see how it applies to the occurrence of TU$_6$.ÉN in our incantation and in some others.

Though we do not wish to convey the impression that the judicial function of the court of the gods of the night in 1-36 is identical with that of the assembly (see below Secs. B-C), it is not amiss, in view of the occurrence of *qabû* in 36 and of our analysis of the incantation, to quote Jacobsen's description of the judicial function of the assembly:

> The competence of the Old Babylonian assembly is in general that of a court of law. A plaintiff may himself "notify the assembly" (*puhram lummudum*), or the case may be delegated to the assembly by the king or other high authority. The assembly investigates the case (inim-inimma igi-du$_8$), hears testimony, and may send one of the parties and his witness to some temple to prove their testimony by oath. Finally, it renders its decision (e or du$_{11}$ and *qabû*).[107]

In lines 34-36 of our incantation the court rules that the witch's magical acts together with their effects are nullified (cf. 4) and that her accusations are without substance and are disregarded (cf. 5). The nature of these lines as an automatically operative court decree explains the use of statives.

In 28 the plaintiff himself asserted that the witch's accusation had been (stative) refuted by the evidence of his own innocence. Since this refutation could follow completely from and be determined solely by his own innocence, the plaintiff used the stative in referring to the refutation. In 35 the judges announce that they accept the plaintiff's refutation of the witch's accusation. They, thereby, accord to the refutation the force of a public legal decision. Hence, the repetition and the use of statives in both lines. In contrast to the refutation, the plaintiff has no power to nullify the acts of magic and their effects, and this power resides solely in the court. The plaintiff can do no more than prove that these acts were a criminal offense and appeal to the court to "release" them (30). In 34 the judges announce their acceptance of this appeal and rule in accordance with it. Hence, the repetition in both lines and the use of the precative in (29-)30, but the stative in 34.

---

[107] *JNES* 2 164.

B. Overview of I 1-36

Before we offer a few observations on the history of this incantation and its relation to other parts of the series, it will be best to first summarize in general terms some of the results of our study. Thus far we have treated M I 1-36 as an integral composition and have recognized its thematic and structural unity, as well as its dynamic quality. The two central concerns of the incantation are the magical acts and accusations which the witch has respectively performed and levelled against her victim. Awareness of the importance and interrelation of these two concerns has allowed us to discern and to understand the structure and logic of the incantation. While these two concerns are of equal importance to the composer and are ultimately balanced within the incantation, the logic of the underlying situation in which they constitute the two main elements determines the dynamic of the text and the emphasis sometimes on one and sometimes on the other.

The plaintiff invokes the gods and watches of the night and petitions them to take up his case on the grounds that a witch has magically silenced him (so as to effectively accuse him), has then accused him and has by her actions caused him to suffer certain injuries. These facts clearly establish that he has suffered injuries at the hand of the witch and therefore that he has a right to a court hearing. However, since the witch's actions are open to conflicting constructions in regard to their legality, these facts do not establish her culpability. When the court convenes, the plaintiff causes the witch-defendant to be present (in effigy) and accuses her of having acted illegally and with evil and malicious intent. The plaintiff then proves that he is innocent of the accusation levelled against him by the witch. He demonstrates thereby that her motives for accusing him were evil and that the accusation was false. Furthermore, since the magical acts performed in the service of a false accusation are illicit and are to be treated as *kišpū*, he asks the court to charge the witch with the crime of *kišpū* and to release its effects. He also expresses the wish that the organs responsible for accusing and bewitching him be destroyed. The court accepts the evidence, argumentation and requests submitted by the plaintiff and rules that the witch's magical acts and accusations are null and void.

C. History of I 1-36

Although the incantation in its present form possesses literary unity, it seems nevertheless possible to discern two literary strata and to suggest that the author of our incantation took an existent, but much shorter, incantation as the basis for his composition.

This suggestion is based on lines 19-20:

šī limūtma anāku lubluṭ
kišpūša ruhûša rusûša lū pašrū[108]

The position of 19-20 in the very heart of the incantation constitutes a structural anomaly, since elsewhere in the witchcraft corpus lines identical with or similar to 19 and/or 20 are always found, as far as we can recall, at or near the end of their respective incantations. For example, line 19 occurs consistently as a member of a fairly common sequence, and it is to be noted that the examples of this sequence listed in *AfO* 18 296[109] are all found near the end of their respective incantations.

---

[108] Contrary to Meier, *Maqlû*, p. 7, the end of 20 should be read *lu pa-áš-ru* and not *lip-pa-áš-ru*. Simply see K 43 + ... (4 *R* 49) and K 3294 + ... (Tallqvist, *Maqlû*, II p. 53). Note that also 82-5-22, 508 (*ibid.*, p. 57) must have read *lu*] *pa-á*[*š-ru*; for the wide blank space between the broken left-hand edge and *pa-á*[*š-ru* indicates that *pa-* was the first sign in the word and therefore excludes *lip*]-*pa-á*[*š-ru*. Cf. 4 *R* 59/1 rev. 18 and duplicate quoted below.

Note, however, that *STT* 78 seems to have [*li*]*p-pa-áš-ru*. If this reading is confirmed by a collation, it should probably be compared with *STT*'s reading *limlâ* in 35 (see notes 105 and 113).

[109] Cf. *BiOr* 14 229. The examples listed are *AfO* 18 294:78f., M II 93-96, *LKA* 154 rev. 10′f. (for this text see above Chapter 3, Sec. A, 2), Laessøe, *Bît rimki*, p. 40:44-47 (// *STT* 76 and 77:47-50). A further example is K 6418:8′-12′:

8′] ⌈*šu*]-*ú lim-qut-ma ana-ku* [*lutbi*
9′ *šu*]-*ú li-niš-ma ana-ku* [*ludnin*
10′ *šu*]-*ú li-mut-ma ana-ku* [*lubluṭ*
11′ *šu*]-*ú li-né-gir-ma ana-ku* [*lūšir*
12′ *šu*]-*ú li-ir-t*[*a-s*]*i*!(text: *i*]*š*)-*ma ana-ku* [*lūbib* .

The force of our observation about the present position of M I 19-20 can best be seen from an examination of the incantation 4 *R* 59/1 rev. 11-20(A) // K 7140 rev. 1′ff.(B):[110]

11 ÉN *ša* MÍ.UŠ$_{12}$.ZU.MU GAZ KEŠDA(*rikis*)-*sa*
12 *ša e-le-ni-ti-ia*$_5$ *su-pi-hi* INIM.MEŠ-*šá*
13 *tir-ra kiš-pi-šá a-na me-he-e* INIM.MEŠ-*šá ana* IM
14 *mim-ma te-pu-ša tu-uš-te-pi-ša lu-bil* IM
15 DIŠ *ku-ú-ru u ni-is-sa-ti lu-bil* U$_4$-*um-šá*
16 DIŠ *hu-uṣ-ṣi u* GAZ ŠÀ-*bi li-qat-ta-a* MU.AN.NA.MEŠ-*šá*
17 *ši-i li-mut-ma ana-ku lu-úb-luṭ*
18 *kiš-pu-šá ru-hu-šá ru-su-šá lu* BÚR-*ru* (B: *pa-aš-ru*[111])
19 *ina qí-bit* ^{d}*É-a* ^{d}UTU ^{d}AMAR.UD
20 *u ru-ba-ti* ^{d}*be-lit i-lí* TU$_6$.ÉN

Not only does this incantation share with M I 1-36 the dual concern with *kaššaptu-riksu* (cf. *kiṣrū*, M I 34[112])/*kišpū* // *elēnītu-amātu*, but it also contains an identical version of M I 19-20. It is therefore significant that these lines occur at the end of the incantation immediately before the concluding *ina qibīt* formula.

We have seen that the latter half of our *Maqlû* incantation contains several literary innovations. Since lines 19-20 are completely unexpected in the middle of the incantation and since the section containing the innovations begins in 21, it is not unlikely that the author responsible for the final version of our incantation took over an already existing traditional incantation more or less identical either with 1-20 or with 1-20 + the *ina qibīt* formula presently found in 36 and wrote by himself only 21ff. Depending on whether the original incantation ended with 20 or whether it also included 36,

---

(To the one example cited in the dictionaries of the N of *egēru* in a non-lexical text, add 11′. Note also that 12′ contains one of the rare occurrences of *rasû* [for other examples and a proposed translation, cf. *BiOr* 14 229f.].) Since K 6418 breaks off with 14′, we do not know how close these lines are to the end of the incantation.

[110] K 7140 rev. 1′ff. // 4 *R* 59/1 rev. 17ff. K 7140 rev. was already identified as a duplicate in the margin of Geers' copy.

[111] The signs *pa-aš-* are transliterated, but without brackets, in Geers' copy. Are these signs on the tablet?

[112] Elsewhere we cite the evidence for the interchangeability of *riksu* and *kiṣru*.

this author would have either written and added 21-36 to 1-20 or written and inserted 21-35 between 1-20 and 36.[113]

This development (1-20 + (?)36 > 1-36) had as its purpose the transformation of an independent incantation (1-20 + (?)36) into one (1-36) which would serve as the introduction to a sequence of incantations and which would find its fulfillment not in itself, but in a later part of the sequence; for while the original incantation (1-20 + (?)36) serves to kill the witch, the incantation constructed from it (1-36) only serves to indict, incarcerate and physically disable her. M I 1-36 constitutes the first stages in the trial of the witch, the final stages of which are to be found in the address to Nusku in I 73ff. M I 1-36, the opening incantation in *Maqlû*, serves as an initial hearing in which the plaintiff's charges are investigated by the gods and watches of the night, who then assign the case to the court of the fire god. While the court in 1-36 does not allow those issues directly affecting the plaintiff to remain unresolved, it does reserve the determination of the verdict and final penalty to be imposed on the witch for the court of the fire god.

Seen from this perspective, the function of the hearing before the court of the gods of the night is as follows: The plaintiff describes the witch's behavior and establishes thereby his right to an investigation. The court undertakes this investigation and requires the submission of evidence so that it may determine (a) whether the effects of the magic on the plaintiff should be eliminated and the plaintiff cleared of the accusation levelled against him by the witch, and (b) whether the witch should be indicted and bound over and the case assigned to the court of the fire god. The evidence submitted by the plaintiff is in the form of an oath whereby the plaintiff establishes his inno-

---

[113] This reconstruction is no more than a tentative sketch of the general lines of development of the composition. Even if it is accepted as generally correct, it will still require further refinement. For example: since it is difficult to explain why a scribe would have changed *malâ* (35) to *limlâ* attested in Sultantepe (see above note 105) and since 4 *R* 59/1 rev. 11ff. attempts to eliminate not only the witch's *kišpū*, but also her *amātu*, is it possible that the incantation which served as the basis for the composition of M I 1-36 was also concerned with eliminating both, that *limlâ* is the more original reading, that 35 was also part of the original incantation, that this incantation ended in the sequence: ... *kišpūša* ... *lū pašrū* (*STT* 78: (?) [*li*]*ppašrū*) *kal amātūša limlâ ṣēra ina qibīt iqbû ilī mušīti*, and that the desire to harmonize 35 with 34 led to the change of *limlâ* to *malâ*?

cence of charges levelled against him by the witch. The court accepts this evidence as demonstrating the existence of a case and as constituting grounds (a) for releasing the magic's effects on the plaintiff and clearing him of the accusation (34-35), and (b) for indicting the witch on a count of having practiced *kišpū* (29) and binding her over for trial before Nusku.

Since the first incantation in *Maqlû* is an investigative hearing and since the final verdict of death by fire is imposed on the witch only in I 73ff., it is understandable why 1-36, in contrast to the original incantation (1-20 + (?)36) from which it was constructed as well as to other incantations against the witch modelled on court trials, does not emphasize the killing of the witch, but rather the destruction of her speech organs. By destroying the witch's speech organs, the speaker seeks not only to avenge himself for injuries previously inflicted by her, but also to make it difficult for her to harm him, to frustrate his efforts to bring her to trial before Nusku and to defend herself properly during the subsequent stages of the legal proceedings.

This understanding of the address to the gods of the night in 1-36 and of its relationship to the address to Nusku in 73ff. is not only supported by the exegetical presumptions inherent in the previously established fact that *Maqlû* constitutes a consecutively recited sequence of incantations;[114] by our exegesis of I 1-36 and 73-121; by the fact that 37-72 become meaningful when interpreted in the light of this understanding of 1-36 and 73ff.; and by the existence of a parallel of sorts in *STT* 256, which text prescribes, among other things, the preparation of statues of a warlock and witch, the recitation of an incantation addressed to the gods of the night (*ilī mušīti*) and the recitation of an incantation in which the speaker states that he is burning his enemy and giving him over to the fire (^{d}Gibil).[115]

[114]For the present see our "Some observations on the series *Maqlû*," which was delivered before the American Oriental Society in 1971.

[115]See above note 35 II 1) for a discussion of *STT* 256. Lines 34-37 of this text read:

34 *te-ri-qam-ma* 2 NU.MEŠ LÚ.UŠ$_{12}$.ZU *u* MÍ.UŠ$_{12}$.ZU ša IM DÙ-[*uš*

35 NÍG.NA ŠIM.LI *i-na* IGI DINGIR.MEŠ GI$_{6}$-*ti* DUB-*aq* KAŠ GEŠTIN(?) BAL-*qí* ⌈x⌉ [

36 A.ESÍR ŠE$_{6}$ *ana* UGU-*šú-nu* ŠUB-*di i-na* GIŠ.PA GIŠ.MA.NU [

Additional warrants for, and further refinment of, this understanding are found in actual legal procedures; for it is well known that in Mesopotamia the adjudication of a case may involve a judicial procedure composed of two stages. Instances are known of criminal charges being brought initially not to the court which will impose the final verdict, but to an authority whose function is to examine the charges and their factual foundations and to assign those cases judged to be sufficient to a suitable court for trial and execution.[116] In *Maqlû* the gods of the night function as the investigating court to which the charges are first brought. These gods investigate these charges and deem them sufficient for allowing the court to rectify certain abuses committed against the plaintiff by the witch and to assign the witch to the court of Nusku for trial and execution.

D. *Maqlû* I 73-121

To fully understand the legal procedure operative in the first tablet of *Maqlû* we must examine more closely the address to Nusku in I 73-121. As we demonstrate elsewhere, this incantation was originally addressed to Šamaš and was re-addressed to Nusku when the text was adapted for nighttime use. In this type of incantation, Šamaš is addressed and functions in his capacity of judge, and Nusku, as his replacement, carries on this function.[117] However, it would be a mistake to infer from Šamaš/Nusku's role as judge in 73-121 and from the law court setting of this incantation that the submission and examination of evidence substantiating the charge against the witch and the determination of her innocence or guilt are part of the proceedings in the court of Nusku in this incantation. In texts

---

37 ÉN 3-*šú ana* UG[U]-*šú-nu* ŠID-*nu* ÉN kúr.kúr gibíl.la kúr.kúr i[n.na.ka. 37a (ÉN 3-*šú* ... ŠID-nu) refers to the Sumerian incantation given in 29-32 (én é.nu.ru an.gi$_6$.a ... dingir.re.e.ne ...), and 37b (ÉN kúr.kúr ...) refers to the bilingual incantation given in 41-44 (én kúr.kúr gibíl ... : *na*!(text: *la*)-*ka-ra* ⌈*a*⌉-[*qal-lu* ...] kúr.kúr šub.ba ^{d}Gibil šub.ba.bi ...), duplicates of which are *ArOr* 17/1 191:25-32 and K 8107:1′-7′.

[116] Cf. Jacobsen, *AnBi* 12 130ff. (now reprinted with corrections in *HSS* 21 193ff.) and especially 139ff.

[117] Cf. Laessøe, *op. cit.*, pp. 87f.

belonging to the same genre as M I 71-121, such as *KAR* 80 and *AfO* 18 289ff., the core of the speaker's address to Šamaš is represented by the simple, though often long, statement by the accuser that he is presenting before Šamaš statues of the witches who have performed witchcraft against him and by his request that the judge pronounce a verdict of death by fire and that the fire god execute the verdict.

In this regard, there is no essential difference between the address to Nusku in M I 73-121 and the aforementioned addresses to Šamaš. Here the accuser identifies the (statues of the) defendants as the ones who have committed acts of witchcraft against him (73-109) and demands that the court of the fire god order and execute a death penalty by fire (110-121). Nowhere in this incantation does the plaintiff attempt to substantiate the claim that the accused did, in fact, perform witchcraft against him, and nowhere is the court asked to determine the innocence or guilt of the accused. The accuser treats the guilt of the witch as a foregone conclusion and demands of the court that it impose the death penalty on her:

115 *qumu kaššāpu u kaššaptu*
116 *akul ayyābiya aruh lemnūtīya*

To all intents and purposes, the accuser himself pronounces the death verdict on the witch. The accuser does not fear lest the court of Nusku declare the witch innocent, does not attempt to prove to the court that she is guilty as charged and feels secure that the court will accede to his demand. The accuser's behavior admits of only one explanation: the court's knowledge of the witch's guilt and the accuser's belief that the court will act in accordance with that knowledge.

Although evidence was previously submitted to the court of the gods of the night in 1-36 proving, or, at least, establishing the presumption, that the defendant had practiced witchcraft, this cannot account for the fact that in 73-121 the facts of the case and the guilt of the witch are taken for granted. Since the guilt of the witch is also taken for granted in the aforementioned Šamaš incantation type, since this type is neither preceded by nor assumes a previous investigative hearing, and since the Nusku incantation derives from a member of this type and agrees with this type in taking the guilt of the witch for granted, the attitude displayed by the speaker in 73-121 and the legal procedure operative in this incantation must have already been present in the original version of the incantation prior to its association with I 1-36 and cannot be explained as a modification introduced into the Nusku incantation as a result of this subsequent association.

Accordingly, we cannot look to the present context of 73-121 for an explanation of the lack of substantiation of the charges and of the assumption of the witch's guilt and must seek that explanation in some datum of the Mesopotamian criminal legal tradition. That explanation is forthcoming if we treat the legal procedure operative in 73-121 and in similar incantations as representing a stage of development in that tradition of criminal procedure discussed by Jacobsen in his analysis of the Nippur homicide trial. We refer the reader to his discussion of the existence and nature of the tradition (*AnBi* 12 142ff.) and simply quote those observations made by him on pp. 141-142. In discussing a homicide case involving an investigation of the charges by the king and the assignment of the case to the Assembly in Nippur for trial, Jacobsen remarks as follows about the trial stage of the case and the situation underlying the tradition of criminal procedure:

> ... the record of a trial for homicide can obviously claim special attention. We find it to be concerned with law to the complete exclusion of facts; it is the record of the formulation of a verdict only. Proceedings in the assembly open with a statement made by a group of nine named men identifying the accused as killers and ordering the death penalty for them; this proposed verdict is followed by a question about the applicability of the term "kill" in the case of one of the accused, the woman, and then comes a ruling on the question by the assembly. The initial statement stands - and is allowed to stand throughout - unsupported by any show of proof, and this complete absence of a detailed establishing of the facts of the case through testimony of witnesses, confession, oath, or otherwise is most striking. Even if one would assume, as we have done above, that a thorough establishing of the facts had already taken place before the king, before the case reached the assembly for trial, the lack of even the briefest presentation of those earlier findings leads again to the conclusion that the assembly was expected to reach its verdict on the basis of its members' personal knowledge and convictions rather than on facts established in court. This is so

> unlike all we know about procedure in the civil trials, where fact-finding looms so large as to constitute the bulk of the average trial record, that the question cannot but arise whether we might not here – since this is a case of homicide – be dealing with a separate and altogether distinct, criminal procedural tradition ....
>
> Rather different [from the situation underlying civil procedure] appears the original situation underlying the tradition of criminal procedure. The early "crime" is an act endangering the whole community, and the community, aroused and scared, is apt to deal with it along lines of lynch-justice. In the emotionally highly charged lynch situation the facts and the guilt of the accused are generally taken for granted (it is the conviction that they are true that has aroused the community to action). At the tense moment when the community faces the accused the salient point is therefore merely the crystallization of the guilt in a precise and poignant formula that will trigger the punitive mass action. This formula fulfills the function of the later "verdict."
>
> If, accordingly, our Nippur trial stands in a specific "criminal" procedural tradition going back to an original situation of lynch-justice its exclusive concentration on the verdict and its lack of interest in the facts of the case would become far easier to understand.[118]

The legal procedure operative in M I 73-121, in the Šamaš incantation from which it derives and in other incantations of the same genre stands in the same procedural tradition as the Nippur trial, and it is for this reason that the accuser is able to take the court's knowledge of the witch's guilt for granted and to base the demand that the god kill the witch simply on his own assertion that she bewitched him. The aforementioned incantations and incantation type represent a further stage of development of this procedural tradition; for in these incantations, in contrast to the examples discussed by Jacobsen, the case is tried by a single judge and not by an assembly.

[118]It will not escape the reader's notice that in the Nippur trial, as in *Maqlû*, the trial stage is preceded by an investigation of the charges (see above Sec. C and note 116) and that Jacobsen's judgment that the "complete absence of a detailed establishing of the facts of the case" during the trial stage is not explained by the fact that "a thorough establishing of the facts had already taken place before the king" would seem to be supported by our having reached a similar conclusion concerning the relation between the hearing before the gods of the night and the trial before Nusku on the basis of an independent and dissimilar line of argumentation.

* * *

We have tried to understand those segments of the proceedings against the witch represented by M I 1-36, the hearing before the gods of the night, and 73-121, the trial before Nusku. Elsewhere we shall discuss the intervening incantations contained in 37-72. We hope that our analysis of 1-36 and of its relationship to 73ff. has convinced the reader of the richness of material contained in 1-36 and has justified the extensive treatment. The scope of our treatment has also been necessitated by the fact that a clear understanding of 1-36 and 73ff. is a prerequisite for the analysis of the incantations contained in 37-72. Since these incantations are quite laconic and their meaning is therefore most elusive, a productive analysis of 37ff. must proceed in part from premises inferred from data found outside of these incantations. Since the incantations in 37ff. are part of a longer sequence and their laconism assumes a knowledge of their background, the best and most valid source of legitimate premises is undoubtedly those incantations which constitute their contextual matrix, i.e., 1-36 and 73ff.

Selected Bibliography

I list here all the published magical and medical texts and studies cited in the body and notes of this book. I also include a few general studies that have been cited.

Biggs, R.D. *ŠÀ.ZI.GA: Ancient Mesopotamian Potency Incantations.* TCS 2. Locust Valley, New York, 1967.

Borger, R. "Das dritte 'Haus' der Serie *bīt rimki.*" *JCS* 21 (1967 [1969]) 1-17.

Caplice, R.I. "The Akkadian Text Genre Namburbi." Ph.D. diss., University of Chicago, 1963.

———. "Namburbi Texts in the British Museum I-IV." *Or*NS 34 (1965) 105-31; 36 (1967) 1-38; 36 (1967) 273-98; 39 (1970) 111-51.

Driver, G.R., and Miles, J.C. *The Babylonian Laws*, Vols. I-II. Oxford, 1952 and 1955.

Ebeling, E. "Assyrische Beschwörungen." *ZDMG* 69 (1915) 89-103.

———. *Keilschrifttexte aus Assur religiösen Inhalts.* WVDOG 28 and 34. Leipzig, 1915-23.

———. *Quellen zur Kenntnis der babylonischen Religion*, Vols. I-II. MVAG 23/1-2. Leipzig, 1918-19.

———. *Keilschrifttexte medicinischen Inhalts.* Berlin, 1922-23.

———, and Unger, E. "Keilschrifttexte aus Konstantinopel. 1. Ein medizinischer Text aus Kujundjik." *AfO* 1 (1923) 23-25.

———. *Aus dem Tagewerk eines assyrischen Zauberpriesters.* MAOG 5/3. Leipzig, 1931.

———. *Tod und Leben nach den Vorstellungen der Babylonier.* Berlin and Leipzig, 1931.

———. "Beschwörungen gegen den Feind und den bösen Blick aus dem Zweistromlande." *ArOr* 17/1 (1949) 172-211.

———. *Die akkadische Gebetsserie "Handerhebung"*. Berlin, 1953.

———, and Köcher, F. *Literarische Keilschrifttexte aus Assur*. Berlin, 1953.

———. "Beiträge zur Kenntnis der Beschwörungsserie Namburbi." *RA* 48 (1954) 1-15; 48 (1954) 76-85; 50 (1956) 22-33.

———. "Ein neuassyrisches Beschwörungsritual gegen Bann und Tod." *ZA* 51 (1955) 167-79.

Falkenstein, A. *Literarische Keilschrifttexte aus Uruk*. Berlin, 1931.

———. "Sumerische Beschwörungen aus Boğazköy." *ZA* 45 (1939) 8-41.

———, and von Soden, W. *Sumerische und akkadische Hymnen und Gebete*. Zürich and Stuttgart, 1953.

Goetze, A. "Cuneiform Inscriptions from Tarsus." *JAOS* 59 (1939) 1-16.

———. "Reports on Acts of Extispicy from Old Babylonian and Kassite Times." *JCS* 11 (1957) 89-105.

Gray, C.D. "Some Unpublished Religious Texts of Šamaš." *AJSL* 17 (1900-1901) 222-43.

Gurney, O.R. "An Incantation of the Maqlû Type." *AfO* 11 (1936-37) 367-68, pl. V.

———, Finkelstein, J.J., and Hulin, P. *The Sultantepe Tablets*, Vols. I-II. London, 1957 and 1964.

Hehn, J. *Hymnen und Gebete an Marduk*. BA 5/3, pp. 279-400. Leipzig, 1905.

Jacobsen, Th. "Primitive Democracy in Ancient Mesopotamia." *JNES* 2 (1943) 159-72.

———. "Mesopotamia." In *Before Philosophy*, eds. H. Frankfort, *et al.*, 137-234. Harmondsworth and Baltimore, 1949.

———. "An Ancient Mesopotamian Trial for Homicide." *AnBi* 12

(1959) 130-50.

———. "Formative Tendencies in Sumerian Religion." In *The Bible and the Ancient Near East*, ed. G.E. Wright, 267-78. Garden City, New York, 1961.

King, L.W. *Babylonian Magic and Sorcery*. London, 1896.

———. *The Seven Tablets of Creation*, Vols. I-II. London, 1902.

Kinnier Wilson, J.V. "An Introduction to Babylonian Psychiatry." In *Studies Landsberger*. AS 16, 289-98. Chicago, 1965.

———. "Leprosy in Ancient Mesopotamia." *RA* (1966) 47-58.

Köcher, F. *Die babylonische-assyrische Medizin in Texten und Untersuchungen*, Vols. I-III. Berlin, 1963-64.

Kraus, F.R "Babylonische Omina mit Ausdeutung der Begleiterscheinungen des Sprechens." *AfO* 11 (1936-37) 219-30.

Kunstmann, W.G. *Die babylonische Gebetsbeschwörung*. LSS nf 2. Leipzig, 1932.

Labat, R. *Traité akkadien de diagnostics et pronostics médicaux*. Paris, 1951

———. *Un calendrier babylonien des travaux, des signes et des mois*. (*séries iqqur îpuš*). Paris, 1965.

Laessøe, J. *Studies on the Assyrian Ritual and Series bît rimki*. Copenhagen, 1955.

———. "A Prayer to Ea, Shamash, and Marduk, from Hama." *Iraq* 18 (1956) 60-67.

Lambert, W. G. Review of J. Laessøe, *Studies on the Assyrian Ritual and Series bît rimki*. *BiOr* 14 (1957) 227-230.

———. "An Incantation of the Maqlû Type." *AfO* 18 (1957-58) 288-99.

———. *Babylonian Wisdom Literature*. Oxford, 1960.

Landsberger, B. "Babylonische-assyriche Texte." In *Textbuch zur*

Religionsgeschichte, eds. E. Lehmann and H. Haas. Leipzig, 1st ed. 1912, 2nd ed. 1922.

———. "Zu den Übersetzungen Ebeling's ZDMG. 74, 175ff." *ZDMG* 74 (1920) 439-45.

———. *Die Serie ana ittišu.* MSL I. Rome, 1937.

———. "Remarks on the Archive of the Soldier Ubarum." *JCS* 9 (1955) 121-31.

Langdon, S. "A Tablet of Prayers from the Nippur Library." *PSBA* 34 (1912) 75-79.

———. *Babylonian Penitential Psalms.* OECT 6. Paris, 1927.

———. "A Babylonian Ritual of Sympathetic Magic by Burning Images." *RA* 26 (1929) 39-42.

Levey, M. *Chemistry and Chemical Technology in Ancient Mesopotamia.* Amsterdam and Princeton, 1959.

Lutz, H.F. *Selected Sumerian and Babylonian Texts.* PBS 1/2. Philadelphia, 1919.

Meier, G. *Die assyrische Beschwörungssammlung Maqlû.* *AfO* Beiheft 2. Berlin, 1937.

———. "Ein Brief des assyrischen Gelehrten Balasī." *Or*NS 8 (1939) 306-9.

———. "Die zweite Tafel der Serie *bīt mēseri.*" *AfO* 14 (1941-44) 139-52.

———. "Studien zur Beschwörungssamlung Maqlû, zusammengestellt nach hinterlassenen Notizen." *AfO* 21 (1966) 70-81.

Meissner, B. "Zu Ebeling's Aufsatz ZDMG. 69, 89ff." *ZDMG* 69 (1915) 412-14.

———. *Babylonien und Assyrien*, Vol. II. Heidelberg, 1925.

Mendelsohn, I., ed., *Religions of the Ancient Near East.* New York, 1955.

Mullo Weir, C.J. *A Lexicon of Accadian Prayers in the Rituals of Expiation.* Oxford, 1934.

Myhrman, D.W. *Babylonian Hymns and Prayers.* PBS 1/1. Philadelphia, 1911.

Nougayrol, J. "Parallèles, duplicata, etc." *RA* 36 (1939) 29-40.

———. "*Sirrimu* (non * *purîmu*) 'âne sauvage'." *JCS* 2 (1948) 203-8.

Oppenheim, A.L. "A New Prayer to the 'Gods of the Night'." *AnBi* 12 (1959) 282-301.

Rawlinson, H.C., and Pinches, T.G. *The Cuneiform Inscriptions of Western Asia*, Vol. IV, 2nd ed. London, 1891.

Reiner, E. "*Lipšur* Litanies." *JNES* 15 (1956) 129-49.

———. *Šurpu: A Collection of Sumerian and Akkadian Incantations. AfO* Beiheft 11. Graz, 1958.

———. "Plague Amulets and House Blessings." *JNES* 19 (1960) 148-55.

———. "La magie babylonienne." In *Le monde du sorcier*, 69-98. Sources orientales 7. Paris, 1966.

———, and Civil, M. "Another Volume of Sultantepe Tablets." *JNES* 26 (1967) 177-211.

———, and Güterbock, H.G. "The Great Prayer to Ishtar and its Two Versions from Boğazköy." *JCS* 21 (1967 [1969]) 255-66.

Renger, J. "Untersuchungen zum Priestertum der altbabylonischer Zeit. 2. Teil." *ZA* 59 (1969) 104-230.

Scheil, V. "Catalogue de la collection Eugène Tisserant." *RA* 18 (1921) 1-33.

———. "Une restitution dans la tabl. VII des Maqlû." *RA* 22 (1925) 154-56.

Schott, A. "Šurpu und Kudurrus." *ZDMG* 81 (1927) p. XLVII.

Speleers, L. *Recueil des inscriptions de l'Asie antérieure des Musées Royaux du Cinquantenaire à Bruxelles.* Bruxelles, 1925.

von Soden, W. "Bemerkungen zu den von Ebeling in 'Tod und Leben' Band I bearbeiteten Texten." *ZA* 43 (1936) 251-76.

———. "Das Problem der zeitlichen Einordnung akkadischer Literaturwerke." *MDOG* 85 (1953) 14-26.

———. "Zur Wiederherstellung der Marduk-Gebete BMS 11 und 12." *Iraq* 31 (1969) 82-89."

Sweet, R.F.G. "An Akkadian Incantation Text." In *Essays on the Ancient Semitic World*, eds. Wevers J.W., and Redford, D.B., 6-11. Toronto, 1970.

Tallqvist, K.L. *Die assyrische Beschwörungsserie Maqlû*, Vols. I-II. ASSF 20/6. Leipzig, 1895.

Thompson, R.C. *Semitic Magic: Its Origins and Development.* London, 1908.

———. *Assyrian Medical Texts.* London, 1923.

———. "Assyrian Medical Prescriptions for Diseases of the Stomach." *RA* 26 (1929) 47-92.

Thureau Dangin, F. "Rituel et amulettes contre 'Labartu'." *RA* 18 (1921) 161-98.

Walters, S.D. "The Sorceress and her Apprentice." *JCS* 23 (1970-71) 27-38.

Yalvaç, K. "Eine Liste von Amulettsteinen im Museum zu Istanbul." In *Studies Landsberger.* AS 16, 329-36. Chicago, 1965.

Zimmern, H. *Beiträge zur Kenntnis der babylonischen Religion*, Vols. I-II. AB 12. Leipzig, 1901.

———. "Der Schenkenliebeszauber Berl. VAT 9728 (Assur)=Lond. K.3464 + Par. N 3554 (Nineve)." *ZA* 32 (1918-19) 164-84.

www.ingramcontent.com/pod-product-compliance
Lightning Source LLC
Chambersburg PA
CBHW022023090426
42739CB00006BA/259
9781930675407